New York, New York

How the Apartment House Transformed the Life of the City (1869–1930)

Elizabeth Hawes

An Owl Book

Henry Holt and Company
New York

Henry Holt and Company, Inc.
Publishers since 1866
115 West 18th Street
New York, New York 10011

Henry Holt® is a registered
trademark of Henry Holt and Company, Inc.

Library of Congress Cataloging-in-Publication Data
Hawes, Elizabeth.
New York, New York : how the apartment house transformed the life
of the city (1869-1930) / Elizabeth Hawes. — 1st Owl book ed.
p.   cm.
"An Owl book."
Originally published: New York : Knopf, 1993.
Includes bibliographical references and index.
1. Apartment houses—New York (N.Y.)   2. Architecture, Modern—
19th century—New York (N.Y.)   3. Architecture, Modern—20th
century—New York (N.Y.)   4. Architecture and society—New York
(N.Y.)—History—19th century.   5. Architecture and society—New York
(N.Y.)—History—20th century.   6. New York (N.Y.)—Buildings,
structures, etc.   I. Title.
[NA7860.H34   1994]   93-46656
728'.314'09747109041—dc20   CIP

ISBN 0-8050-3258-4

Henry Holt books are available for special promotions and premiums.
For details contact: Director, Special Markets.

First published in hardcover in 1993 by Alfred A. Knopf.

First Owl Book Edition—1994

Printed in the United States of America
All first editions are printed on acid-free paper. ∞

3   5   7   9   10   8   6   4   2

New York, New York

for Davis

*There's only one city that belongs to the whole country,
and that's New York.*

—WILLIAM DEAN HOWELLS,
A Hazard of New Fortunes

CONTENTS

ACKNOWLEDGMENTS

THIS VOLUME began as an idea for a Reporter at Large piece in *The New Yorker,* so my first gratitude is reserved for the late William Shawn, who from the beginning encouraged me to write a book. When I decided to expand my original work, the New York Public Library granted me the privilege of residence in the Frederick Lewis Allen Room, a remarkable place that exists only to support writers. I am indebted to a legion of librarians, curators, administrators, and book people there, in particular to Wayne Furman of Special Collections and Stanley Kruger of the Access Department, and also to a company of writers in the room, namely Jonathan Kandell, David Lowe, Gloria Deak, and John Demaray, who helped me in countless ways and became collaborators in spirit. With the same fullness of heart and mind, I also thank Myra Sklarew, who extended an invitation to Yaddo, to which I escaped for a month to write the final chapters of the book, and Jules Feiffer, who insisted I do so.

Many other people helped in the writing of this book. Some of them are attached to institutions: Bonnie Yochelson and Leslie Nolan, who opened up a storehouse of photographs and clippings at the Museum of the City of New York; Vicki Weiner, my assistant at the Avery Architectural and Fine Arts Library; the research staff at the New-York Historical Society and the Landmarks Preservation Commission. Others are associated with apartment buildings: Tom Vitullo-Martin, who really *is* the Belnord; Davida Deutsch, the historian of the Osborne; Juliette Hamelcourt, who shared her years of sleuthing at the Chelsea. There were innumerable and nameless others who offered up exotic bits of information about old apartment buildings, which is a tribute to the New York experience. Harry Forster recalled his early years in real estate and his friendship with Rosario Candela for me; Richard Ferrer briefed me on nineteenth-century apartment houses in Paris; Caesar Pelli talked for hours about residential architecture; Frank Rich offered important thoughts on apartments in film.

I am grateful to the Board of Directors of the Osborne, the New York Public Library, and the Avery Library for their generous permission to publish photographs, and to Megan Weeks for her picture research in the Houghton Library at Harvard. I am deeply indebted to Phyllis Rose, Wendy Gimbel, Ursula Goodenough, and Diane Reverand, who read various drafts of my manuscript and offered invaluable criticism; to my agent, Roberta Pryor; and to my wise editor, Victoria Wilson. Finally, to my sons, Nicky, Jake, and Luke, who can barely remember a time when I wasn't at work on this book, and to my husband, Davis, who has always been my advisor and advocate, I say thank you, which is small recompense for their constancy and spirit.

INTRODUCTION

═══════════

ARCHITECTURAL historians call it "the Great Era of Luxury Apartment Building." The *great* speaks to the era's eminence, the *luxury* to its extravagance, *apartment building* to its accomplishment. Its six decades lie across the year 1900 like a bridge from the past to the present. At the beginning, in 1869, all respectable New Yorkers lived in private houses; in 1929, 98 percent of that same population had been stacked up in multiple dwellings. Phenomenal change had been written in stone.

By anyone's measure, the era between the Civil War and the Great Depression was one of the most boisterous in history. Within those years, Old New York became a city; its citizens became urban people; its leisurely ways became "modern life" with all the social, psychological, and technological ramifications. From the first plainspoken buildings of "French flats" to the last swaggering tower, luxury apartment houses annotated the course of this evolution expressively and comprehensively. The first ones were as awkward and tentative on the street as society was in the city at large. The last ones fit into the Jazz Age with stylish ease. Apartment houses were statistical measures of the process of city building—each one containing hundreds of people and consuming larger and larger chunks of the landscape—but they were also reflections of a state of mind. Beyond their size and style and paraphernalia, they were people's homes.

The saga of the apartment house can be written from an economic point of view. Vertical living was an inevitability in a city with a growing population and a limited landmass. Like the ancient walled cities of Europe, the island of Manhattan was contained by its waters and had to double back on itself to endure. The spiraling cost of living, the need for servants to maintain the regimen of row house living, the added burden of an income tax after 1913—all collaborated with ambitious developers to make the apartment house an increasingly attractive proposition. When builders discovered that a palatial version of a multiple dwelling was even more profitable than an efficiency model, the modern luxury apartment house found its footing and flourished in inflationary times.

Houses, however, are freighted with more meaning than financial data can convey. They have cultural, social, and aesthetic dimensions. They have shapes, styles, decoration, traditions; they have sentimental value. It was historically significant that New Yorkers—particularly well-to-do New Yorkers—gave up their private houses after centuries of cherishing them, and the apartment house belonged as much to the broader mission of reform as to the narrower issue of supply and demand. The campaign to make the apartment house a respectable place of dwelling was a struggle against the stubborn grip of traditional values, and its eventual success with the upper classes, who had the greatest investment in houses and the least inclination to be pragmatic, went hand in hand with the dismantling of the old order that was the way of life.

It is a long way back to the early days when the apartment house represented an incongruous idea, or even to the later ones when it was a Hollywood fantasy. Nostalgia is inevitable, for New York was young and innocent then, and it is thoroughly and matter-of-factly apartmentalized now. The opulence that once served to define a luxury apartment—to give it credibility and respectability—is a virtual impossibility now. The size of a typical well-bred apartment has shrunk to a sliver of its former self. Like apartment dwellings, apartment dwellers have changed dramatically. A century ago, they were inexperienced and wary. The conversion to "gregarious living" was like a process of maturation—slow and uneven, full of resistances and distractions—until, in the end, as the idea of modernity took hold, it was sweeping, like a change of heart.

Hundreds of luxury apartment houses built during the Great Era still stand on the streets of New York. Others reside only in pictures or in memory now, but their facts are still illuminating. They are Queen Anne, neo-Gothic, High and Low Renaissance, moderne. They look like houses, hotels, fortresses, and palaces. They have billiard rooms, jewelry safes, hexagonal parlors, and names like the Garden Gate or the

Cliff Dwellers' Apartments. These buildings are more than mere arti-
facts, and they are more than metaphors. They tell the story of human
use. One by one they annotate the way from 1869 to 1930. Together
they offer a continuum, an explanation of the process of urbanization in
its most intimate terms—of how New Yorkers learned to live in a city,
and of how that city grew up.

New York, New York

OLD NEW YORK

1869–1879

Looking south on Fifth Avenue from Dr. Spring's
new Brick Church at 37th Street, 1859.

1

IRVING PLACE, 1869

WHEN the first apartment house was built in New York City, it was as out of place on the streets as a visitor from another country or another century. The year was 1869, and the idea of sharing a roof, a front door, or a staircase with other families was both exotic and shocking. Frenchmen or Romans or socialists might have found it acceptable to cohabit in large buildings, but New Yorkers, particularly well-to-do New Yorkers, had good reason to demand the privacy, security, and respectability that came with their own address. Strong instincts led well-bred New Yorkers to private houses as single-mindedly as homing pigeons.

From the top of a bell tower or a church steeple, anyone would have seen this fact dotted across the southern face of the city. Single four- and five-story houses radiated out along the lines of the grid like so many rows of social vegetables. They were remarkable for a general similarity of size, shape, and posture, although they represented many generations, and were made by different hands, of different materials. Chocolate-hued brownstone was the dominant color of the day, and had been since the discovery of an almost inexhaustible supply of the building material in the fields of New Jersey. Where Victorian brownstone had not come to prevail, Federal brick still did, just as before the era of brick, colonial wood had too. It was the city's chronology—weathered wood, rosy brick, brownstone. It was the city's tradition—houses.

The neighborhood of Irving Place, where the apartment house had settled, was old and traditional. Houses, predominantly brick, ran up and down its streets, interrupted only by churches, a primary school, a vacant lot. It was a thoroughly residential area, quiet, genteel, convenient for families. The horse car stopped at the corner of Third Avenue; three parks were within a stroller's reach—Union Place, Gramercy Park, and Stuyvesant Square. Like the square, the apartment house was named after Peter Stuyvesant, and its site at 142 East 18th Street was once a field in his colonial farmstead. More directly, it was named after one of the first governor's lateral descendants, twenty-nine-year-old Rutherfurd Stuyvesant, who had commissioned and financed the building. This Stuyvesant had admired apartment houses in Paris and decided it was time to build one in New York.

The Stuyvesant fit its location nicely. It was neither outrageous nor overbearing in appearance, although with small wrought-iron balconies and a mansard roof with triple-dormer windows, it looked very French. It was only five stories high—no taller than some of its neighbors, although four times as wide—and it was built of red brick, lightly trimmed with stone. Its entrance was discreet—double doors up a stoop of four steps—and its windows were in line with those of adjacent houses so it suggested a series of row houses rendered without the usual lines of demarcation. Inside, there were party walls in lieu of house lines, and a series of one-story dwellings strung out en suite from front to back and stacked up four deep. The fifth floor, with its long walk-up and better light, was reserved for artists' studios, in the French tradition.

Irving Place was a canny choice of site for the Stuyvesant. It was respectable upper-class territory, and yet it was not far from Union Place, where residential patterns were changing. Here, what had been a sedate and exclusive park, surrounded by a heavy iron fence that was closed and locked at sundown, was becoming a glittery up-to-date place. Private houses still held the west side of the square, but behind their formal facades, a few of them had been converted to "fashionable" boardinghouses, and a few were being altered for stores. First-class hotels had already claimed corners on the north and east of the square. To the south, the Academy of Music stood strong on 14th Street, a shrine for Old New York society, who appeared in their red-and-gold boxes there every Monday and Wednesday night, but it had been joined by a handful of new theaters, the New York Circus, and Delmonico's Restaurant, which had moved uptown to Fifth from its old quarters near City Hall.

In Union Place, which in a few years would be renamed Union Square (and its fence removed), the forces of change in the city were visible. Not only were new forms being synthesized on the street, new energies charged the air. What a writer in *Harper's Weekly* described as "a certain public frenzy" could be observed in the social behavior, in the fury of the extravagance in public watering places. Dress showed an obsession with ornamentation. Costume balls were the rage. Dinners were longer and proudly epicurean. Entertainments were bolder and more diverse. To some, it was a release from the tension of war; the postbellum scene had opened to enormous speculation, political corruption, the flaunting of industrial wealth. To others, it was the inevitable product of progress and prosperity. The northern advance of commerce reflected economic growth; the hotels, restaurants, and theater, the new public life; the boardinghouses, the cost of living in a city.

In a way, the Stuyvesant was no more or less revolutionary a piece of architecture than the boardinghouses or hotels on Union Place, in which many respectable middle-class people had taken to living in inflationary times. It gave itself the new name of "apartment house," however—the first such building in America to do so—which made it recognizable as something new. Furnished apartments had never had an institutional character before; they were only rooms to let. This apartment house was known as "Stuyvesant's Folly" among the upper classes, whose regard for Stuyvesant kept them from stronger ridicule. (Stuyvesant was actually Stuyvesant Rutherfurd by birth, the son of the learned astronomer Lewis Rutherfurd, but had reversed his name to comply with the terms for inheriting the vast Stuyvesant landholdings on his mother's side.) Certain patriarchs of society thought that the idea of "cohabitation" was a shocking, even immoral proposition, for it offered no more privacy or propriety than the tenements inhabited by the poor. Others, like George Templeton Strong, a well-to-do lawyer, found the small six- or seven-room suites quite charming, and innocuous as a housing idea. Strong visited friends in the building out of curiosity and reported back, with unexpected pleasure, "This substitute for householding seems to work well, and Rutherfurd is a public benefactor, especially to young people who want to marry on moderate means. Nothing could be brighter, more comfortable, or more refined-looking than these tiny, cosy drawing rooms." It was not surprising, he added, that all the suites in the Stuyvesant had been rented before its completion to young couples, widows, and "artistic people."

Strong, an active and principled gentleman, and a blueblood too, kept a diary of his times, in which he expressed his thoughts and concerns about the evolution of the pleasant, peaceful, simple-minded city of his youth. When he had begun his daily notations, as a Columbia College sophomore in 1835, the northernmost outposts of fashionable residence were at Bond Street, a short block that ran from Broadway to the Bowery, and Lafayette Place, which ran from Great Jones Street to Astor Place. In the years since, the downtown commercial areas had expanded, and the city had pushed north on the average of a block a year, by the end of the Civil War reaching 42nd Street, above which the streets remained ungraded and unpaved. The fashionable domestic quarters had been displaced to quieter fields accordingly, from Stuyvesant Square to Washington Square, to lower Fifth Avenue, and then up that street, "the Middle Road," toward 42nd Street.

In the late 1860s, Strong's diary reflected a physical and psychological uneasiness in the city, as he began to note, along with the details of his law practice, a dinner at the Schermerhorns' or a first public reading by Charles Dickens at Steinway Hall (where five thousand people had waited for the ticket window to open), a building going up or coming down here and there. In May 1866, he told of much building above 42nd Street, and much tearing down. On August 6 of that year, he entered, "Another material change in the aspect of Broadway. Taylor's showy restaurant becomes the office of the American Express Company. Chapin's Universalist or Unitarian Church (east side of Broadway between Prince and Spring Streets, built some twenty years ago, used of late as a picture gallery) is being demolished. So things go. Let em go!" On October 22, 1866: "To Fifty-ninth Street this afternoon, traversing for the first time the newly opened section of Madison Avenue between Fortieth Street and the College, a rough and ragged track as yet, and hardly a thoroughfare, rich in mudholes, goats, pigs, geese, and stramonium." In the course of the next two years, Strong voiced particular concern about the rising cost of living and the fifty thousand unemployed in the city—"Should be helping them. But fine houses and social position use up all one's money, and more."

On the surface, New York had an air of recklessness. Beneath the glitter, however, it was barely metropolitan. Physically, the city of 1869 retained the character of a small town, an English cathedral town, or a French *ville de province,* as the novelist Edith Wharton suggested. Its population, which numbered almost 900,000, was still huddled at the lower end of the island. Almost two-thirds of the gridiron of streets laid down on the island as far north as 96th Street was empty except for scattered shantytowns and outlying inns, hotels, and country homes. Below 96th Street, it contained more than twenty-five thousand vacant lots. The tallest structures were church steeples, of which there were hundreds.

The most prominent one belonged to Trinity Church, Richard Upjohn's Gothic Revival structure at Broadway and Wall Street. When it was built in 1846, it was declared the first monument of the modern city. So it had stood, quite alone and uplifting, with few other monuments to even suggest new times or new aesthetics. There were some exotic architectural shapes in the streetscape—the Croton Reservoir, the massive truncated pyramid on the west side of Fifth Avenue between 40th and 42nd streets where the city stored its water supply; the new Harper Brothers Building and the Haughwout Building downtown, two incongruously elegant commercial structures constructed of cast iron. The A. T. Stewart Department Store, at Broadway and 9th Street, which was also built of cast iron, painted white, was a source of great civic pride. Stewart's private house was also a popular showcase, but it was considered a distinct oddity. Stewart, the largest landowner in the city after John Jacob Astor, had demolished a brownstone in order to erect a vast and heavily ornamented white marble mansion on the northwest corner of 34th Street and Fifth, decidedly north of the fashionable sector. It was a singular exception to the old rule of thumb about houses—the greater the wealth, the more the discretion. No one but Stewart had ever indulged in the frivolity of porticos and pillars and a private picture gallery. Other rich men were content with filling the interiors of their brownstones with fine furnishings and adding a stable, for a horse and carriage, nearby. The Stewart house was judged vulgar by architectural critics. Society dismissed it as ostentatious, although it was made a point of interest on Sunday strolls.

NEW YORK had been planned for single-family houses of regular dimensions, so it was no surprise that the cityscape was uniformly low and orderly. In 1811 newly appointed city commissioners had imposed a gridiron scheme on Manhattan, ruling the empty terrain from 14th Street to 155th Street into a rectilinear system of streets and avenues. It was designed for greater economy and convenience in building, and it had in effect ironed the kinks out of the topography. Only below 14th Street, where the city had taken form without the benefit of commissioners, was there a sense of the unruly natural contours of the island—the tidal estuaries and reefs, the ponds and swamps, and the ubiquitous outcropping of rock. Here, a maze of streets had grown along the random lines of the least resistance. Development had veered to the east to avoid the Collect Pond and its feeder streams in the middle of the island. Commerce had centered on the East River, which, as an arm of the sea, was not supposed to freeze.

In order to create a uniform surface, the commissioners filled in watercourses and leveled hills and ridges. (Second Avenue had been so precipitous that extra horses were always posted at the bottom of hills to help stagecoaches reach the top.) Then they laid out two-and-one-half times more east-west streets to accommodate the expected river-to-river traffic, and broader north-south avenues to serve as formal thoroughfares. Only Broadway was retained on a diagonal. Open land was reserved for a marketplace, a parade ground, a reservoir, and four square parks; the "eternal respite of the sea" was to counterbalance the meager allotment of green. Otherwise, blocks were subdivided into forty to sixty lots that uniformly measured twenty-five feet by one hundred feet.

The grid plan offered a regulating harmony to the city, as well as the infrastructure for real estate speculation. It also removed the opportunity for architectural drama and diversity. Seen through the grid plan, the city appeared to be caught, contained, and diffused behind fine netting or grating. And as it grew, as streets opened in northbound sequence and the little numbered lots began to fill with the only houses appropriate to such sites—narrow and deep, without recourse to alleys or courtyards, with explicit boundaries and a sense of enclosed space—the image was sustained. New York had a rational but uninspired orderliness, which was clearly stated in parallel rows of one-family row houses, solid, genteel, and unprepossessing.

Montgomery Schuyler, a nineteenth-century architectural critic, pronounced the commissioners "unconscious vandals" for what they had stolen from the city to come. Edith Wharton too, in her novels about the nineteenth-century New York, decried the "straight up-and-downness" of the city, the monotony of its endless rows of brownstones, the ennui of a town without towers or perspectives. Yet this landscape suited New York of the 1870s, and the predictable patterns of conventional houses reflected the upper classes accurately. Mrs. Wharton, who was seven years old when the Stuyvesant was built, had grown up in a brownstone on West 23rd Street, and she knew the well-to-do quarters around Irving Place, Stuyvesant Square, and lower Fifth Avenue well. An old-line aristocrat, née Jones, she had a clear idea of how faithfully houses, decoration, modes of speech and dress all expressed society's concern with respectability; of how, in a way, a proper home was no different from a gardenia in the lapel or a calling card. Even in New York, where the social world was changing as new fortunes sprang up and a new breed of fashionable commercial people came onto the scene, the stablest and most influential portion of society was still a tightly knit tribe of first families, bearing old Dutch and English names like Schermerhorn, Van Rensselaer, Rhinelander, and Jones. This narrow aristocracy—perhaps the only aristocracy New York has ever known—staunchly upheld a traditional code of values in which morals and manners mattered more than money and imagination, and decency outdistanced display. These families' pieties filtered down through the social pyramid, and while the age was decorous—even gaudy—its proprieties were firm and circumscribed behavior.

It was the Age of Innocence, as Mrs. Wharton titled a novel about the time, a phrase that has stuck with historians and come to stand for the postwar era when Old New York was still able to maintain its traditions in the face of change. The world of fashion was still conservative and conventional; scandal was to be dreaded, and innovation had dangerous overtones. This all showed in the attitude toward housing. In 1870, when Mrs. Isaac Jones, Wharton's aunt, built herself a large white marble Empire house in lonely isolation on Fifth Avenue between 57th and 58th Streets, she astonished her set, for "brown sandstone seemed as much the only wear as a frock coat in the afternoon."

In a fictional treatment of this real-life move, a character named Mrs. Mingott, who was based on Mrs. Jones, further insulted New York's sense of propriety. Heavy with flesh, and unable to climb stairs, she established herself comfortably on the ground floor of her new house, where the view from her sitting room caught the vista of her bedroom, her huge low sofa bed, her lacy toilet table and gilt-framed mirror. "Her visitors were startled and fascinated by the foreignness of this arrangement," Mrs. Wharton reported, for it "recalled scenes in French fiction, and architectural incentives to immorality such as the simple American had never dreamed of. That was how women with lovers lived in the wicked old societies, in apartments with all the rooms on one floor, and all the indecent propinquities that their novels described."

That it could be a stage set for adultery was one of the challenges the apartment house had to face. While Europe was full of apartment houses, New York was still provincial in its attitudes, still rooted in small-town agrarian traditions. There were few established cultural institutions in the city to elevate thinking—the Astor Library had been completed in 1858, but it was small and gentlemanly; the Metropolitan Museum of Art was organized in 1870, but its permanent home in Central Park was not fixed for a decade—and few established canons of taste to rely on. Artists and writers talked of the need to develop the arts, to find new modes of expression appropriate to the political and social conditions of the young nation. Artistic people were regarded warily, however, as if their ideas might be decadent. "Good" society was probably the least intellectually adventuresome of all the classes, for it was very homogeneous, and it had a vested interest in the status quo. Life had changed little in the domestic pieties over the course of the century. Members of society met one another every day, on promenades or at parties. They dined punctually at seven, to allow time for after-dinner calls. They talked about "pleasant" things.

Outside this citadel, the air was less rarefied. In the late 1860s, according to George Templeton Strong, "burglaries, highway robberies, and murders—have been of late many and audacious beyond example." Brothels and saloons existed in such numbers that preachers took to the pulpit to decry the decline of morality. The "foreign element," as guidebooks discreetly referred to the heterogeneity of language, custom, and costume introduced by immigration, was more and more conspicuous. New York was a study in contrasts, as a popular 1872 book titled *Lights and Shadows of New York* had illustrated for those who did not know all its dimensions firsthand. Low life annotated the high life, tenements and sweatshops and homeless children served to counterpoint cotillions and gentlemen's clubs and jeweled combs. Tenements had been introduced in the city in the 1830s, with the first waves of immigration. Since 1865 more than a million homeless people had arrived in New York, and tenements had spread over vacant lots on the Lower East Side like weeds. Cheap, hasty, barracks-like constructions without adequate light, air, or sanitation, they invited overcrowding, filth, and general misery, and soon became slums.

To many people, this underbelly of violence, depravity, and poverty only confirmed their inherent feelings about cities. An anti-urban bias was as American as Thomas Jefferson. Writing in *Notes on the State of Virginia,* he said, "I view great cities as pestilential to the morals, the health, and the liberties of man. True, they nourish some of the elegant arts, but the useful ones can thrive elsewhere, and less perfection in the others, with more health, virtue, and freedom, would be my choice." Throughout the nineteenth century, as the industrial revolution began to take effect and towns grew bigger and noisier, writers like Emerson, Thoreau, Melville, Hawthorne, and Poe—American's pre-eminent voices—also painted cities as negative forces. "Cities force growth and make men talkative and entertaining, but they make them artificial," Emerson wrote in an essay titled "Farming." "In cities, families rise and burst like bubbles in a vat," Melville, who had grown up poor in New York, admonished in "Pierre." Only Walt Whitman, whose *Leaves of Grass* was banned for its passion and free expression, celebrated the city in all its lowly glories, the street life, the flow of humanity, good and bad.

To the conventional New Yorker, the postbellum scene was bewildering and disorienting. The term "wicked city" came into the argot of the 1870s. And as crass politicians, big-time gamblers, and shortsighted industrialists claimed the spotlight, the upper classes retreated into private worlds that received little sustenance from the real city around them. While the scourge of war and public corruption had shaken confidence and shattered ideals, the continuum of established traditions offered security, the established codes of behavior the integrity that came with minding one's manners. The home assumed great importance in these times; it was the stronghold of tradition, where the household gods were kept safe and sacred.

A painting by Eastman Johnson provides a glimpse into the snug interior of a typical well-to-do house of this time. It is a family portrait, commissioned in 1871 by Alfred Smith Hatch, who was president of the New York Stock Exchange, and lived at Park Avenue and 37th Street. Parents, in-laws, and eleven children pose informally about an ornate Victorian table and a marble fireplace in the parlor of their home. Small children with toys sit on the floor in the foreground, while behind them Mr. Hatch poses at a desk, his father reads a newspaper, and his mother-in-law knits. The room is wide and high and implies the presence of other such rooms, sedate and opulent. The carpet is thick, and the fringed and swagged draperies are heavy, admitting only a narrow vista of a neighboring house, presumably similar. Repose, even languor, hangs over the scene; there is a sense of well-being, security, position, and permanence. On the countenances of the family lie calm, confidence, and perhaps a touch of arrogance or ennui.

2

Richard Morris Hunt

I T WAS to this city of expanding new energies and restraining old forces that the architect Richard Morris Hunt brought the apartment house in 1869. Hunt had been drawn to New York by its vitality and its sense of promise. As the nation's largest, wealthiest, and most cosmopolitan city, it was the obvious ground to do his work. The first American to study architecture at the Ecole des Beaux-Arts in Paris, Hunt had arrived in New York in 1855 like an ambassador of the arts, with a mission. "It has been represented to me that America is not ready for the Fine Arts, but I think they are mistaken," he had written in a Christmas letter to his mother before his return. "There is no place in the world where they are more needed or where they should be encouraged."

At the age of twenty-seven, Hunt had training and education such as no American had ever enjoyed. The United States did not have an institution for training architects until the Massachusetts Institute of Technology opened its doors in 1868, and until Hunt forged the way abroad, an aspirant learned his profession through an informal system of apprenticeship. By contrast, the Ecole des Beaux-Arts, which traced its origins to the seventeenth century and its ideals to Roman antiquity, was the most prestigious and competitive training ground in Europe. Physically, it was a romantic, hallowed sort of place, occupying the site of a medieval cloister just off the Left Bank of the Seine, and embracing an array of buildings, portals, courtyards, and architectural fragments rich in historical significance. Its curriculum was divided between academic study in the classroom, where a distinguished faculty lectured on architectural history and theory, and design competitions, which were carried out primarily in a private atelier under the supervision of a successful architect. Hunt had joined the atelier of Hector Martin Lefuel, who in 1854 was appointed architect to the new emperor, Napoleon III.

Beyond his formal education, Hunt also had the enlightenment of a decade at large in Paris, and—with frequent lengthy forays accompanied by his brother William to the south, into Italy and the Mediterranean, his sketchbook recording everything of interest—over much of continental Europe. "If other countries teach you as France has taught you," Lefuel had told his young protégé, "you will do great things." The years in France had a profound effect on a youth who was fifteen years old when his mother packed the family off to Europe, and eighteen when he entered the Ecole des Beaux-Arts. It was a remarkable time to be *en scène,* a time when he could partake of the mellow Old World, a vainglorious New World, and the process of change that tied them together.

Upon his arrival in the 1840s, Paris had been a pre-eminently medieval city of narrow twisting streets, of ancient palaces and churches, of lofty old houses, crowded apartments, and tenements, all packed colorfully but uncomfortably behind its ring of fortified walls. By the end of the decade, however, major architectural projects were altering the face of the city—the building of the Bibliothèque Ste-Geneviève, the Gare Montparnasse, and the Gare de l'Est, and the decoration of the Place de la Concorde, the Champs-Elysées, and the Place de l'Etoile. Then in the fifties, Louis Napoleon (Napoleon III) and his zealot master sergeant, Baron Georges Haussmann, the prefect of the Department of the Seine, embarked on a plan to rebuild the city, or in Haussmann's words, "to make a capital of Paris." In a seventeen-year program that essentially extinguished medieval Paris, Haussmann tore down the city walls, opened the clogged grid with long new avenues, planted them with architectural masterworks—the new Opéra, the Bibliothèque Nationale, Les Halles, the central markets, a completed Louvre—and filled the spaces in between monuments with hundreds of fine apartment buildings.

The scale of change was truly impressive, and by the end of the Second Empire Paris would realize Napoleon III's vision of a great imperial city. As a young man, Louis Napoleon had expressed his great desire to be like the emperor Augustus, who had turned Rome into a city of marble, and to reclaim for Paris the splendor and glory of the days of his uncle, Napoleon I. This massive endeavor, which also embraced new schools, hospitals, railway stations, parks, bridges, aqueducts, and an elaborate sewer system, resulted in the creation of a great modern city, for half a century the model for urban planners around the world. It made of Paris a splendid unity. The city flowed down its grand, wide boulevards and celebrated at its important plazas; its population was lodged in the long stands of apartment buildings along the way like attendants to a great parade. The apartment buildings themselves gave the city a harmony, for their facades had been matched with older elements on the street, their height limited according to the width of the street, and their decoration—gilded iron railings, carved caryatids, consoles and crowning medals—made uniform. The Second Empire, in the end, provided Paris with its lasting image—a city that was elegant, ornamental, and monumental, and also livable, pleasurable, and popular. "Paris now had the space to look at herself and see that she was no longer a village clustered about a few grandiose palaces, nor merely a city of bustling commerce and exchange. She had become a stage, a vast theater for herself, and all the world."

Hunt was not only a witness to the transformation of Paris but also a contributing party. For at the conclusion of his formal studies, his patron, Lefuel, newly elevated to imperial architect and engaged in the extension and completion of the Louvre Palace, made him an *inspecteur des travaux* and assigned him the design of the facade of the Pavillon de la Bibliothèque, opposite the Palais-Royal. It was practical training in the French school of academic architecture, and firsthand involvement in one of the great building projects of the nineteenth century. During his first decade in New York, Hunt made several lengthy pleasure trips back to Paris and kept up with the work in the city and his old colleagues.

It was on the strength of his work in France and his familiarity with France that Hunt won his first large commission in New York. The Studio Building, erected in 1857 at 15 West 10th Street, showed where the architect had been and also where he was going. In addition, it introduced a type of building that was, in essence, a precedent for the apartment house. Modeled on French ateliers, the Studio Building (also known as the Tenth Street Studios) was built specifically for artists, and combined studios and gallery space with living quarters in an arrangement that imitated the apartment hotel, the duplex apartment, and the courtyard buildings of the future. The ornamental brick and stonework

Richard Morris Hunt's Tenth Street Studio Building was designed specifically for artists, but it later would inspire studio apartments.

building was planned in the form of a hollow square, with a domed, skylighted two-story exhibition room placed at center like a courtyard, and surrounded by three floors of large and lofty studios, many with adjoining bedrooms at half-level. With serious and elegant workrooms, cheap and convenient domestic accommodation, and a built-in social aspect—the doors connecting studios could open to provide a flowing space for the gala receptions and open houses that soon characterized life within—the building was an immediate success and filled quickly with the amazing nucleus of New York's art world. Hunt was held in great esteem by painters like John La Farge, Frederic Church, Albert Bierstadt, Eastman Johnson, and Winslow Homer, who were grateful for their congenial new quarters. Hunt was closely identified with his building in the public mind, for he established his own studio and office there.

Settled in amidst the rich clutter of architectural volumes, photographs, and relics he had amassed in Europe, Hunt produced a variety of commissioned buildings—Second Empire and neo-Grec city houses, picturesque Newport "cottages," commercial and public buildings that encouraged a new urban style. By the very nature of his training, Hunt was an urbanist. The Beaux-Arts tradition tied architecture to city planning, for in its philosophy, the greatest architectural achievement was not a single building but a complex of buildings. Hunt had returned home with a vision of the city that had not existed in America.

Hunt also organized an atelier in which he offered architectural instruction based on the Beaux-Arts tradition. His students, who included Henry Van Brunt, George B. Post, Frank Furness, and William R. Ware, were inspired by both his teaching and his example, for he opened up a whole new realm of experience to them. He believed in the art of composition and the ability of the architect to create and enhance the sense of place. He demanded order and discipline, and amidst the general confusion of contemporary American building practices, he offered a firm new sense of direction. His students would subsequently make important contributions to American architecture— William Ware would organize and direct the first professional architecture school in the country at M.I.T. and the department of architecture at Columbia University—and through them, Hunt would influence the course of architecture and architectural education in the United States.

A coincidental meeting with Rutherfurd Stuyvesant in Paris lay directly behind Hunt's commission for the Stuyvesant Apartments. Both Hunt and Stuyvesant were familiar with the French apartment house and both thought the form might satisfy American housing needs and enhance the immature urban landscape of New York. Apartment houses in France, particularly those built by Haussmann, represented a refinement of the private house, and they provided a very satisfactory and sophisticated form of city living. Haussmann's apartment houses were elegant affairs, generously articulated private spaces within, dignified imperial structures without. They also had a signal importance in the city's plan. Physically, the long stands of authoritative buildings defined the shape of the city, both uniting and dividing its space. Spiritually, they symbolized the comfortable urbanism of Parisians who lived together but separately, *chez soi* and *en ville*.

In contrast to New York, however, apartment living was not new in France or indeed in most of Europe. In Europe, the tradition of communal living was as ancient as prehistoric man. The nomenclature had cropped up with the *appartimenta*—from the Latin verb *partire,* to divide or to share—of the great cities of the Roman Empire. Faced with a population growing apace with the prosperity of the first centuries after Christ, the city planners of Rome erected thousands of multiple dwellings called *insulae,* or islands—at the height of the empire, some 46,000 *insulae* against 1,800 *domus,* or private houses—so many in fact that the orator Aelius Aristides calculated that if the dwellings of the city were reduced to one story they would reach Hadria on the upper Adriatic. Cicero spoke of his city borne aloft on the tiers of its apartments.

Typically three or four stories tall, but occasionally six, seven, or eight (a giant apartment house, called the Insula di Felicula, was one of the great sights of the city, rivaling the Pantheon and the Columns of Marcus Aurelius for crowds, who came to contemplate its fall), the *insulae* housed both patricians and plebians in a comfortable melee. Elegant buildings like the Casa dei di Pinti—six stories, duplex living room and dining room, balcony overlooking formal gardens, the whole awash with light and air from oversized windows (built in Ostia in A.D. 127)—stood side by side with simpler dwellings, each a maze of suites of small unparticulated rooms up flights of stairs above street shops. Sometimes a single framework housed different classes in closer proximity, with a gilt-ceilinged domus on the ground floor and humble quarters overhead. Building facades were commonly picturesque, relieved by a variety of balconies or loggias entwined with climbing plants or, as at the luxurious Casa dei di Pinti, "the House of Paintings," decorated with tiles and mosaics and tinted with color. Water carriers, porters, and sweepers were attached to each apartment house. Heat and sanitation were insufficient, and construction faulty, however, and according to the lamentations in Roman literature, a tenant lived in constant fear of fire and the imminent collapse of his home. When Livy told of the ox from market that had scaled the stairs of an insula and thrown itself off the roof, he was presumably pointing out the contradictions in tall buildings in an old-fashioned city.

Over the early course of Western European history, the upper classes established patterns of living together, of sharing a general space according to the social conditions of their times. In the Middle Ages, they inhabited the feudal castle, which sheltered an extended community from armed attack and social isolation. During the Renaissance, when life became more secure, royalty abandoned the rugged regime of the castle and returned instinctively to the Roman ideal of civic life. In Italy palaces like the Farnese and the Vatican were built like covered forums, with courtyards, public galleries, and private apartments reserved for the royal family and for those in attendance. French royalty in turn imitated these models with the Luxembourg, Tuileries, and Louvre palaces. Behind this architecture was an incipient urbanism, a tacit understanding that private life must be organized with a view to public duties and diversions, and to the very spectacle of public life.

The supreme example of this architecture was the Palace of Versailles, which Louis XIV had envisioned as the nucleus from which his power would radiate. In 1682, long before his plans for the site were fully realized, Louis invited his then itinerant court and government to live at Versailles, intending to mold the monarchy and aristocracy into the framework of Versailles and, not incidentally, to gather any stray rebellious elements of the nobility under his wing. The king's state apartments occupied the exact center of the palace and comprised fifteen chambers, including the salons used for consultations and receptions. (Three times a week, Louis offered a ceremony of music and games he called *une appartemente*.) They were decorated sumptuously and arranged in a long string, or enfilade, of spaces that followed, one upon another, without any particular pattern. North and south of this hub stretched two great wings of three stories that contained other suites of apartments, with those on the ground and first floors, overlooking the courtyards and gardens, allotted to the queen and family members designated the Princes of the Blood. Above ran a dismal labyrinth of small rooms, staircases, kitchens, and entresols to which the nobility flocked, willing to endure cramped quarters and discomforts if only to share in the pageant of court life. Madame de Staal, the lady-in-waiting to the Duchess of Maine, recalled, "I was astonished at seeing the dwelling-place assigned me. It was an *entresol,* so low and dark that I had to stoop when I walked, and feel my way about. One couldn't breathe for want of air, or warm oneself for lack of a fireplace. . . . We had only one garde-robe between four of us. . . . I used to shut myself up in my 'cave' and console myself by reading." Versailles grew larger as the empire reached its height, and by 1710 it held 226 dwellings, twice as many single rooms, and some 10,000 people in residence.

The palace was itself a small rarefied city. It was also an early and extravagant example of an apartment house, which would inspire the apartment houses in Haussmann's Paris at least indirectly. In fact, the baroque court influenced many aspects and institutions of modern urban life. As the aristocracy of Paris aped the manners and amusements of royalty, so they built their private mansions like scaled-down versions of the palace. These *hôtels particuliers* were centered on courtyards and organized in an enfilade of chambers and antechambers—rich, lofty rooms on the *étage noble* and smaller, more modest ones on the floors above. (The *étage noble* was the *premier étage,* which Americans think of as the second floor. The first floor, or ground floor, which housed only the concierge, was called the *rez-de-chaussée.*) In the eighteenth and nineteenth centuries, when the tide of fashion swept the nobility into other quarters of the city, their *hôtels* were divided up into apartments for other classes, who arranged themselves within according to their station in life, prosperous to poor, in a vertical order.

By the time of the Second Empire, a variety of new apartment houses had been introduced in the effort to contain Paris's exploding population. Haussmann, however, institutionalized the palatial example that had evolved on the street, for it was still the best example at hand. Like the old *hôtels particuliers,* his apartment buildings, called *immeubles* or *maisons de rapport,* opened through prominent carriageways onto inner courtyards with stables and gardens. Six or seven stories high, they were arranged into large apartments of six or seven rooms and a large entrance

OPPOSITE: The Stuyvesant, at 142 East 18th Street, was seen as a small historic event by the city's chroniclers. Neighbors who ventured inside the building found the lobby dark, the mahogany staircase grand, and the number of wood-burning fireplaces impressive.

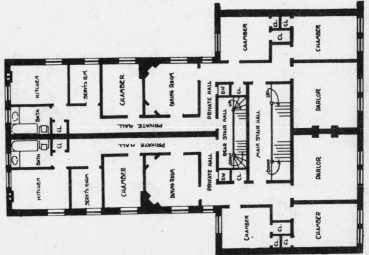

gallery on the *premier étage,* with smaller apartments of three to five rooms above; maid's rooms were tucked under the roof. Sometimes an extra story was provided by the addition of a mansard roof with dormer windows, where rooms modest in rent and generous in light were commonly let to artists.

While he was a student at the Ecole des Beaux-Arts, Hunt had lived in a converted *maison de rapport* at 1, rue Jacob. He had incorporated its basic shape into the Tenth Street Studios. Judging from preliminary drawings, he had considered using this form for the Stuyvesant Apartments too, but had rejected it for practical design reasons and because he was aware of the uncertain ground upon which he was treading. His friend and fellow architect Calvert Vaux had warned against it, noting that "American ladies . . . think it far more lively and cheerful to look out on a busy thoroughfare than on a monotonous quadrangle, however elegantly it may be decorated," and judging that courtyard apartments would be harder to rent. The Stuyvesant had a distinctly French presence, and was christened the first example in America of "French flats," but Hunt in fact had altered the French street model to suit New York as he saw it, and to make the apartment appealing to a society that resided in private single-family houses.

The Stuyvesant was a compromise between the mansarded brick-front row houses already existing in the city and Haussmann's *maisons de rapport.* While the Gothic details of its facade were probably inspired by recent work in Paris, its dominant lines conjured up a series of row houses that would keep happy company with the New York street scene. The interior layout of the building paid little heed to the established French hierarchy, although a space on the ground floor was reserved for a concierge, and the top floor was obviously meant for artists. Instead, it was divided into two wings, centered on a tiled Romanesque lobby, which held four equal-sized seven-room apartments per floor. Each apartment had a parlor and two chambers in the front, a dining room and a third chamber issuing off a long hallway that led to a kitchen, a maid's room, and a bath in the back. Each apartment had ample light, well-proportioned rooms, two wood-burning fireplaces (including one in the big square kitchen), a dumbwaiter, one water closet, and was served by front and back stairs.

3

THE TRADITION
OF HOUSES

THE LABEL "French flats," which the Stuyvesant wore, left no question in the public mind about its foreign ancestry. It was an exotic label, meant, perhaps, to capitalize on the undeniable allure of things French at the time. Since the 1850s, New York had been tentatively trying on French style; a few new houses sported mansard roofs, a few new banks and hotels Empire facades. Dinner entrees carried French names. Society women followed the lives of Napoleon III and Princess Eugénie, and showed off "the Josephine look." When Anthony Trollope visited New York in 1860–61, he had marveled at the taste for French conversation and French comforts, and ventured a guess that French art was next. The growing affection for Second Empire ornamentation was very different from one for shared housing, however. In a deeper vein of thinking, French flats was an unfortunate label—*flats* with its spare and homely image, and *French* awaking puritanical suspicions about debauched European cultures—and it could only serve to feed the ready hostility to these new structures. As it happened, as long as the label stuck, the apartment house made little headway with a society still centered in its traditions in the English mother country and still feeling the hereditary instincts for a private house.

The settlers of America had brought with them the tradition of the private house and the notion that no one above the laboring class should share the roof over his head. There was little in the short history of the country to challenge this notion. The fact that ancient Indians had built

25

sophisticated communal houses—the ruins of one of the great houses of the Anasazi Indians had been discovered in Chaco Canyon in 1849—or that the immigrant poor lived in tenement houses on the Lower East Side, did not offer valid precedents. From this perspective, an upper-class apartment house was in fact a revolutionary notion, renouncing principles engrained in the American way of life.

The first tenants of the Stuyvesant were by nature and by need an adventuresome lot. They were fashionable young couples, like Mr. and Mrs. Burton Harrison, and solitary women, like the mother of Edwin Booth, who lived nearby on Gramercy Park. General Custer's young widow moved into the building after the battle of Little Bighorn, in 1876. These people found in the small concentrated residences practical solutions to their respective stations in life. Most of them were friends or relatives of Stuyvesant himself, and the list produced "a very old Knickerbocker sort of effect upon the outside mind," Mrs. Harrison noted, wondering at the number of "people one knows" who lived in the building. For Mrs. Harrison, it was a charming first home—with children came a move to a house on Gramercy Park. She delighted in "the simple quarters," but she also took care to call it an "apartment," thinking that "flat" had a vulgar sound.

Mrs. Harrison belonged to a lively and progressive young set that was caught up in the first emanations of "a city of wondrous progress" and that did not regret the passing of "odd, provincial, pleasant little old New York." Although she was by birth and breeding a gentlewoman (Thomas Jefferson was a great-grand uncle), she was critical of the posturing ways of the old guard. Her commitment to a richer and more "broad-visioned" urban culture was evident in her various musical, theatrical, and charitable activities. She also wrote essays, stories, and novels about New York life. Later in her career, she would contribute an important chapter to a history of New York and write *The Anglomaniacs,* a comic portrait of America's social climbers, which was the succès fou of 1890.

As Rutherfurd Stuyvesant's impeccable social credentials attracted tenants, so Richard Hunt's reputation as the architect of the Tenth Street Studios preceded him, and the Stuyvesant Apartments also drew a conspicuous number of artistic and literary people. A disdainful establishment would explain that these were people who were notoriously indifferent to the conventions of society anyway. However respectable, they had odd ways and had always seemed to prefer to keep to themselves, to dwell in unfashionable quarters of the city in Greenwich Village and Chelsea, in neighborhoods of "dressmakers, bird-stuffers, and people who wrote." "These scattered fragments of humanity had never shown any desire to be amalgamated with the social structure," a matriarch in *The Age of Innocence* concluded rather wistfully; they stood beyond the rule of old New York society.

Among those who quickly signed leases in the building were the painter Worthington Whittredge, the writer Bayard Taylor, Col. W. C. Church, editor of the magazine *The Galaxy,* the publisher G. P. Putnam, and the architect Calvert Vaux—a highly respectable and rather impressive assembly of "bohemians." The gracious accommodations and the fine appointments—the high ceilings and brass doorknobs and mahogany staircases—when combined with the reasonable rents, were responsible for their early allegiance to the apartment house. But their practicality was visionary too, for their independence of mind placed them on the cutting edge of a new society. It was characteristic of this group of inadvertent urban pioneers that many of them were also actively engaged in promoting social change in their professional lives. Taylor's novels, peppered with satire, were critiques of nineteenth-century life. Church, in *The Galaxy,* published an impassioned series of lectures advocating apartment living.

It was particularly appropriate that Calvert Vaux took up residence in the Stuyvesant, for more than a decade earlier he had introduced the idea of apartment houses into the New York architectural consciousness. In June of 1857, in a paper concerned with "The Adaption of Houses à la Française to This Country," he had lectured the members of the newly revived American Institute of Architects on the advantages of the "Continental Plan of Housing" and even proposed specific designs for use in New York. The structures should be no more than four stories high, he explained. "Two or three flights of easy stairs may be readily surmounted and the freedom from dust and noise obtained by those who might live in the third or fourth stories would be found to compensate, in a great measure, for the trouble of traversing an extra flight or two of stairs; and thus people of about the same standing in society could, in all probability, be readily induced to occupy comfortable apartments as high as the fourth floor." (Higher and cheaper rooms would attract a lower class of tenants, which would, "in all probability, be thought very disagreeable in an American city.") Furthermore, they required large frontage, with flats facing the street; an attractive entrance; and a majestic staircase. "To be suitable to New York needs, the public staircase, which is the unusual feature to which we have to be accustomed, must be made light, airy, and elegant, and if possible, lighter, airier, and more elegant than other parts of the house, or a prejudice will be likely to be excited on entering the premises against the whole effect, and this it is all-important to avoid."

Vaux, with all his "probabilities," had been wary of the popular response to the "Continental Plan," which, up to this time, had been confined to "the inadequate shape known as tenement houses." But he had charged his fellow architects to respond creatively to the unsatisfactory state of housing in the city, pointing out that the existing alternatives were smaller houses on smaller lots (where people would "live, as it were, on a ladder"), residential hotels or boardinghouses ("distasteful as a permanent thing to heads of families, who have any taste for genuine home comforts"), or suburban residences.

Vaux was familiar to all New Yorkers as the co-author, with the landscape architect Frederick Law Olmsted, of the great "people's park" taking shape on the ragged terrain above 59th Street. In his principles, his ambitions, and his zeal, he was typical of a new generation of architects who were attempting to forge architecture into a valid and respectable profession. With a public that barely differentiated between an architect and a carpenter, with no common training or body of thought and ethics or community of interest, the architect in mid-nineteenth-century America held an uncertain position. The AIA had been duly founded in 1836 to work for improvement in architectural education and to enhance the perception of the profession—in the words of Alexander Jackson Davis, its first chairman, "for the proper appreciation of this noble art." But the fledging professional society—with members like James Renwick, Leo Eidlitz, Detlef Lienau, Joseph C. Wells, Richard Upjohn, and Henry Van Brunt, each with a sustained vision of the needs and possibilities of the profession and of the city—had made little progress toward its goals.

Looking back on the period between 1850 and 1875, most New York historians have agreed that the architecture of that time was the most tasteless and least aesthetically successful in American history. Noting the medley of historical styles on the street, some critics have deemed it "eclectic." Others have seen a lack of coherence, imagination, utility, and anything resembling the expression of a national style. Lewis Mumford delivered his appraisal full force: "When the Civil War broke, architecture in America had been sinking steadily for a generation. Order, fitness, comeliness, proportion, were words that could no longer be applied to it, construction was submerged in that morass of jerry-building, tedious archaeicism, and spurious romanticism that made up the architectural achievement of the 19th century. . . ." He concluded, "Looking back over the previous hundred years to the time when there was but one professional architect in the whole country, one might have made the generalization that, as the number of architects increased, the number of satisfactory buildings had proportionately diminished. The generalization might be misleading; but the facts were indisputable. Architecture, on the downgrade since the twenties, had by 1860, touched bottom."

This indictment appeared in a book called *The Brown Decades,* which was named for the prevalent color of the time—brown was the color of a growing industrial society, Mumford said, the color of mourning for Abraham Lincoln, the color of frock coats and row houses. Surveying the art and architecture of late-nineteenth-century America, Mumford singled out the state of housing in New York as a particular concern. Partly under the pressure of higher land values, the rooms in city houses were becoming narrower, he noted, and the interiors dark and airless, sometimes three and four rooms deep on lower floors. Even the upper classes were "gaily and rapidly building slums of their own, with almost as little concern for their hygiene as they showed in their tenement properties." Vaux had sounded the same cry, and in 1865, the *New York Times* had written that New York furnished the worst place of residence of any city in America.

Despite a superficial complacency, few people other than the very wealthy were in fact satisfied with their domestic situations. George Templeton Strong grumbled about the cost of keeping up his home. Others perceived that beauty existed only in one's visible possessions. Edith Wharton found the brownstone in which she grew up so grim, so monotonous and oppressive that she took artistic vengeance in writing *The Decoration of Houses,* a book on house aesthetics. In it, she bemoaned the estrangement between architecture and decoration that turned nineteenth-century houses into stuffy labyrinths of upholstery and bric-a-brac, citadels of cheerless domestic ritual and outworn taste. Built almost exclusively on speculation, New York houses were designed to a general taste that suited no one in particular. As a result, many households inhabited them like hermit crabs in other creatures' shells, adapting their lives to dwellings that didn't quite fit. The rigidity of the standard New York plot dictated an awkward stratification—the dark cellar floor, the ceremonial and rarely used parlor floor, the distant bedrooms—and a rigorously vertical living, which created an undesirable dependence on servants. Increasingly, the upper middle class was pinched by the cost of maintaining the basic requirements: cook, chambermaid, children's nurse, carriage, and summer home. In quest of greater economy, a more graceful fit, or merely a more fashionable address, those who did not own their houses moved—hopefully, haplessly, and as predictably as the arrival of the first day of May.

Thousands of New Yorkers changed households on May 1, the sanctioned moving date since Dutch days. In 1859, *Harper's Weekly* published a satirical drawing called "May-Day," showing medieval bedlam in the streets, and commented, "It has long been an axiom that food and rest are out of the question on May-Day in this city. Every one is moving; no one has a house; every one is miserable except the licensed cartmen, who are in their seventh heaven, and make $25 a day easily at this season." Mrs. Frances Trollope, who had spent four years observing American life, chose this event to describe for the curious citizens of the mother country in her *Domestic Manners of the Americans*. "On the first of May the city of New York has the appearance of sending off a population flying from the plague, or of a town which has surrendered on condition of carrying away all their goods and chattels. Rich furniture and ragged furniture, carts, waggons, and drays, ropes, canvas, and straw, packers, porters, and draymen, white, yellow, and black, occupy the streets from east to west, from north to south, on this day. Every one I spoke to on the subject complained of this custom as the most annoying, but all assured me it was unavoidable, if you inhabit a rented house."

To many observers, the restlessness and rootlessness of city people indicated a readiness for change. The apartment house was perceived as a possible solution to their ills. Although it was an old European way of life, many New Yorkers saw it as a vision of the future. It was in fact a form of city planning based on a concept of New York larger than a series of separate households, of its urban life as more interlocking than isolating. Behind its broader mass was the intent to serve a community of interests; if there were compromises embodied in a single public staircase, there was, in the same staircase, the promise of a new sociality.

Few architectural forms had been generated in New York suitable to an urban setting. There were several groups of houses in the landscape, however, that suggested a more cohesive view of urban living. In Colonnade Row, on Lafayette Street, nine single houses had been made into an architectural ensemble by adding an arcade of Corinthian columns on the street. On West 23rd Street, Alexander Jackson Davis had designed a long suite of houses—called London Terrace, for its resemblance to residential squares in England—which were also uniformly pilastered to effect the splendid unity of a colonnade. Uptown, in an even bolder departure from the norm, in 1856 Davis had designed the House of Mansions, on Fifth Avenue between 41st and 42nd streets, which gave eleven self-contained row houses the appearance of a grand turreted fortress.

In nonresidential areas of the city, a discerning eye could identify a more forthright expression of the new public conviviality. In Central Park, where by 1870 the first phase of building was nearing completion, all classes of society met in a vast spectacle of pleasure and sport. As many as twenty thousand people skated on the lake on a winter evening; forty thousand people regularly attended the band concerts in summer. Both the success of the department store and the emergence of the hotel as a fashionable watering place were early manifestations of a public culture created expressly by city conditions. In both institutions one could detect, along with a vibrant new sort of social energy, a certain blurring of the old republic distinctions between proper and improper behavior.

A shopping spree at A. T. Stewart's, for example, was one of the few occasions when a respectable woman could venture forth unaccompanied. A Fifth Avenue matron lunched in the tearoom in the company of strange men and women, rubbed shoulders with all ranks of society, and shared with them a common interest in the merchandise on display. Shopping was a classless activity. The promise of the better life represented by the bazaar of goods was accessible to all; everyone paraded as equals and shared an illusion of luxury. For a fleeting moment, the middle class identified with the upper crust, who in turn felt the clamor and color of communal activity. Shopping was a form of enlightenment, and also of emancipation for women, for it allowed the unencumbered enjoyment of what Henry James called the most "down-towney" aspects of the city.

A store like Stewart's embraced within its walls a novel form of downtown life. In a similar way, the large new luxury hotels that had

replaced the old inns on Madison Square, with their vast halls for promenading, lounging, and dining, fostered the communal activities that were flourishing within. At the opulent Fifth Avenue Hotel, considered too far uptown to succeed as anything but a summer resort when it was built between 23rd and 24th streets in 1859, a quaintly domestic social life was giving way to more flamboyant behavior. Although traditionalists continued to deplore the ostentation ("the tendency to live in herds, and the absence of a subdued and harmonious tone of life and

The House of Mansions looked romantic and unlikely in the company of stooped brownstones, even Levi Morton's at 42nd Street, which had a mansard roof, and a private ballroom. To the north are the new Temple Emanu-el and Ye Olde Willow Cottage.

manner") and warned against exposing women and children to the "demoralizing influence of public houses," the hotel had prospered from the start, inaugurating the era when Madison Square became the center of metropolitan public life. During and after the Civil War, prominent Republican politicians gathered at the hotel. Wall Street financiers met there after work. Public figures like Jay Gould, Christine Nilsson, and the Prince of Wales made late-night appearances. Society itself had taken to gathering in the resplendent public rooms for extravagant dinners and midnight suppers where they were seated at "family tables" that accommodated twenty or thirty.

Whereas eighteenth-century inns and early hotels had been conceived to provide food and shelter for travelers, the Fifth Avenue and all the hotels that were appearing on Broadway above Madison Square, and on Fifth Avenue as far north as the 40s, offered luxury and elegance as well. To a society with a growing fondness for gilt and glitter, there were glimmerings of status in the European silks, rosewood furniture, and crystal chandeliers that appointed the public rooms, and in the palatial marble structures themselves. Such settings conferred social dignity upon everyone present. They created a situation of make-believe, like playacting, that was intensified by their public character, the sense of collective experience built into the walls, the potential adventure of the present.

The private accommodations of the new New York hotels redefined transient living. They offered the settings of stately homes, rather than extemporized lodging, and the services attendant to such homes, magnified into public facilities. Paran Stevens, the owner of the Fifth Avenue Hotel, had initiated this transformation of standards, advertising more than one hundred suites of apartments, each combining the convenience and luxury of parlor, chambers, dressing and private bathing rooms with "a perpendicular railway intersecting each story." While the old "downtown" hotels like the Metropolitan and the St. Nicholas remained strictly "commercial," the Fifth Avenue Hotel, the Albermarle, the Hoffman House, the Clarendon (where the Grand Duke Alexis of Russia stayed during his visits), the Brunswick (which the aristocratic Coaching Club had made its social headquarters) were considered suitably and respectably "residential." Visiting royalty, international opera stars, and theatrical celebrities stayed in these establishments for weeks and sometimes months on end. To the dismay of the old-fashioned, a small number of New Yorkers of unquestionable gentility were also giving up conventional housekeeping to live in these colossal buildings, cities in themselves, won over by the grace, the space, and the convenience of their apartments.

4

FRENCH FLATS AND OTHER FIRST THOUGHTS

THE STUYVESANT Apartments remained alone in a landscape of houses for less than a year. In 1870, less than a half-mile to the south, an entrepreneur named Dr. David H. Haight rebuilt two fine houses at 15th Street and Fifth Avenue into a more refined rendition of a multiple dwelling. Taking advantage of the invention Elisha Otis had first publicly displayed at the Crystal Palace in 1852, Haight added a safety elevator for passengers as well as a general kitchen staffed by a first-class cook. Hunt's second apartment venture, designed for Paran Stevens, appeared that same year. The Stevens House, which was eight stories tall and occupied the whole block between Fifth Avenue and Broadway on 27th Street, was larger, bolder, and more patently Parisian than the Stuyvesant. It was oddly shaped, tall and very narrow on its avenues and broad on the cross street, which reflected the irregular pattern of the streets in the area but also recalled Haussmann's buildings in Paris. With its iron balconies and stone trim, a two-story mansard roof full of finial-topped, hipped pavilions, variously shaped dormers, and heavy chimneys, it looked more like one of the new crop of luxury hotels than a home, which suited hotelier Stevens. Its ground floor was given over to shops and a restaurant; there was a communal dining room and an elevator. The eighteen suites of apartments each contained a parlor, dining room, kitchen, butler's pantry, as many as five bedrooms, dressing rooms, and bathrooms; quarters for servants were tucked into the attic. All these innovations inflated the early prototype for the

apartment house into something quite grand. Even before its completion, the New York *Illustrated* judged that the Stevens House was "the
most truly picturesque architectural pile in the city." Other critics,
however, thought "it aimed to be chic," and, although admiring of its
"finely frescoed and harmoniously tinted" walls, were overwhelmed by
its "monster" size, which made it one of the largest buildings in the city.
The Stevens in fact suffered from its ambitions, as well as from the effects
of the financial panic of 1873, because in 1874 it was reconstructed as an
apartment hotel for bachelors, and then five years later revised into the
Victoria Hotel, serving the traveling public.

Like the Stuyvesant, the Haight House was an example of French
flats, which was the form that proved profitable in the 1870s and proliferated. By 1876, several hundred versions of French flats existed in New
York City, for the postwar years had ushered in an era of crazy speculation. In the nineteenth century, speculation in land was America's most
popular gamble, and apartment houses were surfacing as a promising
new outlet for capital investment. With John Jacob Astor and August
Belmont purchasing vacant lots in the wilderness around Central Park,
and with old downtown commercial buildings giving way to taller
restatements of themselves, enterprising builders saw good reason to try
out a form that would expedite the growth of the metropolis. It was
symptomatic of the heightened interest in building, and even architecture, that the *Real Estate Record and Builders' Guide,* a modest trade
weekly founded in 1868, grew steadily in size, circulation, and scope to
the point where in 1891 it would publish a seçond journal called the
Architectural Record. The *Real Estate Record* and the *American Architect and
Building News,* launched in 1876, kept tabs on the expanding cityscape.
Systematically, with registers of land sales, mortgages, and projected
buildings, as well as market reports on lathe, lime, and lumber, these
journals offered a running account of a city trying to break out of its
mold. From their detailed discussions of new buildings, their surveys,
censuses, essays on the state of architecture or rental markets, and frequent notes from foreign correspondents, a distinct new voice emerged.
It was the voice of the city in motion. It was eager, impatient, uncertain,
moralistic, idealistic, ambitious, full of hopes and worries.

From the beginning, the *Real Estate Record* had expressed allegiance
to a system of apartments, persuaded that it would play an important part
in the future of the city. But as it watched buildings poke up around
Ladies' Mile, the new shopping district that stretched from 18th Street

to 23rd on Broadway, and off Fifth Avenue up to 42nd Street, it also found no "beau ideal" among them to light the way. The 1870s was an era of experimentation, an era of first efforts, and inevitably, an era of irresolution. The number of French flats constructed, or reconstructed, from existing buildings staggered upward during the decade: after a temporary halt following the financial panic of '73, 112 appeared in 1875, 115 in 1876, 121 in the first half of 1879. But "French flats" was a term popularly used to describe any multiple dwelling that was not conspicuously working-class housing. Most of these buildings were hasty endeavors from the "slop-shop" of architecture, and they were deemed "improved tenements" or "plainer flats," and excluded from serious consideration by the self-appointed overseers of the new domestic architecture.

Although the tenement house provided the conceptual bridge between the private house and the apartment house, its association with lower-class living was a formidable obstacle to the success of the apartment house. Critics, however, had begun to perceive a hierarchy among multiple dwellings. They saw that the most expensive models of French flats were a class of buildings unto themselves. They spoke of them as "specialties" at first, and then, tentatively, usually employing a qualifying hyphen like a hedge against permanent status, they began to call them "apartment-houses." They put the Stuyvesant, the Haight House, and briefly, the Stevens House into this class and named them the noble exemplars, the models to study and perhaps to duplicate.

The Stuyvesant was notable for a "good plan" and "charming spaces." The Haight House was more elegant and had more service, which placed it midway between an apartment house and a family hotel in the public mind. Its appointments were lavish. The design was conceived to guarantee a tenant's security and privacy. Tucked under the grand black walnut staircase in the lobby, a porter's lodge had a view to all persons entering the building and was equipped with bells and speaking tubes to each apartment. Individual staircases led to each of the five suites of apartments per floor, which made them "entirely distinct from each other." Each was laid out with an antechamber, a parlor, and a dining room to seat eighteen (both with carved-wood mantelpieces), three main bedrooms (the master's with a marble bath), two servant's rooms, a kitchen, and a butler's pantry complete with a dumbwaiter to the basement, where the kitchen provided meals upon request. This last feature plus a house steam laundry promised to reduce the cost of housekeeping by a third. Providing both economy and comfort was an untried experiment in New York, the *New York Times* noted cautiously.

The top floor of the Haight House provided two- and three-room suites for bachelors. In the past, their lot had been cast with the boardinghouse, for there were few other choices outside home. During his visit to New York in 1867, Charles Dickens had commented that there were "300 boarding houses in West 14th Street, exactly alike, with 300 young men, exactly alike, sleeping in 300 bedrooms, exactly alike, with 300 dress suits, exactly alike, lying on so many chairs, exactly alike, beside the bed." A few years later, his words seemed to articulate new fears about apartment houses.

As artists and writers and an atelier full of eligible bachelors settled into its suites, the Haight House took on the air of an elegant clubhouse. It was only five stories tall and fit easily into the streetscape, but inside, it accommodated almost a hundred people. Appraising the building with an eye to the progress in domestic reform, *Scribner's Magazine* found its character appealing. "The internal history of this house neatly illustrates what promises to be a characteristic feature of New York life under the coming *régime*—that is, the clustering of particular social sets about particular centers. From the first, the Haight House has been the chosen refuge of artistic and literary people, who are able to find home, society, recreation—almost everything that serves to distinguish civilized life— without passing from under their own roof."

The Haight House had a Fifth Avenue address in addition to its other conspicuous assets, although its wide entrance was sited on 15th Street so that it did not intrude on the old-fashioned avenue. Only a few other early apartment houses would also be found on or near Fifth Avenue, for that was the fashionable quarter and it was effectively occupied. The elite Fifth Avenue corridor, which stretched from Sixth Avenue to Park Avenue in breadth, and from Washington Square to 59th Street in length, contained a mere handful of vacant lots below 42nd Street and, above it, only dozens where recently there had been hundreds. Resolutely, the well-to-do were staking out their territory, focusing in their exclusive and gregarious way on this one area of the city and leaving the rest in limbo. This practice effectively defined and determined the law of expensive growth in New York, the *Real Estate Record* noted. Given the number and the costliness of its new homes, "it is no wonder," it said, "that all eyes are turned to operations in this quarter as furnishing the concert pitch for the entire real estate symphony."

Society was "Fifth Avenue mad." Above 42nd Street, the broad cobblestone roadway, with its steady procession of carriages rattling to and from the park, had a ragged transitional look. It was not yet "the Avenue" about which New Yorkers spoke with casual hauteur, and yet the process of domestication had begun there too. Several new hotels, considered remote but refined, had broken into a landscape dominated by churches, five in all, as well as a splendid synagogue at 43rd Street, across the way from Boss Tweed's brownstone manor. At 50th Street, opposite a large and flourishing vegetable garden, St. Patrick's Cathedral was nearing completion; roofless and spireless, it was already a major monument, its Gothic Revival formality and morality almost too big and too important for the bland Manhattan grid.

Only a handful of private houses declared the area's residential capabilities explicitly. Millionaire Levi P. Morton, newly elected member of Congress, had bought the brownstone on the northeast corner of 42nd Street, which boasted one of the few private ballrooms in the city; in 1879, Edith Newbold Jones made her debut into society there, a situation her family considered far more discreet and decorous than the fashionable but ostentatious public room at Delmonico's, although it was still considered "uptown." (Later that same year, Morton, who objected to the presence of the reservoir across the street, decided to convert his property into a hotel or French flats.) Farther up the street, a large old-fashioned brownstone at 54th Street belonged to Mme Restell, the wealthy abortionist, who had refused to be dislodged from her home. At 55th Street, across from St. Luke's Hospital, there was a block-long terrace of Empire row houses designed by Detlef Lienau, a distinguished Danish-born architect who, like Hunt, had studied in Paris and then transplanted the classic French forms he loved to this country. (It was Lienau who, in 1852, had provided the first example of a Second Empire town house for the city, which duly launched both the mansard roof and a wave of Francomania.) Two blocks beyond that, a second row of attached houses with a marble face and mansard roof virtually duplicated the first.

Both the Colford Jones Row and Marble Row, as these blocks were known, had a monumentality that reminded those who had been abroad of the streets of Paris. Lienau had in fact modeled his design for the former on the French apartment house, even though inside, it provided eight separate and proper dwellings for various members of the Colford Jones family. Marble Row, designed earlier by Robert Mook, also had

A view from Madison Avenue and 55th Street northwest toward Fifth Avenue and Central Park, 1870. The landscape was rugged—unpaved roads, a new church, shanties, speculative houses. The first house in Marble Row, where Mrs. Isaac Jones lived, had just been erected on the northeast corner of Fifth and 57th Street. The new apartment district would soon crop up to its west.

a unified facade and held seven separate dwellings, the first and grandest of which was the house that had been erected for Edith Wharton's aunt, a cousin of Colford Jones's. The civilized world effectively ended here at 59th Street, where Mrs. Jones lived in her stylishly French confection, like her counterpart, Mrs. Mingott, "watching calmly for life and fashion to flow northward to her solitary doors. She seemed in no hurry to have them come, for her patience was equalled by her confidence. She was sure that presently the hoardings, the quarries, the one-story saloons, the wooden greenhouses in ragged gardens, and the rocks from which goats surveyed the scene, would vanish before the advance of residences as stately as her own—perhaps (for she was an impartial woman) even statelier; and that the cobblestones over which the old clattering om-

nibuses bumped would be replaced by smooth asphalt, such as people reported having seen in Paris."

The Jones blocks marked the northern boundary of respectability; above them the avenue was paved with wooden blocks, and quail and partridge still had their rights. The whole upper half of the island was nearly empty. On a city insurance map of the day, which was color-coded to indicate the character of its buildings—a wash of rose for residences, green or blue for industry, golden brown for wooden structures—upper Manhattan showed up as a field of paper white, marked only occasionally by a malthouse, a country house, an inn, or a cluster of angular little wooden shanties that looked like flotsam in the sea of white. The grid was ruled in, but it was theoretical, a geometry of possibilities and probabilities. Few people seemed to know how the city was going to grow once it began to move out from its safe, low, central hollow. The *Real Estate Record* guessed that fashion would follow the avenue north to 72nd Street and Park. The land around Central Park was of questionable value, however, for the prospect of facing a vast tract of uninhabited green was a lonely one. A sure system of rapid transportation was needed to join the upper and lower halves of the island, to point the way north and east or west, to unloose the city from its old moorings.

For the moment, society was hemmed in. Sixth Avenue was becoming commercial in nature. Fourth Avenue had the railroad. Colonel Vanderbilt's new Grand Central Terminal between 42nd and 45th streets, which the *New York Times* called neither "grand" nor "central," marked the practical northern boundary for residence on that street, for above it the wide boulevard was laid with railroad tracks, which meant steam, soot, and noise. The terminal deliberately faced south, for the city was there, and it turned its unapologetically dreary back wall on the north, for only freight yards and warehouses held the ground for the foreseeable future. Farther east of Fourth and west of Sixth, industry and tenements limited luxury development. On the shoreland, breweries, stone yards, and slaughterhouses prevailed, and noxious enterprises like fat rendering and bone boiling warded off development like the plague.

APARTMENT HOUSES, or first-class French flats, hovered around the edges of the fashionable quarters. Most of them looked like houses, which was an appropriate disguise, and they tentatively stretched out the residential parameters. A handful of buildings appeared downtown around Ladies' Mile, among all the shops and restaurants and clubs: McLittle's Apartment House, Griswold and Darlings, and Spinkler's Wellington Apartments by Griffith Thomas on 23rd near Sixth. Another handful appeared uptown, west of the fashionable district, in quiet sections of Broadway or Sixth Avenue, at first near 42nd Street, and then, as if lured by the prospect of green, closer to Central Park: the Albany and the Saratoga on Broadway near 51st and 52nd; the Windsor at 54th; the Vancorlear on Seventh between 55th and 56th; the Bradley facing the park at 59th Street. New neighborhoods seemed to form naturally around these buildings. The process of accretion worked like a geological law. Each new building brought not one but a dozen new families to a locality. Since a colony of families made an area more sociable and more respectable than a single family in a single house ever could, other buildings arrived, and clusters of apartment houses became the cores of new residential districts.

Like watchful fathers, the architectural journals passed immediate judgment on buildings that seemed promising—solid or imposing or worthy of a reader's attention. Meticulously, they noted every facet of a building's composition down to the copper pipes, the bronze door-knobs, the water boilers, the filagree staircases, and the marblework, carefully recording even the names and addresses of the contributing plumbers, ironmongers, cabinetmakers, and stoneworkers. "The fireplaces show the characteristically fine work of Mr. Field and his son," they would say, reassuringly, or "The elevator work was supplied by Murtaugh's well-known establishment on Broadway, and can be relied on as staunch and solid." There was great eagerness in their voices—an eagerness that often found expression in superlatives or produced a pronouncement on a building even before its completion. The Knickerbocker, on the corner of 14th Street and Fifth, and the Osborne, on Fifth between 52nd and 53rd, both erected in 1876, were heartily welcomed while workmen were still putting on their finishing touches. Like the Haight House, the Knickerbocker was a reconstruction of a prominent residence on a prominent corner. The architects, D. and J. Jardine, who had already attached their name to the Jardine apartment house on West 56th Street, provided generous two-bedroom apartments for nine families, double floors for soundproofing, and laundries and extra servant's rooms in the attic. Here, the *Real Estate Record* said, was "everything requisite for housekeeping in the most convenient style," in "one of the most eligible apartment houses in New York" and in "a district of the city most convenient to those who prefer healthful exercise when going downtown to being crammed in a horse-car."

Six months later, the imposing six-story Osborne had emerged as "the finest apartment house in New York," for the architects, Duggin and Crossman, had "taken advantage of the most recent improvements, not only in the general construction of the building, but also in the minor details so far as they promote the comforts of tenants." These new assets included an external window in each of an apartment's nine rooms (including one in the bath and the larder), a kitchen that confined the disagreeable fumes of cooking, a separate service entrance, and a general aura of quiet good taste. Dutifully, the *Real Estate Record* promised to report further on the building, "to show that considerable progress had been made even in this year of depression in improving the homes of our people."

Both idealism and naiveté colored these reports, for the reporters who were educating their audience were innocents. Like the rest of the city, they were merely watching an experiment that might or might not have important implications for city life. Their ideas of what constituted the best or the most convenient or the most luxurious flat had to be subjected to constant revision, for there was no body of experience or literature to guide either architects or architectural critics through these times, and perspective came in direct proportion to the number of buildings on the street. The latest example of an apartment house was inevitably the paradigm of the moment, for better or for worse. One year a critic might state that the apartment house had been perfected, and the next that the apartment house had failed. There was, after all, great confusion about what an apartment house was, and should be.

According to a lead article in the *Real Estate Record* in the spring of 1877, the apartment house system had already failed, for the prophecy that it would rival private houses and attract the patronage of "the better class of people" had not been fulfilled. In expensive buildings like the Albany and the Osborne, chronic vacancies were the rule. Ominously, a costly apartment house planned for a site at 57th Street and Fourth Avenue had been abandoned in favor of private dwellings. Exorbitant rents were partly to blame for the perceived stalemate; in anticipation of wealthy patrons, an elaborate flat often leased for the same sum of money as a fine and proper brownstone. Furthermore, would-be tenants commonly found fault with the construction—the small rooms, the awkward layouts for dining and entertaining, the inadequate heating and ventilation—as well as with the management of even the best French flats. According to one critic, the most serious objection to the apartment, "threatening miscarriage of the whole plan," lay with the concierge, an ill-chosen character capable not only of annoyances like "despoiling the linen basket" but also of espionage, blackmail, and petty theft. Servants, too, objected to living in apartments because the presence of the concierge threw a household into disarray.

In the estimation of the *Real Estate Record,* the apartment hotel offered a more popular and more promising new system of city living. The Stevens House, although originally called French flats and ultimately proved unmanageable, had been the pioneering example of this hybrid, which offered the domestic features of the apartment house in combination with the managerial and gastronomic features of the best European hotels. The apartment hotel resolved, or at least sidestepped, the most common problems of the apartment house. It eliminated the kitchen in favor of a communal kitchen, which furnished either private meals or a bill of fare in the house restaurant. It replaced the concierge with a manager, "clothed in autocratic authority," to maintain "harmony, homogeneity, and a wholesome atmosphere" among tenants. Even while negotiating convenience, the apartment hotel preserved certain aristocratic niceties—structure, service, a semblance of ceremony—that suited the times. While it offered the luxuries of the hotel that so captured the social fancy, it did not carry its stigma, its reputation for high and risqué living. Its increasing popularity was interpreted as a sign that the wealthy were not seeking economy so much as ease, and that if they indeed had to forgo private dwellings, they would then choose to escape the burdens as well as the traditions of the old-fashioned home.

Commentators made the apartment hotel sound quite dreamy—the combination of quiet secluded rooms, service that included meals expedited to private dining rooms in felt-lined boxes, and freedom from all thought of servants and daily provisions. They spoke of "an absolute perfect homelife, exempt from petty annoyances and costly cares, and replete with a measure of luxury, comfort, and convenience not attainable under any other system." On the subject of the Grosvenor, the first so-called apartment hotel in New York, which appeared on the corner of 10th Street and Fifth Avenue in 1871, they praised the proprietor for his clear understanding of the wants of the upper class, a group described as "possessing wealth, culture, refinement, and love of ease, and desiring the security and comfort of home life, with none of its cares." Not surprisingly, this "nest of elegant homes" was built for a Frenchman, a well-to-do importer named Francis Cottenet, and designed by Detlef Lienau, who seemed intent on jolting New York out of its brownstone rut. Its immediate success—and long waiting list—prompted the construction of a fraternal twin named the Berkley, across the avenue at 9th Street, where it claimed the site of the neighborhood ball field.

Perhaps the most unequivocal success among apartment hotels belonged to the buildings designed exclusively for bachelors. In nineteenth-century New York, respectable unmarried women resided obediently at home. Until French flats like the Haight House had set aside separate floors of suites for them, however, unmarried men had few prospects of proper lodging without exorbitant rent or annual May Day moves. "The discomfort of his rooms may have a good effect in precipitating him into matrimony, out of Scylla into Charybdis," a critic forewarned. In 1876, a paper presented to the annual AIA convention outlined the requirements for a building in which a bachelor would find "a permanent and real *home,* where he could expand beyond his previous narrow limits, and accumulate around him 'works of art,' and the hundred and one things which conduce to personal comfort and intellectual growth, and give rise to the attachment and sentiments of home." These were a central location, suites for fifty to sixty young men (providing a parlor, bedroom, bath, wood-burning fireplace, and "heavy substantial finish"), a roof garden (balconies were known to annoy neighbors), a restaurant, and a general laundry. Within several years, buildings like the Benedict on Washington Square, designed by the young firm of McKim, Mead and Bigelow, had met these conditions and were filled to capacity.

In late 1877, the appearance of the Bradley, on 59th Street between Fifth and Sixth avenues, revived enthusiasm for the so-called housekeeping apartment. Its location, more than anything else, gave the city a new perspective on this questionable breed of building. It was a handsome brick-and-stone building with new design elements—a low stoop instead of the high one associated with brownstones (which made it possible to build a full basement, with a full-time janitor instead of a concierge), two large light courts instead of numerous small air shafts, an important front door. With eight- and nine-room apartments, furnished in "correct good taste," it was classified as expensive, the contemporary synonym for luxurious. It also offered a host of new technical paraphernalia—passenger, furniture, and provision elevators; water hydrants on each floor; ash chutes; electric bells; and noiseless radiators. In all these details, the Bradley represented an advance in the form. Yet, in the end, it was its position before the park that caused people to think in a different way about the building. It had a presence there before the 250-acre preserve that a small private house could never have maintained. It seemed distinguished rather than diminished by the open space, and it had intimations of a European manor set before endless gardens.

The Bradley effectively opened the Central Park territory for settlers. "No grander field can be imagined for the expatiation of the apartment house than the margins of the Park," the *Real Estate Record* now de-

The Bradley Apartment House, located a few doors west of Fifth on 59th Street, and designed by John S. Prague, helped to establish a new neighborhood at the edge of Central Park. Buildings like Mr. Peter's Apartment House and the Dalhousie gradually filled out this block, and in 1891, Carl Pfeiffer's Plaza Apartment House took the Fifth Avenue corner.

clared, extolling the possibilities for light, ventilation, and heroic views. "The lonesomeness which a large unoccupied space naturally suggests is entirely overcome by the congregating of a number of families under one roof." An assortment of French flats cropped up along 59th Street to inaugurate the new apartment district. The promise of Central Park, however, such as the Bradley had suggested, took hold with buildings that were grander than would-be row houses, and had more physical stature than a house.

Together with the Bradley, the Windsor, at the corner of Broadway and 54th Street, and the Vancorlear, a blockfront on Seventh Avenue between 55th and 56th, were the cornerstones of a new neighborhood. They were larger, more imposing, more ornate, more evolved, and more daring than earlier apartment models, and they looked more like hotels or commercial buildings than row houses. In summer, wearing colorful striped awnings, they looked like European resorts. The Windsor, designed by James Giles, the architect of the elegant new cast-iron Lord and Taylor on Ladies' Mile, was a brick pile framed by bay windows that simulated towers. The Vancorlear, which was described by its young architect, Henry J. Hardenbergh, as "pure Renaissance with considerable of the Queen Anne features about it," was a double building, and its two main entrances were located on the side streets to allow the full flow of its front facade. Its courtyard, which was spacious enough for a carriage entryway and a spouting fountain, was the first one worthy of the name as Parisians used it. Its apartments, all well il-luminated by the courtyard and all lavishly appointed with marble, mosaics, and fine woodwork, offered at least nine or ten rooms, supple-mented by coal and wine cellars and drying and laundry rooms. After seeing the Vancorlear, a lady returning from Paris expressed astonish-ment at New York's progress with the apartment in recent years.

Henry J. Hardenbergh, who had studied at the Ecole des Beaux-Arts and served a long apprenticeship with Detlef Lienau, designed the Vancorlear, his first apartment house, for Edward Clark, one of the prin-cipals of the I. M. Singer Company. Clark, who was known as a bold and shrewd businessman, believed in the future of the West Side; he had bought land from August Belmont and had other construction plans besides the Vancorlear on file. As he told a meeting of the new and zealous West Side Association late in 1879, he thought a new era in building was about to begin, and that a superior version of the apartment house would figure in it prominently. Clark advocated large apartment houses for all the principal streets of the West Side, declaring that "there was hardly any limit to the rate of expenditure and style of social splendor to which the apartment house might not easily be adapted."

Clark had a vision of the city of the future. It would be a careful composition rather than a mere accretion of single buildings on single lots. Architects would plan whole blocks together, uniting small buildings with the large. Clark's thoughts were not stray ones, and they were reported in the *Real Estate Record* under a big banner headed "The City of the Future." Many magazines and journals were showing a heightened curiosity about the new age that was dawning. Both the *Real Estate Record* and the *American Architect and Building News* were working hard to present a broader and more informed perspective, including in their pages relevant news from abroad—"Aquariums are the rage in England and may be the wave of the future," and "The French build buildings to last, not out of wood"—speculating about life in the next century. The editors of the *Real Estate Record* ran a regular column called Our Prophetic Department.

The American Centennial had prompted much of the musing about the future, for it celebrated the beginning of a new century. The event had officially opened in Philadelphia in May 1876 with an exposition that ended the Victorian Age, as the chronicler Isaac Stokes declared. Laid out in seven great halls, this exposition paid tribute to "the unparalleled advancement in science and art and all the various appliances of human ingenuity for the refinement and comfort of man" that had happened in the one hundred years since the United States was born. Nothing on so grand a scale, so exotic, or so "euphoric with culture," had ever been seen in America, or indeed in the world. The vast artistic display from many nations—paintings, sculpture, and "industrial art" (the furniture, carpets, hangings, and bric-a-brac produced by machine)—had an enormous impact on the country. It aroused a new public interest in the fine arts; it brought the aesthetics of Queen Anne architecture, William Morris handicraft, and Charles Eastlake furniture into the public ken; and it made the shape, dress, and decoration of the house a subject of critical interest.

"There never was a time when so many books written for the purpose of bringing the subject of architecture—its history, its theory, its practice—down to the level of popular understanding, were produced as in this time of ours," recalled Clarence Cook, who was the author of a popular 1876 volume titled *The House Beautiful*. The *Real Estate Record* responded to the fair with a new regular column, Home Decoration. Ironically, although critics now speak of the centennial as an artistic calamity—all pomp and virtuosity and the epitome of the self-conscious bad taste of the Gilded Age—it inspired a phase of tastefulness known then as the "Artistic Craze." Across the country, heads and houses were cleared of sentimental and conventional clutter, filled with new ideas. Critics saw in the new broadened appreciation of art and architecture—in the art consciousness—the seeds of a Renaissance in America.

As a result of the centennial, architects grew thoughtful about the past too, and they indulged in retrospection about how America had been built, about the hard task of creating an architecture. Looking back, the *Real Estate Record* noted that New Yorkers had first built "as they dressed, dined, did business, and worshipped, as much like Englishmen as they knew how in the absence of mail three times a week and an Atlantic cable." With the Greek Revival, they displayed their "decent, solid, God-fearing, bourgeois aspect." Finally, the Brownstone Decades showed them to be "a community of vulgar adventurers," greedy, ostentatious, and callow. "A man's house in spite of him will express his way of thinking," they concluded, "and the brownstone house is not a flattering likeness of the New York man."

If a new age demanded a new image and a new type of residence, the specifics were as yet unclear. Eclecticism prevailed in the city, so that architecturally, as one critic put it, "everything was afloat." "The new streets seem to be arrayed as for a masquerade. The young architects have ransacked all times and all countries, not only for hints and suggestions, but for copies and caricatures and for completed types. Now, besides Gothic and Renaissance, and vernacular brownstone, count Colonial, Queen Anne, Florentine Renaissance, English Renaissance, French, Transitional Gothic, French Renaissance, Dutch Renaissance, Hispano-Moorish, Neo-Grec, and 'Old New York.' " "We are like children in a toyshop," another voice said, "dazed with the multitude of our opportunities, and for the present, incapable of fixing our choice."

To this general confusion could be added the dilemma of the apartment house, which was, if not a fixture, at least a growing presence in the streetscape, hulking at prominent corners of Fifth Avenue and Broadway, gathering in numbers along the southern face of the park, both a promise and a threat. Critics were in a quandary about the apartment house, for it was still in a state of becoming. Faced with a variety of models, from the simple housekeeping suite to hotel quarters European-style, and a wide variety of problems and promises, they issued tentative forecasts. "We expect that there will be sufficient patronage to warrant future production." "Future development may be marked by the increase in stories to seven, eight, or ten." "Perhaps one day there will be apartment houses set in gardens and lawns." One end-of-the-decade survey noted that the formation of "a cultivated and traveled class, not only among the money-making rich, but much more largely among those of inherited and more moderate means, and the rapidly increasing and disproportionate value of land, have combined with other causes to make a market . . . for a large number of compact dwellings . . ."; therefore, it was "probable" that the apartment had taken permanent root in New York soil. The *Real Estate Record* for all its usual passion and proselytizing, concluded that the great majority of people would prefer to live in their own homes.

Symptomatically, the term "apartment house" was sometimes hyphenated, sometimes not. It had emerged, however, as a classification distinct from and elevated above the term "French flats," which was now used to describe the modest and standardized so-called improved tenements that were filling in the cracks in unexceptional neighborhoods along transportation lines. In 1878, when an East Side matron filed suit to stop the conversion of nearby houses into an apartment house, under the provision that her neighborhood was zoned against "tenements," a judge ruled against her, advancing the cause of the apartment house one measured step. Nonetheless, a year later, when two apartment houses rose at 56th Street and Fourth Avenue in a setting of unpaved streets, modest farms, and errant livestock, an irate citizen complained to the builder that he was ruining the prospects for the neighborhood. "Gentlemen will never consent to live on mere shelves under a common roof," he said.

Nonetheless, the New York apartment house had potential grandeur. Although many voices complained about the high rents, it was a sense of extravagance that made buildings like the Grosvenor, the Osborne, and the Vancorlear popular. This aspect also served well to distinguish a special luxury class of apartment house from ordinary French flats or even decent brownstones. Owners of the highest rank of building were very sensitive to the matter of securing the favor of their tenants in this time of trial and error; among the upper classes, they had deciphered a peculiar need for a show of status, an illusion of wealth, an aura of prestige. Looking long and hard at the great piles here and there on Fifth Avenue, some critics were distressed at the pretensions. They faulted architects and builders who "overwhelm and embarrass a new idea in the expectation of enhancing its value." They faulted shortsighted tenants too. "Those who were willing to be lost in the common run of brownstone fronts when keeping up on a separate establishment require, when they look about them for a French-flat apartment, an exterior which to their eye is palace-like. It must be gorgeous . . . it may have a thousand faults, may be inconvenient, cramped, and in some degree unhealthy, but given a few showy items which may be seen at a glance, then all is well." This architecture—all gloss and veneer—they identified as "the wretched New York ideal."

This concern with external appearances was a reminder that these first attempts to rehouse the well-to-do belonged to an era that was variously named the Gilded Age, the Tragic Era, the Flash Age, the Dreadful Decade and the Pragmatic Acquiescence. It was a time of change and confusion, of a general insecurity that was handsomely masked behind a facade of pomp and glitter. "Mind your complexion, my dear," Edith Wharton had said was the abiding concern of those years; keep up appearances, even as the discreet order and harmony of the colonial city was breaking down.

5

THE COOPERATIVE
EXPERIMENT

O F ALL the early forms the apartment took during these years of
experimentation, the most ambitious, the most promising, and
the least abiding was the cooperative apartment. From the beginning,
there was a particular excitement to such buildings: they were idealistic
in purpose, they were economical in plan, they were extravagant in
nature. They first turned up in the early 1880s, graced with the very
descriptive name of Hubert Home Clubs. The name expressed its time;
it might have come out of the centennial, or one of the home beautification books, or out of the head of an urban visionary. *Hubert* was for
Philip G. Hubert, a Frenchman. *Home,* with its intimations of permanence, was for reassurance. *Club* was an invitation to elitists of the day.

Philip Gingembre Hubert, who had added his mother's anglicized
surname to his own upon emigrating to this country, was an energetic,
resourceful, iconoclastic man. The son of an architect, he had taken a
circuitous route to the profession, eventually financing his studies with
the sale of his patent for the first self-fastening button, an item that
interested the U.S. Army. It was the first of many inventions, most of
them directed toward improving apartment life. In 1879, he formed a
partnership with an American, James L. Pirsson, another mid-life
prodigy, who had turned to architecture himself only after establishing
a name in music and art. After an abortive pilot project downtown on
Lexington Avenue and 18th Street, the firm erected the first Home Club

in 1881 on West 57th Street, adjacent to the site where Andrew Carnegie's "Music Hall" would stand. Planned as a residence for artists and duly named the Rembrandt, it was a meaningful beginning, particularly for Pirsson, for like Hunt's Tenth Street Studios, it represented a happy convergence of private and public interests. Other buildings—the Hubert and the Hawthorne, both in the newly created apartment district on 59th Street; the Chelsea, on West 23rd Street; three unnamed buildings on Madison Avenue; and the Central Park Apartments—followed in rapid succession, creating a lively stir of interest in both the new firm and its chosen form.

To the members of a Home Club, Hubert, Pirsson and Company proposed sharing far more than the controversial common roof. Under the terms of a cooperative home association, as it was formally known, tenants—"a number of gentlemen of congenial tastes, and occupying the same social positions in life"—formed a club, or joint stock company, to share the cost of land and a building, with each associate receiving a proprietary lease on a suite appropriate to his investment, and with an excess of suites to be rented to pay the mortgage and running expenses. Soon after the appearance of the Rembrandt, for example, a group of eight families projected a building of six stories on three lots; it would translate into apartments that provided each family with a ten-room apartment of 2,200 square feet: reception room, library, dining room, hallway, three bedchambers, kitchen, servant's room, butler's pantry and trunk room, with extra servants' rooms and drying rooms on the top floor. In addition, adjacent to this apartment house, which was only 56 feet wide, a small four-story English-basement house was to be constructed as a rental property, to supply the funds to pay for a janitor, a fireman, three elevator youths, one hall boy, property and water taxes, repairs, and the maintenance of the front walk.

In concept, Hubert Home Clubs were designed for the wealthy. Hubert had learned from experience that people of limited means could not enter into an arrangement that called for assets and economic risks. His first building, a plain but substantial structure in a neighborhood of clerks, had been planned for the moderate middle classes, but it filled with well-to-do entrepreneurs. Beginning with the Rembrandt, Hubert recognized the cooperative scheme as an opportunity to create fine, increasingly large and extravagant apartment buildings, in effect, to work to perfect the form. The collective animus of a building—the collective desire for comfort, for service, for security—encouraged him. Knowing the class of New Yorkers for whom he was articulating and elaborating the idea of "cohabitation," he could plan facilities that would be as socially acceptable as they were fiscally sound. Engineering economies in some aspects of his buildings, he could afford to indulge architectural excellence in others.

From the beginning, a Hubert Home Club was regarded as a superior building. A recognizable physical type quickly evolved, as could be seen from the Hubert, the Hawthorne, and numbers 121 and 80 Madison Avenue. Its exterior was decorative—subject to bays, balconies, and ornamental brickwork. It was tall—eight, ten, and twelve stories in height. Its interior included duplex apartments, ingeniously arranged on what Hubert called his mezzanine plan, which gave greater height to the public rooms on the lower floor than to the bedrooms above. Three stories of bedrooms corresponded to two stories of public rooms and provided a half more bedrooms than in an ordinary plan. The layout was thus both expansive and compact. The entertaining rooms on the first floor—the reception room, the drawing room, parlor, and dining room—were large and lofty and lined up to create a grand sweep of space connected by sliding mahogany-and-etched-glass doors. The bedrooms were snug and intimate, and in Hubert's mind more sanitary, for he championed the notion that low ceilings allowed impure air to rise and depart more rapidly. Usually, a spiral staircase linked the two floors—an improvement in some minds over the monotonous "ladders" serving private houses, and an allusion to the mansions of the rich. Just as the Home Club nominally offered a permanent "home," it conceptually preserved, even aggrandized, the image of home as defined by a vertical house.

Hubert's thoughts were not focused on the past, however. He believed that the cooperative apartment had advantages that made it a compelling substitute for a private house, and he was a proselytizer, a promoter, and a reformer. He looked forward to a new era in human society, and was constantly tinkering with ideas to pave the way. As an inventor he was irrepressible. When his buildings were criticized as being too tall—too far from the street, too much dangerous "altitude," people said—he devised the first fireproof plaster blocks to allay fears of fire. He invented a self-propelling elevator, and cold-air boxes to refrigerate food before the advent of refrigerators. His 1882 building at 52nd and Madison waxed particularly eloquent with invention, and the New York *World* described its "special features" with perceptible awe. These included a basement located above the sidewalk, a fireproof mansard roof, a summer garden where fountains and sprinklers kept tiles cool, an appliance for cremating vegetable refuse, and in the bedrooms, bedsteads that were designed with steampipes in lieu of slats that could be connected to steam coils for heat.

Philip Hubert was in fact a utopianist. He was an enthusiastic follower of Henry George, an economist whose book *Progress and Poverty* challenged the complacencies of bourgeois economics. In 1879, the year that book swept New York, Hubert himself had published an ambitious pamphlet extolling cooperation and explaining his venture into this form of housing. His first unsuccessful building on lower Lexington Avenue was meant to be a mutual benefit society, and in principle, his grander buildings, too, were like "friendly societies," the social organizations that the followers of George and Charles Fourier championed. Fourier, a French socialist writer who early in the century had advocated cooperation over competition and union over individualism, had laid the philosophical foundations for the cooperative movement in the United States. His proposed division of society into "phalanges," or small communities, which inhabited phalansteries, or common buildings, had struck the principle behind the new home associations.

Cooperation in general and Fourierism in specific had waxed and waned in the 1840s. In the last third of the century, Americans were again exploring the concept of the nonprofit management of economic ventures, as they began to experiment with credit unions, burial societies, food co-ops, and cooperative housing. Andrew Greeley had opened his newspaper, the *Tribune,* to new ideas, and published a regular column of the writing of Albert Brisbane, an ardent and influential Fourierist. In 1888, Edward Bellamy illustrated the rewards of cooperation in his enormously popular novel *Looking Backward,* set in Boston in a society blissfully free of crime, poverty, and prejudice. It was "the age of concert"; the year was 2000, when people lived in large apartment houses where cooking was done in central kitchens, and meals were taken in communal dining rooms. "A very important cause of former poverty was the vast waste of labor and materials which resulted from domestic washing and cooking, and the performing separately of innumerable other tasks to which we apply the cooperative plan," a happy apartment dweller explains. "To save ourselves useless burdens, we have as little gear about us at home as is consistent with comfort, but the social side of our life is ornate and luxurious beyond anything the world ever knew before."

Cooperation was a powerful notion, particularly in times that were characterized by ever-deepening divisions in society. Its principles were noble, its goals humanitarian, its methods pragmatic. Many dwellers in Home Clubs looked upon themselves as quasi-utopian pioneers on the brink of a luminous new era. Their habitations were seen as not-too-distant relatives of Bellamy's communal buildings, although according to its author, *Looking Backward* was a "fairy tale of social felicity," and his model apartment was not a practical contrivance, but "a cloud palace for ideal humanity," a fantasy "hanging in midair, far out of reach of the sordid and material world of the present."

Looking Backward exerted a strong influence on a generation's thinking, for it stirred up intellectual hopes. Home Clubs did too, for they offered bold new solutions to the domestic and economic ills of city life; in many aspects they resembled cloud palaces. They were as widely cooperative as Hubert could make them; he purchased coal and ice in bulk and passed on the economies to tenants; he talked further of communal cooking, laundry details, and bootblacking. The Home Clubs were architecturally and technologically innovational—with roof gardens and newfangled incinerators and generators—almost futuristic. They were luxurious too, so luxurious in fact that some critics wondered what Fourier might have thought of this version of the socialist dream. Contrary to the usual post-capitalist scheme for utopia, they were also proving profitable.

As reports circulated that Hubert Home Cooperative Associations were doing a flourishing business, a furor developed for this new kind of investment. A few buildings in which income had exceeded expenses had declared dividends. A number of "associates" had resold their apartments for handsome sums of money. "Promoters," who encouraged and organized cooperative ventures, proliferated. Buoyed by his own success, Hubert himself enlarged the scale of his enterprise, and gave his architectural imagination free rein. He experimented with new combinations of accommodations, he elaborated upon decoration, he added startling structural innovations.

The Home Club called the Chelsea, erected in the middle of the block between Seventh and Eighth avenues on 23rd Street in 1883, was greeted as Hubert and Pirsson's most novel building, and became its

The Chelsea at 222 West 23rd Street overwhelmed its neighbors but matched their gables, eleven stories above the street.

most popular and profitable as well. At eleven stories, it was the tallest apartment house in the city, towering above the three- and four-story houses at its feet and providing a view from atop that ranged far beyond its own neighborhood, beyond the department stores, beer gardens, and theatrical houses, beyond even the bustle of the waterfront, to take in the harbor and the sea. The Chelsea was also one of New York's first Victorian Gothic structures, as critics were calling the new rendition of the Gothic mode celebrated so fervently by John Ruskin. Made of red brick, the Chelsea had a roof full of gables and dormers and wide manor-house chimneys, and its facade was covered with tiers of ornate cast-iron balconies.

The balconies, floral filigree from the foundry of the Cornell Brothers on Center Street, tipped off the public to the quality of decoration within. Marble, onyx, and polished hardwood were the materials of choice—marble dadoes and floors, onyx mantelpieces, polished hardwood floors and doors. In the public hall or lobby, the sweeping cast-iron staircase, the elevator cage, and even the giant andirons in the fireplace all carried rosettes to match the balconies outside. In the manager's office, the ceiling was painted with pink angels on white clouds and trimmed with gilt. A uniformed doorman presided over the front entrance, a French maître d'hôtel over the private dining rooms, a French chef over the kitchen.

The Chelsea had a rich, almost baroque quality, inside and out. According to its original plan, the building offered a variety of accommodations that was unique in the city, and it attracted a wide spectrum of society, from bachelors, bohemians, and young couples to full and extended families. Its ninety apartments, of which two-thirds were cooperative and owned by members of the Home Club and one-third rented for revenue, were sized from three to twelve rooms. They were spacious, decorative—finished according to the individual taste of the cooperative tenants—and accommodating. Servants' quarters were generally included, although few of the apartments had full kitchens, given the house culinary facilities; a private ballroom under the roof was available for lease by tenants. On the tenth and eleventh floors there were also duplex studios, which attracted a long line of resident artists, for on the north side of the building they caught a painterly light, and on the south they opened directly onto the large roof garden, where evening concerts were held during the summer. The roof itself was the first fully fireproof model in the city.

The Central Park Apartments, seen from the park drive, 1884.

Despite its uniqueness, the Chelsea was not Hubert and Pirsson's most ambitious building, although it would prove the most enduring. The same year the Chelsea opened, the half-completed Central Park Apartments was already being proclaimed the most elegant apartment house in New York, the largest apartment house in the world, and the most important building project ever undertaken, in terms of its novelty, magnitude, and cost. Designed by Hubert and Pirsson but also called the Navarro, or Spanish Flats, in reference to its builder, José F. de Navarro, it occupied a half-block between Sixth and Seventh Avenues, from 58th to 59th Street. It stood eight stories tall, towers, gables, and turrets notwithstanding, and rising above the trees of the park, it looked like a fortress, or a whole Moorish kingdom.

The Navarro was a single mass divided into eight separate apartment houses, which were arranged around a central courtyard and connected internally only on the first floor. Each house had a separate name and address—Navarro named them the Barcelona, the Salamanca, the Cordova, the Tolosa, the Grenada, the Valencia, the Madrid, and the Lisbon, after his favorite places—and each was distinguishable by an entrance of triple arches. Inside, each held twelve apartments of extraordinary dimensions. The largest provided a drawing room (23 by 29 feet), a reception room (14 by 29), library (14 by 29), dining room (20 by 23), kitchen (18 by 20) with several roomy pantries, six bedrooms ranging from 22 by 24 to 14 by 18, three baths with tubs, and three rooms for servants. It was munificent space, distinctly more generous than an entire three-story row house. There were not ten houses in New York with such facilities for entertainments or occasions of ceremony, where public rooms opened onto one another, like the French nobleman's enfilade, and included a covered balcony that could be converted into a formal conservatory when necessary.

The general design of the Navarro was even more impressive. Its suites were not only lavishly decorated but also ingeniously arranged into simplexes, duplexes, and triplexes (the first in the city), which were stacked up, in an interlocking scheme similar to Hubert's mezzanine plan, to occupy two stories in the front of the building and three in the rear. The taller and grander public rooms on the main floor were set before the park vista, and the kitchen and bedrooms overlooked the interior courtyard, where there was quiet and an abundance of light and air. The courtyard of the Navarro was vast, 40 by 300 feet, a luxuriant space filled with trees, flowers, and fountains. To ensure the flow of fresh air there, and to harness the breezes that swept off the river and down across the park, Hubert had also incorporated open archways into his building, perforating its mass every second story between each of the eight sections with a passageway that was loggialike, and decorative, as well as utilitarian. Beneath the courtyard another subterranean courtyard, accessible by means of a vehicular tunnel leading directly from the street, allowed carts and wagons to deliver their supplies and provisions and to remove garbage and ashes in a manner that was inaudible and invisible to tenants. It was the most original feature of Hubert's technical design, which also included an apparatus to create steam heat, a generator for electricity (electricity was as yet an independent and expensive proposition in the city and therefore a luxury item in housing), and an artesian well to supply private water to the building.

Ironically, the Navarro was ill fated as a cooperative. As critics were extolling Hubert as an extraordinary architect of apartments, famous for "striking a mean between profusion and parsimony," the bank was foreclosing on his mortgage. It took over and completed the project as a complex of rental buildings, for only half of it was finished and functioning as a cooperative by 1885. Hubert's "parsimony" was misplaced in this venture; his downfall was a scheme by which he had planned to lease the land, temporarily, to the building owners in order to limit their cash investments, an idea that was untenable in the face of construction costs that ranked as high as those for St. Patrick's Cathedral and the Plaza Hotel. Hubert's success would be an artistic one, for while his building was unanimously praised as the best planned and best appointed in the city, it would prove uncomfortably expensive to operate, even as a rental. Cooperative buildings, with their tendency to extravagance rather than efficiency, were for rich subscribers or profit-seeking speculators. Years later, however, after it had been demolished, historians would sigh at the very fact of the building, which arrived too early to succeed.

In the annals of architecture, there is another Hubert and Pirsson building that served to extend the form of the modern luxury apartment house still further, even though it was never built. It was a larger, more elaborate, more inventive version of the Navarro, designed for the square block between 26th and 27th streets on Madison Square Park, a property that was optioned from William H. Vanderbilt in 1884. As the architects described it, the building resembled a layer cake, thirteen stories high, with a ground floor of stores and six tiers of small two-story houses, 22 feet by 50 feet each, or 40 houses per tier and 240 houses in all. Even more than its predecessor, it resembled a vertical village around a central green. Its courtyard was twice the breadth of the Navarro's, and on alternate floors, airborne walkways, which gave free and open access to the parlor floors of each house, encircled the building, like public sidewalks.

Here, in concept, was a building that was aerial, that celebrated a new spatial dimension. Here, in principle, was a building that was traditional, a pileup of old-fashioned houses. Such a hybrid might have served its times well, had it not been defeated by them first. In 1885, new height regulations outlawed buildings of its size, and five years later, Stanford White's new Madison Square Garden rose on the site.

HUBERT AND Pirsson's buildings were the most exemplary cooperative buildings in town, but they were not the only ones. As the interest in the Home Club plan had spread, a handful of other ambitious buildings had cropped up: on Fifth Avenue, the Plaza at 59th Street and a new Knickerbocker at 28th; on Madison Avenue, behind St. Patrick's Cathedral, the Berkshire and the St. Catherine; on fashionable Gramercy Park, the Gramercy. Of these buildings, the Gramercy, a ten-story red brick tower with turreted corners, was the most conspicuous new arrival, for it had broken into a self-contained landscape of houses. Samuel Ruggles, the original developer of the English-style residential square, had restricted what could be built around his private park, specifying materials and a minimum height to ensure its gentility, but he had not foreseen the challenge of a tall apartment house. To the relief of the nine households already living on the square, the Gramercy made a respectable neighbor. It was a handsome structure, designed in the stripped-down Empire style favored by Richard Hunt, and it had a magnificent lobby, with a marble staircase, and large tasteful apartments. Discreetly positioned on the eighth floor (far removed from the sensitive noses of all but the maids and bachelors at home in the attic), a Louis Sherry restaurant offered, as the lease specified, style and quality equal to Delmonico's.

Despite all the talk about collectivism, the cooperative apartment was not really a radical concept. It involved a novel financial arrangement, but architecturally it was an experiment with houses. In a changing city it was an attempt to preserve the status quo. Hubert and Pirsson made that clear in their plans for Madison Square. According to them, the apartment system was merely a geometric rearrangement of reality.

To those who believed in the value of multiple dwellings, however, the cooperative apartment was a fresh vision of the future of the city. George W. DaCunha, the architect of the Gramercy, predicted that one day five million people would be living in great apartment houses in Manhattan. He felt sanguine about the apartment house. Its present form was to its potential what the log cabin was to the Vanderbilts' new mansion. "We are feeling our way," he said.

The cooperative struck a different note than had earlier versions of the apartment. There was something so hopeful, so purposeful and uncompromised in its nature that it cast city living, for a moment, in a radiant new light. It afforded luxuries and conveniences unknown in ordinary family life. It disclosed people of a new social want—people who "like to live in a crowd—to see their fellows daily and hourly"—"modern man and woman," as they were identified. A few critics drew

The Gramercy was built in 1883. It stood directly across town from the newly constructed Hotel Chelsea.

even grander conclusions from the success of the cooperative. They moralized and sermonized about its social significance in prose that owed its epic tone to Oscar Wilde, who had recently lectured New York on the aesthetics of the beautiful. "The very fact that a dozen to one hundred families can dwell together in harmony under one roof should be inspiring to the nineteenth century architect," an editorial in the *Real Estate Record* read. "He should seize the idea of their unity, of their solidarity, and express it in stone and bricks and iron. He should build tremendous stairs for his brave one hundred; splendid cities with pillars and arcades; front doors as wide as those of a cathedral and as rich in carved tracery. He should provide marble pavements, frescoed halls, gardens full of statuary and fountains. He should never forget that he is working for an entity that is more sacred and more powerful than any one human being can be, for a corporation or at least a congerie of individuals. The corporation should be first, the individual last in his thought, and so it must become with the inhabitants of apartment houses themselves. The system will engender a new sentiment—the apartment house sentiment, which will take the place of civic pride, of family feeling, perhaps even of patriotism."

These were inflated sentiments, born of yearnings for a brave new world and a heroic new social order. The old-fashioned dream of owning a house ran deep, however, and the idea of the tall collective building was as threatening as it was inspiring. Hubert received anonymous warnings to desist from his work. Negative feelings about communality were clear in the exaggerated efforts to guarantee privacy and to make public spaces glamorous. By 1900, economics as well as image defeated the cooperative. Very few high-class cooperatives were able to balance their revenues with running expenses. In a tradition-minded society, home was not a joint investment.

A new height-control law, imposed by the Buildings Department in 1885, was, indirectly, a barometer of feelings about the apartment house such as it had evolved over a decade and a half of efforts. The so-called Daly Law, which, like Napoleon III's regulations in Paris, limited the height of new residential buildings to seventy feet on side streets and eighty feet on avenues, was adopted in response to the growing fear of the future. To many eyes, eight- or ten-story buildings loomed menacingly above the landscape and insulted respectable old buildings. It was difficult to identify with them, to relate to their unfamiliar and inflated proportions. Anxious citizens projected themselves into a future of aggressive towers casting deep canyons of shadow over the land. They questioned the effect of earthquakes on such structures, remembering that their city was located in a vulnerable zone. They were worried that disease might thrive in long communal halls and crowded elevators. Before its passage, advocates of the Daly bill had focused their attack exclusively on apartment buildings, painting them as unwieldy and unhealthy structures, calling physicians to present evidence that their tenants were more liable to symbiotic and contagious diseases than ordinary householders. In the end, by providing an escape clause for hotels and office buildings, the bill effectively singled out apartment houses for reproval and redress.

Architects like Hubert and Pirsson, who were typical of the energetic and idealistic new breed of city builder, thought that the Daly Law seriously checked progress. In fact, many dozens of buildings would be retracted or would remain on the drawing board until 1901, the year it was repealed. The few tall buildings in existence would be granted the special status that belonged to the exceptional and the privileged. The Daly Law, however, was an honest expression of a time before a vision of the future had come into focus, before the growth of the city had achieved a force, a momentum, an excitement of its own. Men were still not confident that elevators were safe, that tall buildings would stand strong in a wind, or that life in a big luxurious apartment house could be either healthy or harmonious. The bill was meant to keep New York "pleasant," to safeguard its old character, to exert control over a place that was beginning to run wild.

It was increasingly difficult to know how much influence to yield to the future, how best to honor the past. The city was noisy and unruly with change. Neighborhoods were rocked regularly by explosives preparing sites for new buildings. As rapid transit made advances, the heavy skeletons of the elevated invaded many of the avenues; trains thundered overhead, scattering ashes and sparks below. A tangle of telegraph and telephone wires already confused the streets downtown in the business district. To many New Yorkers, the poles and the lines, like the tall buildings, were symbols of incongruous change.

The most dramatic symbol of new times was the Brooklyn Bridge, which had opened, after thirteen years of intense public anticipation, in the spring of 1883. A miracle of modern engineering, one of the wonders of the world, the bridge offered literal and figurative passage to a new world, to Brooklyn and beyond. Suspended from cables that swung down from two great granite towers across the wide and turbulent East River, it was a triumphantly modern structure. The poet Hart Crane said that it liberated the eye. It set forth over the water like an experiment in time and space and motion, like a mechanical sculpture, or a defiant work of art. Its aesthetics had nothing in common with the Gilded Age, for it was spare, steely, and unadorned, arrogantly so. When one crossed the bridge (riding over the water, relieved forever of the prosaic problems that beset ferry travel—fog in the morning, devilish currents, ice blockades in the winter), the pattern of cables that spun by the eye, a dizzy geometry of straight lines in motion, was almost otherworldly. It was frightening and exhilarating, both.

If the Brooklyn Bridge was "both a fulfillment and a prophecy," as Lewis Mumford later suggested, this meaning was not widely understood by a generation that expressed itself in silk and feathers, marble and mahogany. For the moment the bridge was a mere wonder, a great big crude and fascinating toy. Photographs taken from the top of its towers provided amazing new panoramas, wide stereoscopic perspectives on a city that looked like a stage set. The bridge announced a new kind of beauty, and even portended a new kind of architecture, but it would take many more years of industrialization and urbanization before that message made any particular sense.

THE GILDED AGE

1880–1899

Fifth Avenue looking north from 51st Street, 1879.

6

THREE NEW MANSIONS:
VANDERBILT, TIFFANY,
VILLARD

In 1879, ten years after introducing the notion of multiple dwellings to the city, Richard Morris Hunt designed a building that offered society another, more glamorous and more ambitious alternative in housing. This was the new residence William K. and Alva Smith Vanderbilt commissioned for themselves on the corner of 52nd Street and Fifth Avenue. So dramatic was the house that Hunt's early lessons in communal living would be forgotten. So successful was Hunt's rendering of patrician taste that his lot would be irrevocably cast with the new class of millionaires. Many critics would overlook the significant innovations of Hunt's early work—the studio apartments, the French flats, and the pioneering commercial buildings—and date his career from the moment Vanderbilt walked into his office. With this commission, Hunt laid the cornerstone of his reputation as the father of American classicism. He crowned the times with an appropriate emblem, and he became an official figurehead of the Gilded Age.

Hunt's creation was a small-scale château inspired by the example in Blois, France, and fashioned in the late French Gothic–early Renaissance mode after Francis I. It was massive, rich, regal, and powerful. Its exterior was a cool gray Indiana limestone, which made the warm brownstone of neighboring houses look extremely dull. Its mansard roof raised gables, pinnacles, and finials to the sky like bits of royal insignia.

Its most striking feature was an elaborate entrance porch, which rose the full height of the house and was dominated by a delicate corbeled tourelle, topped by a steep conical roof and a finial that marked the highest point of the building. It might have been flying a king's banner. Instead, there was a large stone figure of Hunt, dressed as a stonemason, perched on the roof nearby, an *hommage au architecte* carved by his staff.

The Vanderbilt house was immediately deemed "the plum of the season." It was officially opened on March 26, 1883, with a house-warming costume ball, one of the most lavish parties of the day, which succeeded in establishing the Vanderbilts, four generations removed from the first Dutch merchant Van Der Bilts, in New York society. Alva, who had directed the design of the house as single-mindedly as she had plotted her attack on the social citadel ruled by Mrs. Astor, had determined that the house would illuminate her as a new social force, which it did. The ball itself recalled an affair at Versailles. It began with an elaborate "Hobby Horse Quadrille," in which the dancers were costumed to appear to be mounted on real horses, with genuine hide and flowing manes and flashing eyes. Alva dressed as a Venetian princess out of a painting by Cabanel. Mrs. Paran Stevens appeared as Queen Elizabeth, while Mrs. Cornelius Vanderbilt, in white satin trimmed with diamonds, called herself "The Electric Light." Guests saw a brilliant new display of wealth that night, for the mass and splendor of the facade of 660 Fifth Avenue was more than equalled by the sumptuousness of its interior. There were great halls and a grand, richly carved Caen-stone staircase; banqueting rooms and billiard rooms; chandeliers and sculptured nymphs and graces, painted and beamed ceilings; medieval panels of stained glass; white, pink, and green marble from Italy. Both the architecture and the interior decoration of the house set new standards for luxury and sophistication. Every heroic detail was the talk of the town—the breakfast room with Flemish tapestries and Rembrandt's *Portrait of a Turkish Chief;* the white drawing room with a secretary and commode made for Marie Antoinette; even Alva's bathroom, which was wainscotted in marble, with mirrored walls above, overpainted with flowering vines.

In size, bearing, and aesthetics, the Vanderbilt house was different from any other house in America. In sheer showmanship it shared lineage with A. T. Stewart's mansion. But in the artistry of its rendering and the force of its image, it was in a class by itself. It was so grand and so palatial that is seemed to stand outside American culture, to confer on

Hunt's house, at 52 Street and Fifth Avenue, built in 1879 for William K. Vanderbilt, made society aware of the social advantages of European architecture.

its residents worldly status. It was more than a home, a pleasant and appropriate place in which to live and bring up a family. It was a monument; like a monument it represented the material expression of something abiding, and it inspired awe and wonder in the city.

THE VANDERBILT house was the first public monument of the Gilded Age. To those who had not yet noticed that the solemnity, the respectability, and the innocence of one age had given way to the frivolity, sophistication, and dissolution of another, Hunt's masterpiece sounded a call. Clearly, this French Renaissance château, sitting self-importantly on the main street of New York, was a product of a new mood and new ambitions. Clearly, this beautiful ostentation, created by the greatest fortune ever amassed in America, represented the ultimate expression of the recent appetite for glitter and vainglory.

A taste for display had in fact been flourishing in New York society since before the Civil War. The richly decorated steamboats on the Hudson River, all plush carpet, tasseled curtains, and tinted windows; the Pullman Palace Cars that took passengers from New York to Chicago in a giddy atmosphere of elegance; the opulent new hotel lobbies and opera houses all attested to society's growing weakness for luxury and appetite for riches. Private amusements, too, had become inordinately frivolous. Hostesses achieved social momentum by hiring a Cordon Bleu chef, proffering a rare port, staging a string of extravagant little dinners, or, more historically, a big dinner, one "with a hired chef and two borrowed footmen, with Roman punch, roses from Henderson's, and menus on gilt-edge cards." On an occasion that made social history as the Swan Dinner, a host transformed a table at Delmonico's into a forty-foot lake over which four swans from Prospect Park glided for the duration of an eight-course dinner.

Such were the fashionable vanities. While voices of reason spoke out against sham and show, society flitted from one fad to another: truffled ice cream mousse, gilded French furniture, Worth dresses from Paris. They were carefully chosen fads, however, and as fads they didn't interfere with proper behavior. The Worth dresses were kept in the closet for at least a season, so as not to be too new and conspicuous upon first wearing. The gilt bamboo jardinieres and anonymous Italian busts were arranged in sedate drawing rooms inside brownstone fronts. Old-fashioned decorum ruled that home was the base of serious taste, and serious taste was still traditional and conservative. While the centennial had inspired new thoughts about interior decorations, the immediate effects were purely ornamental.

The Gilded Age got its name from its superficiality. The traditional standards of respectability had not been substantially altered, but overlaid with an exuberant glitter. With all the new fortunes accruing in the pitch of the industrial revolution, there were nearly four thousand millionaires in the city in 1880, whereas in 1870 there had been forty, and the example they put forth was expensive and showy. They staged musical teas, masked balls, dinner parties for dogs; bought silk stockings for their footmen and hothouse flowers for the drawing room; collected oriental rugs and European statuary. They had money to squander and a standing to secure.

The new millionaires were in a class by themselves, distinct from the closely knit, monied but not rich social and intellectual elite. They formed a new stratum in society. If they did not yet have the *droit de cité,* they were at least recognized as a powerful social force. Their presence in the city fascinated and disturbed. To members of the old guard who inhabited a quiet and honorable world of "faint implications and pale delicacies," bold and intrepid characters like Mrs. Paran Stevens or the Vanderbilts were disruptive forces. Typically, Mrs. Stevens had broken the unspoken law about entertaining on the Sabbath. Nonetheless her Sunday-night parties were dazzling affairs, with opera stars in attendance and a brilliant artistic flavor. Mr. Vanderbilt, whose rejection by high society had been confirmed by his inability to obtain a box at the Academy of Music, had almost single-handedly effected a transfer of power by engineering the construction of the larger and opulent Metropolitan Opera House, on 39th Street, to which he subscribed and society flocked without noticeable fuss. Such was the power of money, ambition, and innovation, commodities rarely even discussed in polite company.

In an era before radio or cinema stars, millionaires were the new celebrities. Their manners and amusements caught and held the public eye, for they were grander and more sophisticated than anything America had known. The wealth amassed, the extravagance with which it was dispersed, had no precedent in this country. It was a product of new energies, new ambitions, which were themselves products of new technology, new times. For all that it did or did not imply, to be rich was in itself an interesting occupation. Coming to

New York from a more staid and more mannerly Boston at the end of the 1880s, William Dean Howells, the new editor of *Harper's Monthly Magazine,* was overcome by the show of wealth. Reflecting on the course of American history, he concluded that the millionaire had replaced the soldier, the literary man, and the statesman as the national hero. It was the man with the most money who now took the prize in the national cakewalk, he said.

Of all the accoutrements of wealth in a millionaire's life, none elicited more interest than his habitation. The decoration of houses had become a national obsession, and the millionaire's house, for all intents and purposes an aesthetic debauch, was like a museum. It was symptomatic of the universal interest in the home that the new art of photography was trained on houses. Books like *Stately Homes* and *Artistic Houses,* a four-volume portfolio issued to subscribers in 1883, offered intimate views of the most beautiful rooms in the country: J. P. Morgan's library, with a carved honeycomb ceiling (its light fixtures dangled naked bulbs, for Morgan had just been lit with the first private electricity in the city); H. G. Marquand's neo-Grec music room; William H. Vanderbilt's library, bedroom, and Japanese parlor.

From the beginning, the William K. Vanderbilt house received an extraordinary amount of attention. Almost unanimous praise came from architectural, artistic, and social authorities, who named it the most beautiful house in America. One lone dissenting voice was raised in the Midwest by a Chicago architect who had a different vision of ornament and beauty. Louis Sullivan, now acknowledged as the father of the modern skyscraper, and then about to embark on a decade of building "proud and soaring things," found the Vanderbilt house foolish, and poked fun at the silk-hatted Vanderbilt and the feather-hatted Hunt. "Must I show you this *French chateau,* this little Chateau de Blois, on this street corner, here in New York, and still you do not laugh! . . . Have you no sense of humor, no sense of pathos? Must I tell you that while the man may live in the house physically (for a man may live in any kind of house physically), that he cannot possibly live in it morally, mentally or spiritually, that he and his home are a paradox, a contradiction, an absurdity, a characteristically New York absurdity; that he is no part of the house, and his house is no part of him?"

Sullivan was distressed at the pretentiousness that he saw displayed in the architecture of his age. He believed that "what the people are *within,* the buildings are *without;* and inversely, what the buildings are objectively is a sure index of what the people are subjectively " He was a populist of sorts, a spiritual kin to Walt Whitman; he embraced the forces of science, industry, and democracy. For him, art or architecture was a social manifestation, and the Vanderbilt house manifested something distracted, dishonest, and decadent in the society.

The old guard of New York society—the Knickerbocker families who resolutely continued to inhabit the dark corridors of brownstones downtown—the "cave-dwellers," the smart young set called them—felt much the same way about the Vanderbilt house and the other millionaires' mansions that soon rose in its image. Supercilious and showy, they represented an assault on the old order of the city and its code of values. In the face of changing patterns of behavior, the erosion of tradition, and the threat of invasion by new people, society had grown self-conscious and defensive—more rigidly circumscribed than ever before. It identified itself as the Four Hundred, which was allegedly the number of fashionable people who could fit into Mrs. Astor's ballroom. It closed ranks with formula events like the Patriarchs' Balls, Mrs. Astor's subscription balls that took place at Delmonico's every Monday night after the opera. Ward McAllister, her social advisor, had devised this scheme by which the twenty-five leaders of society, called Patriarchs, decided "whom society shall receive and whom society shall shut out," and issued invitations accordingly. That it was arrogant and artificial was a measure of society's perceived need to protect itself. "If we don't all stand together, there'll be no such thing as Society left," Mrs. Archer says in *The Age of Innocence.*

Behind the question of who was who in society was the deeper question of security. It was a confusing time in a country that had no established class system and staunchly upheld the democratic myth while celebrating individual achievement. With the city population expanding in number and diversity, and the social scene changing accordingly, many New Yorkers were losing their sense of place and well-being. In the face of the growing sophistication and materialism, they were uncertain who they were and where they belonged.

Given the psychological makeup of the day, the Vanderbilt house was a brilliant solution for a time of social transition. It was ideally suited to Vanderbilt, an American captain of industry whose fortune was secure and whose social standing was not. It relieved his insecurities. It projected an image that served to identify the owner as a man of wealth, power, and station. It was both an emblem of taste and a vehicle for

social ambition. At a time when appearances were of the utmost importance and all visible effects—a top hat, a Worth dress, or a fashionable
address—were clues to who one was, this classical dwelling provided a
public statement of worth. It was so effective that even before completion of the house, the young Vanderbilts received an invitation to the
Patriarchs' Balls, and the William H. Vanderbilts were admitted into
high society.

The public character of the Vanderbilt house made it distinct from
other houses in New York, and also from earlier works of Hunt. During
his first decades of practice, Hunt had received most of his residential
commissions from family members and friends in the old-guard elite. He
had designed houses for Thomas P. Rossiter on West 34th Street and
William Osborne on Park Avenue near 30th, for example, that were
private in nature and expressed a quiet, refined, rather hermetic architectural taste. Beginning with the Vanderbilt house, when Hunt's work
became associated with the new circle of plutocrats, his aesthetic turned
almost civic in character. His houses were recognized as New York's
"public possessions," as palaces in the true sense. They defined a new
echelon of the social order.

With this domestic palace, Hunt expected to elevate taste, to bring
the grandiloquence of classicism to bear on both the Vanderbilts and
their neighborhood. In the pursuit of beauty, his goals were as lofty as
Oscar Wilde's. But Hunt was also consciously flattering the Vanderbilts
by associating them with the great architecture of the past. The classical
tradition was something to look upon with awe and reverence. The
grandeur of Rome and the glory of France were there, written on
facades in medallions and turrets and flying buttresses. The life-styles of
dukes and counts were spelled out in reception rooms lined with statuary, in ballrooms imported directly from châteaux in Bordeaux.

A literal rendering of "a man's home is his castle," the Vanderbilt
house set an example for New Yorkers of wealth and fashion to emulate,
and it seeded a trend in patrician housing that was far more compelling
than either the homely and egalitarian brownstone or the practical and
democratic apartment. New York society was ripe for the noble ideals
of classical architecture. Here, in the imperial order, it could express its
taste for ornament and display without sacrificing the virtues of dignity,
formality, propriety, and tradition. Here, in an age-old architectural
style, it could associate itself with an aristocratic past. It could promote
its new aesthetics, and indulge its yearning for culture, status, and pur-

pose. An architectural critic said that the Vanderbilt house was destined to shock a city of brownstones into realizing that architecture could, in itself, further the ambitions of the Four Hundred. In a city where millionaires had been content to live side by side in identical houses, the door had been opened upon a new world in which rivalry and social ambition would manifest themselves visibly in architecture.

IT WAS not surprising that American millionaires turned to the building of great domiciles to express their social and cultural ambitions; their European counterparts had erected châteaux and palaces to assert their own social supremacy. In a country without a class structure, there were no other formulas for would-be aristocrats to follow, and there was no easier way for families like the Vanderbilts to spend their money than on houses. It may have been paradoxical to have a French Renaissance château sitting on a small corner lot on Fifth Avenue, but it was natural that a young transitional society would take cues from Old World culture.

The rapidity with which the New York rich accepted the new architectural idiom was startling, however. Almost overnight, an expensive and magnificent house, especially one designed by Richard M. Hunt, became a sign of culture and a badge of success. In a growing city where there were still fortunes to be made and where prestige could be bought, entrepreneurs turned avidly to palace building. They seemed to be celebrating the opportunity to display their wealth as keenly as the fact of the wealth itself. Most of the financiers, landlords, and merchants who had amassed fortunes in the city built great houses here. Industrialists from far-flung corners of the country came to New York to build what they regarded as their ancestral seats.

It looked like a parade of crown princes, the lineup of great houses. In 1884, a neo-Renaissance double brownstone by John B. Snook and the Herter Brothers was finished for William Henry Vanderbilt, the paterfamilias, at 640 Fifth Avenue. William Waldorf Astor erected a cream-colored Touraine château several blocks north, at 56th Street, before emigrating to England. On the northwest corner of 57th Street, Cornelius II, another Vanderbilt son, commissioned a house from George B. Post, a pupil of Hunt's, which looked like a small version of Fontainbleau. Hunt's design was judged the best of the Vanderbilt holdings, but the competition was not strictly a family affair.

Before his death in 1898, Hunt would design "superb privacies" on Fifth for the Goelets, the Gerrys, and Mrs. Astor too. By then, Fifth Avenue was an almost uninterrupted mile and a half of palazzi, châteaux, and fortresses, "a visual summary of free enterprise and the history of architecture."

Never before had Americans built their homes as showcases—to bedazzle, inside and out. Never had such wealth been expended on the external trappings of life. One historian calculated that between their New York houses and their country estates, the Vanderbilt family had invested as much money as any of the royal families in Europe, with only the Bourbons excepted. Never had New York architects been so busy, so prosperous, so purposeful. The handful of classicists who had followed Hunt's pioneering road to the Ecole des Beaux-Arts came home fervent. For a new breed of clientele, they designed adaptations of the French Renaissance, the Italian Renaissance, the Romanesque Revival. Like Hunt, they dispensed taste, culture, and a sense of place.

The architecture of these houses encompassed far more than shape and style. Hunt, for example, found himself designing family heraldry for Alva Vanderbilt to display on mantelpieces and firebacks. In the classical mode, the architecture of a room was its interior decoration; therefore, the ceiling friezes, wainscotting, chandeliers, and sculpture all fell under the architect's eye. In the tradition of the Ecole des Beaux-Arts, architects like Hunt, Post, H. H. Richardson, or McKim, Mead and White supervised all aspects of design and construction and worked closely with their artisans and craftsmen; they discovered and sponsored sculptors and painters and collaborated with interior decorators. Sometimes they served as antiquarians, and scoured Europe for medieval mantelpieces or Roman gates.

In the 1890s, a visiting Frenchman sought to explain these amazing New York reproductions. Paul Bourget, a novelist and journalist, had been commissioned to write a series of "impressions" on America for the New York *Herald*. He had been to Newport and seen the summer cottages of the wealthy set. "The American spirit seems not to understand moderation," he observed from there. He had commented on the grid system of New York: "This is not even a city in the sense in which we understand the word, we who have grown up amid the charm of irregular cities which grew as the trees do, slowly, with the variety, the picturesque character of natural things. This is a table of contents of unique character, arranged for convenient handling." Bourget was par-

ticularly struck by the "mad abundance" of money in the city and by a
Fifth Avenue that had "visibly been willed and created by the sheer force
of millions." In its houses he saw irrefutable signs of the American spirit:
the expression of individual will, the desire for refinement, a hunger for
long ago. "This desire for a deeply prepared soil," he explained, "is just
what a tree would feel on being transplanted to a new place with its roots
too near the surface. This unconscious effort to surround oneself with
the past, to ennoble oneself by it is what saves these homes of millionaires from being coarse . . . [and gives them] an unexpected bit of
poetry."

In 1885, the Senate Committee on Education and Labor considered
a bill to limit the amount of money that could be spent on a house—a
direct response to the Vanderbilts, and a sign that New Yorkers still
could be moralistic. Pulpits in the city, too, rang with attacks against the
grand and palatial houses, calling them indulgent, wasteful of resources,
conducive to selfishness and sloth. The litany of reproaches grew louder
a decade later, as ever more costly houses were completed at a time of
economic stress. Great houses were alien to American manners, experience, and culture, the critics scolded. They were "socially inappropriate." They were evidence of "conspicuous consumption." Nonetheless,
most New Yorkers of the Gilded Age liked the way the new houses
looked on the street. They were beginning to take pride in the gathering
spectacle of beauty on Fifth Avenue, which suggested a whole new
urban character. It was the first show of American taste, they said, the
first glimpse of an American style. All that had been needed for the free
flow of artistic expression was a class of patrons who, like the Medicis,
could fund a cult of art.

One of the great admirers of Hunt's Vanderbilt house was a young
architect named Charles McKim, who had formed a partnership with
William Mead and Stanford White in 1879. McKim, who was also a
product of the Ecole des Beaux-Arts in Paris, professed that he was
soothed by the mass and the stability of the building—by its intimations
of immortality—and that he liked to take a stroll up Fifth Avenue to gaze
upon it before he went to sleep. McKim was an urban soul; he enjoyed
the city, and was excited by its growth, its gaiety, its accelerating
rhythms. His partners shared his positive view of urban life, and his firm,
after early years designing picturesque Shingle Style cottages in the
country, shifted its focus to the urban center. The firm's positive view
of the city was a progressive one. Traditionalists, holding fast to the

Jeffersonian view of the city as negative, seemed to want to impede urban growth, to preserve order and innocence. Progressives, on the other hand, were optimistic and energized in the face of change; they felt the tug of the future.

As a firm, McKim, Mead and White formed a near-perfect union. They had been shaped by the best minds in architecture: McKim by the Ecole des Beaux-Arts; Mead by his studies with Russell Sturgis, a committed Ruskinian; White, by an apprenticeship with Henry Hobson Richardson. Their disciplines and temperaments were complementary; together they had a breadth of vision and purpose. They were like a sailing vessel, White's son, Lawrence, would say—patient and idealistic McKim, the hull; artistic White, the sails; and level-headed Mead, the anchor and rudder. Their motto was "Vogue la Galère," a nautical idiom that was translated as "Here Goes." Over the next twenty-five years, they would escort the city, mentally and physically, into the twentieth century.

IT TOOK almost a decade for McKim, Mead and White to find the proper footing in the city. During this time, as the partners were looking for their discipline, they designed a variety of fine town houses, mainly for Knickerbocker families; a bachelor apartment house named the Percival; and two unusual domestic structures that fell somewhere between the prototypes drawn for the private house and the communal apartment buildings.

The Charles L. Tiffany house, which was erected on the northwest corner of 72nd Street and Madison Avenue between 1882 and 1885, looked like it might have been Stanford White's homage to his mentor, H. H. Richardson. It was a huge brick fortress on a heavy, parapetlike stone base, with a steeply pitched gable for a roof and a wide semicircular arch and grille for a front door. While the massive masonry and the authority of expression were reminiscent of Richardson, the design was in fact part White, part Louis Comfort Tiffany. Tiffany, an artist whom White admired and with whom he had already collaborated on interior decoration, had been delegated by his father to oversee the project, and he had sketched the shape of the building and the design for his own quarters under the roof. The Tiffany house was divided into three apartments,

OPPOSITE TOP: Tiffany's house, on the northwest corner of 72nd and Madison, 1885. OPPOSITE BOTTOM: The vestibule of Tiffany's studio.

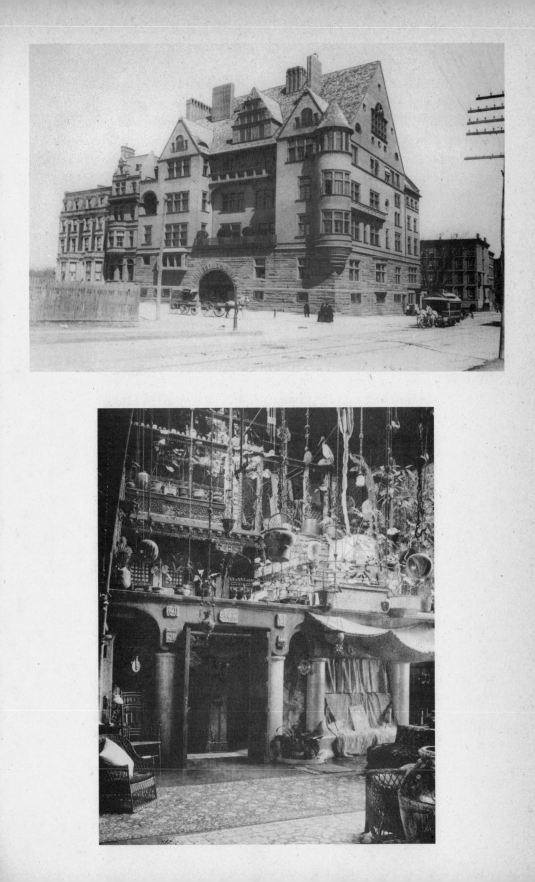

which provided homes for three families. Charles was meant to occupy the two floors above the base; his married daughter and her family, the third floor; and Louis and his family, a duplex studio apartment above. In concept the scheme recalled the twin brownstones William H. Vanderbilt had built for himself and his daughters at 51st Street, although it was vertical. Like Vanderbilt, the senior Tiffany, founder of the New York silver company that bore his name, was making a patriarchal gesture; he wanted to offer support and security to his exotic son, who had been widowed and left with three young children.

The six-story fifty-seven-room mansion on 72nd Street excited constant comment in New York. Given Louis Tiffany's reputation as America's leading decorator and the ever-growing interest in the field, his own apartment was of particular note. From the street, it looked like the crown of a palace. Inside, it was a grand and theatrical place of residence, with long perspectives on Central Park and the sleepy East Side. Tiffany had provided himself with spacious family quarters, which included a breakfast room, a formal dining room, and a ballroom, as well as a vast studio. He installed a portion of a two-thousand-year-old Indian palace in one room and decorated the mantelpiece of another with his collection of Japanese sword guards and Pompeiian glass. In his studio, located at the top of a palatial staircase, Tiffany indulged his decorative genius further, setting his glasses high in the walls, where they were lit by outside light; suspending lamps of many shades of red, rose, cream, and yellow from the twenty-foot-high ceiling; carving four immense fireplaces from a central chimney, painted black. "It was a dream: *Arabian Nights* in New York," a visitor recalled. Thirty years later, Tiffany would stage his famous Egyptian Pageant here, the most lavish costume fête ever seen in New York, according to the *New York Times,* which gave it a full page of pictures in the Sunday edition.

Tiffany's house suited him well, for it was both of and ahead of its time. "It is a style of its own—one which must be judged by intrinsic standards and not by reference to bygone fashions and antiquarian dogmas," a perceptive critic noted. It was a mansion like Vanderbilt's and an apartment building, a private house, and a multiple dwelling. (His father, in fact, never moved into the space on the lower floors, which was divided into self-contained rental apartments.) Tiffany had no nasty preconceptions about communal housing; never a conventional figure, he had lived in an apartment before and made it a model for urban living. In 1878 he had moved his family into the top story of the Bella Apartments, a modern building across from Madison Square, and spent the next years redecorating the rooms in the profusion of patterns and blend of Eastern and Western styles that he loved. When it was done, the suite stood as the earliest example of his work in interior design, and was the only apartment included in *Artistic Houses.*

With the appearance of the new Tiffany home, the idea of sharing houses made a tiny inroad into high society. Here was an instance in which several generations of a fine family had chosen to dwell under the same extended roof, and while it was all the same family, the arrangement was nonetheless a departure from the aristocratic rule of one house to one patriarch. While it was an experiment, and a one-of-a-kind commission for an unusual and artistic client, the Tiffany house posed an interesting parallel to another group of houses that McKim, Mead and White had designed and put into construction at the same time, twenty-two blocks to the south.

To a casual observer of the street scene, the Villard Houses at Madison Avenue between 50th and 51st streets looked like an alternative solution to the question of how a gentleman of means might share space in the city. Rather than a great vertical pile of private residences, it was a horizontal arrangement of six fine five-story houses, joined shoulder to shoulder and side to side to form a classical U around a formal courtyard. Henry Villard, the German-born publisher of the New York *Post,* who was in the process of consolidating a transcontinental railroad, had conceived the idea for this house group himself; he planned to occupy the largest house, sell the others to friends, and shape a sort of residential forum. The scheme would not only create a pleasant neighborhood unit, he thought, but it would also enliven the urban landscape and perhaps even inspire better domestic architecture.

Architectural historians could find a gentle precedent in the city for the idea of architectural ensemble. In some respects, the Villard Houses were merely a more artful arrangement of row houses than usual. It was another variation on the traditional English terrace housing that began with Inigo Jones's Covent Garden in the seventeenth century and took modified form in Colonnade Row and London Terrace in New York. The House of Mansions and the Jones blocks also may have influenced Villard and his architects. In all these run-on residences, there were shared walls, a shared purpose, and a shared image and identity.

The Villard Houses looked grand and imposing. Although they were no larger than many clusters of town houses, they seemed considerably

The Villard Houses, seen from St. Patrick's Cathedral, 1885. The church lawn and the courtyard created an oasis almost as large as Gramercy Park, as Villard himself had envisioned.

more important. The courtyard lent them drama and dignity and created a shape and a unity. A host of Renaissance details, repeated in moldings, windows, and entrance architraves, emphasized the harmony of the design. The design itself announced McKim, Mead and White's conversion, once and for all, to Renaissance classicism, for it was an Italian palazzo, reminiscent of the Palazzo della Cancelleria and the Villa Farnesina of fifteenth- and sixteenth-century Rome.

Joseph Morrill Wells, who had been Stanford White's principal assistant, was responsible for pushing the firm into a commitment to classicism, and he had personally articulated the form the Villard Houses had taken—he rose to the status of full partner thereafter. It was Villard

himself, however, who had the inspiration for the house and who, against the wishes of his architects (who had a fancy for the fine pallor of limestone), insisted upon New York brownstone for its cover. He also initiated the courtyard arrangement, which, Villard reasoned, would secure his privacy (his neighborhood had two orphan asylums, three hospitals, and aggressive industrial enterprises on Fourth Avenue) and guarantee him tranquillity and light.

Villard was a cultured European, and he had experience with cities. He had seen at first hand how people lived in a quiet and secluded way in the midst of an urban area. He had seen French *hôtels particuliers,* Italian *palazzi,* and the block-long apartment houses under construction in Vienna and Berlin. They all looked like important family houses on the outside, but on the inside contained half a dozen or more separate dwellings. The home in which Villard grew up in Zweibrücken, several buildings at the University of Munich where he studied, his favorite palaces in Frankfurt, all bore a resemblance to his own new complex.

It was a fortuitous collaboration between a strong-minded client and a strong-minded young architectural firm, for the Villard Houses caught the principles that expressed them both best: ambition, optimism, urbanism, a respect for order, discipline, and decorum. Villard had had ample reason to turn confidently to McKim, Mead and White: through a labyrinth of coincidences, he was already bound to the firm by family ties and liberal sympathies. As a young reporter, he had followed the Union cause fervently, which had drawn him into a circle of abolitionists dominated by William Lloyd Garrison and Miller McKim, the father of Charles. He had married Garrison's daughter, Frances, whose brother was already married to McKim's sister, Lucy. Together with Miller McKim and Richard Grant White, the father of Stanford, Villard had founded a liberal literary magazine called *The Nation,* which he purchased in 1881. Before commissioning his new city residence, Villard had engaged McKim, Mead and White to realize a large body of other work for him. Most of it annotated the enlarging horizons and fortunes of an energetic builder of empires—extravagant passenger and freight terminals, hotels, hospitals, and line depots planted along the route of the Northern Pacific Railroad from Minnesota to the Great Northwest. One reason, it seemed, that Wells had been chosen to do the elevation of the Villard Houses was that the founding partners were always out West, inspecting building sites and pursuing railroad dreams.

Villard's apartment, 451 Madison Avenue, which was entered to one side of the courtyard, occupied the southern wing along 50th Street and contained dozens of rooms, on four floors, plus a basement with a kitchen, a laundry, wine room, servants' dining room, billiard room, and a cellar for the mechanical plant. The scale of the house was magnificent. It was borrowed from the great classical houses of Europe, where proportion itself created style, and ornament was organic rather than incidental or imposed. On the first floor, which lay at the top of a short flight of marble steps and resembled the row house parlor floor in elevation, there was a great groin-vaulted "living" hall, a two-story barrel-vaulted

OPPOSITE: From the drawing room of the Villard Houses through the hall to the music room (as seen in the lower right of the floor plan).

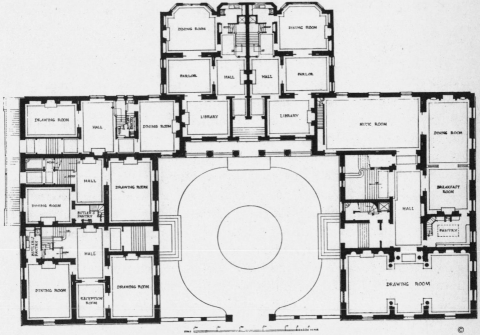

FIRST FLOOR PLAN

HENRY VILLARD, RESIDENCE, NEW YORK CITY. 7
1885

music room decorated with biblical panels copied from Della Robbia's *Cantoria* in Florence, a baronial dining room of richly carved English oak (which could be subdivided into a breakfast room), a triple drawing room, arranged enfilade. Upstairs, there were bedrooms and sitting rooms for the family, and Villard's library, which was en suite with a guest room, dressing room, and baths.

The interiors had been planned as the culmination of the whole architectural experience of the Villard Houses. Accordingly, the terms of sale stipulated that each owner had to engage McKim, Mead and White to complete his apartment. The work was consistently rich and expressive. The materials were of the highest quality—marbles, mosaics, marquetry and parquetry, gilt, custom-made furniture, embroidered silks and gold-threaded brocades for the walls, electrical fittings that were the first to be designed to be compatible with city power when it arrived. The appointments were exquisite. Stanford White had engaged his friend the sculptor Augustus Saint-Gaudens, the painter Frances Lathrop, and both John La Farge and Louis Tiffany to work on the interior in a collaborative fashion. For the smaller-scale ornamentation, he had orchestrated a legion of local craftsmen.

Ironically, for wealthy New Yorkers, the Villard Houses set an example of restraint. Compared to the Vanderbilt house, the group was thought to be merely decorous. *Artistic Houses* photographed the house for its fourth volume and noted "a chaste simplicity" and "a profound loyalty to what is delicate and self-repressive." Nonetheless, when Villard's plans for the railroad failed, an angry public, thinking the entire building was his, came to his doorstep to taunt him for his greed. In early 1884, with only several weeks of residence in an unfinished house, Villard left his complex to trustees for completion and sale, and retreated to his country house to live.

By the time Whitelaw Reid, a fellow journalist and publisher, bought Villard's residence in 1886, the house group was a conspicuous landmark. It was the first Roman High Renaissance palace in the city. Moreover, it was a unique place to live. Although it was really a millionaire's mansion, it was as different from the houses rising on Fifth Avenue as the respective avenues and the respective owners were different from each other. Fifth Avenue houses like the Vanderbilts' or the Goulds' were all ego. The Villard Houses group had a more sedate, more temperate bearing. From the street it was difficult even to know how to divide the mass into its components, so well were house lines disguised behind the design. It was easier to see a single house occupied by a number of well-to-do people. The building radiated a sense of integration.

The Villard Houses were important buildings, for they had a strong effect on architectural fashions of the day, and they intensified the appreciation of classicism that fueled the movement to come. As a model for upper-class living, however, they were admired in theory and never duplicated in fact. The wealthy of New York had ideas about gracious living that had little regard for neighbors. "Most nineteenth-century millionaires courted fame, not anonymity; what they considered to be an ideal personal monument wasn't a fraction of a house on Madison Avenue but the whole of a house on Fifth Avenue." Nonetheless, the Villard Houses exerted a psychological influence by their mere presence in the city, for they took command of the street, and they struck a pose of eminent sociability. They were row houses of unparalleled elegance, and they were also cooperative apartments of a very special order. In hindsight, like the Tiffany house, they would look like part of the slowly maturing revisionist movement in housing.

7

Two Communal Palaces: The Dakota, the Osborne

Ｎew york had rich new taste, and a rich new emblem of that taste—the palace. Hunt's splendid image of domesticity stuck in the city. It had a sense of fitness; it was authoritative, and it was seductive too. Nathalie Smith Dana, the daughter of the rector of St. James Episcopal Church on Madison Avenue at 68th Street, who grew up on the East Side of New York in the 1880s, recalled how she tried to catch a glimpse inside the new houses when a butler opened the door to a caller, or the woman of the house left for an outing. Walking down Fifth Avenue in the afternoon with the sun in her eyes was a reminder of the blinding light of prosperity, she said. For such a promenade, she dressed in a long full gown with a laced waist, a high collar, and a heavy veil. According to the popular decree, she walked on the west side of the avenue, where the most splendid houses were located, for "they created an atmosphere which attracted stylish people to walk on the sidewalks in front of them instead of on the other side. We liked to walk there though we would never enter the world the mansions represented."

That world was a new and a narrow one, populated almost exclusively by the highest order of capitalist. Mrs. Dana herself had been a proper young lady, from the respectable upper-middle-class Smith family from New England. She had been comfortable, enlightened, privileged. As a young girl, she lived on 71st Street, on Lenox Hill, a neighborhood east of Central Park that was too undeveloped for the first families, too remote for the fashion-minded, an unresolved terrain of churches, institutions, brownstones, farmhouses, shanties, and open fields. Then in 1884, her family moved to a larger house on the corner of Park Avenue and 69th Street, one of a brick row designed by a builder, but finished inside by the architectural firm McKim, Mead and White. Architects, Mrs. Dana noted, were rarely used for private houses in 1884. She had been proud of her home, with its mansard roof, stained-glass windows, and grand dining room, but she also understood that it was not socially ambitious.

Almost directly across Central Park from the St. James parish, a new variation on the domestic palace made a conspicuous appearance that same year. The building was a vast and dignified château set on the high ground above the park and the lake at West 72nd Street. Constructed of two different colors of brick, set on a heavy high stone base, and finished with an expressive roofline of gables and chimneys, it resembled the Tiffany house in general shape and impression. It, too, was massive, and overpowered a street scene that included wandering goats and small truck farms. It looked both important and unlikely, a sophisticated stranger in a one-horse town.

The Dakota, as the building was known, sat virtually alone on the still rural Upper West Side, all the more imposing and iconoclastic for its regal isolation. For all appearances the colossal new home of some tsar of untold wealth, the building in fact contained homes for scores of ambitious families. It was a new version of a luxury apartment house, and it was planned like the cornerstone of a new city. Edward Clark, its builder, was confident about the future in store for the West Side, for the population of New York had doubled in a decade, and a million and a half people could not be contained downtown much longer. Clark had named the building, eight years before either North or South Dakota was admitted to the Union, in response to a friend's mockery that West 72nd Street was Indian territory: "Why don't you go a few blocks more and build it out in Dakota?" The Dakota was also known as Clark's Folly, and an Indian head was prominently carved on its facade.

The Dakota was a daring building and a daring venture. Although its situation seemed enviable—the peace and quiet, the unobstructed light, the country air, the boundless vista—many New Yorkers thought that a view to a vast greensward was a lonely prospect. Others condemned the intrusion of a bulky nine-story silhouette into the precious arcadian landscape of the park. There was, in fact, no other significant shape on the western horizon. The Upper West Side was still a patchwork of small sleepy settlements and vacant lots, interrupted here and there by a country house, an inn, an asylum or a saloon. In 1880, the Sixth Avenue Elevated had been extended up Ninth Avenue to 155th Street, which Clark hoped would spur development in the area. That year, Riverside Drive had been officially opened too. To further encourage settlement in the area, Egbert Viele, the other strong voice in the new West Side Association, had suggested that above 59th Street, Eighth Avenue and Eleventh Avenue be given the new names of Central Park West and West End Avenue. Viele, who lived in a large house on the Hudson, thought that the West Side had natural topographical advantages. His names were meant to conjure up the great capitals of Europe to which it compared favorably.

The most daring aspect of Clark's scheme was the extravagance of his building, which his architect, Henry J. Hardenbergh, designed for the well-to-do. While apartment living was beginning to gain favor among the middle classes, there was nothing in the air to suggest that people of wealth and standing were ready to give up the dream of private houses. Vanderbilt's example had served to renew other ambitions, to inspire grandiosity and encourage pretension in the single home. Yet the Dakota was a direct response to Mr. Vanderbilt. "There are but few persons who are princely enough to wish to occupy an entire palace," Clark had lectured the West Side Association back in 1879, "but there are many who would like to occupy a portion of a great building, which would be more perfect in its arrangement than any palace in Europe."

The Dakota was just such a building—"One of the Most Perfect Apartment Houses in the World," the New York *Daily Graphic* proclaimed ecstatically in a headline on opening day, October 24, 1884. It presented a very different proposition than the discreet Stuyvesant, Albany, or Bradley. It had a noble bearing, projecting high above any building on the West Side, and an imposing style, gleaned from various beloved schools of the nineteenth century. Behind a facade described as Brewery Brick Victorian neo-Gothic Eclectic, the building was shaped like a huge hollow square, with a large open courtyard, 55 by 90 feet, planned as a carriage drive at center, and separate entryways to its

OPPOSITE TOP: Looking north to the Dakota, designed by Henry J. Hardenbergh in 1883. Surrounding the building were farms, shanties, and a few brownstones. Some of the streets had not yet been graded. OPPOSITE BOTTOM: The ground floor plan. Note in the lower right (southeast corner) the layout for a restaurant, café, and private dining room.

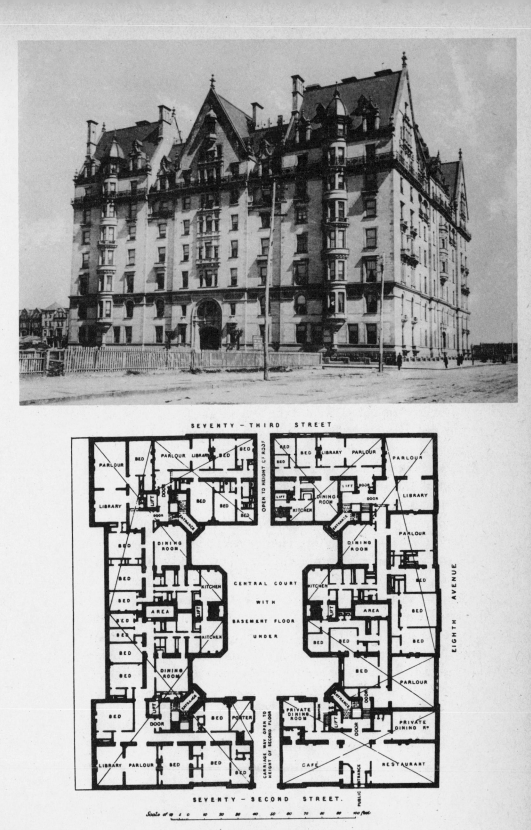

THE DAKOTA APARTMENT-HOUSE, NEW YORK.

GROUND FLOOR PLAN

apartments at the corners. Inside, the building was immense and contained 65 suites and 623 rooms in all. "A visitor is lost . . . room after room is passed, until their number appears legion," a reviewer reported after an inspection tour. The largest room was the public dining room on the ground floor, which was fashioned after an example in an English manor house, with a baronial fifteen-foot fireplace, an inlaid marble floor, and an elaborately carved, quartered-oak ceiling. Adjacent to this, "the handsomest dining room in Manhattan," according to the newspapers, was a smaller private dining room, fitted with mahogany and large beveled-glass windows, and a ladies' reception room, which was "the gem of the House" and featured a frieze of clematis painted by the famous Greatorex sisters.

The sixty-five apartments in the Dakota ranged in size from four to twenty rooms. Although Hardenbergh had originally planned for "Suits [sic] of Apartments for forty two families besides Janitors" and designed six roughly equal apartments on each of the seven main floors, Clark had begun to rent his "French flats," as the records described them, to friends and acquaintances while the building was still in the early stages of construction. As a chronicler of the Dakota's history has recalled, "This meant that Hardenbergh's floor plans for the building changed almost daily, as apartments were enlarged and divided to suit tenants' wishes. Walls came down and doorways were created as the architect tried to fit individual apartments together like pieces of a jigsaw puzzle. In the beginning he had planned to place the largest apartments on the lower two floors . . . because elevators were still something of a novelty and not entirely trusted. . . . Also, Hardenbergh reasoned that lower-floor living would seem more familiar to New Yorkers who were accustomed to living in town houses. The eighth and ninth floors were to be used exclusively as laundry rooms, service and storage rooms, and servants' rooms. Then Hardenbergh hit upon the idea of turning the second floor into hotel-style guest rooms that could be rented to tenants to put out-of-town friends. And in each of the four corners of the eighth floor he designed four smaller apartments." For Clark's personal quarters, which had been allocated to the sixth floor in the hope of popularizing upper-story living, Hardenbergh designed an eighteen-room suite, which held the building's second largest room, a ballroom-like drawing room with twin fireplaces and Baccarat chandeliers.

The scale of the Dakota was grand, its ornamentation extravagant. One look at its roofline told a passerby that it was not an ordinary apartment house—the two-story copper-trimmed slate roof seemed to break out irrepressibly into a fantasy of expressive features: turrets, towers, chimneys, flagpoles, finials, and windows of every conceivable style, size, and shape. Inside, the voluminous rooms, the fifteen-foot ceilings, the one-of-a-kind carved marble mantelpieces bespoke luxury that was unknown even to wealthy householders. Scale and ornament were Hardenbergh's particular strength, as Clark had learned in the course of building the Vancorlear with him. In the Dakota, the young architect extended the form he had set down three years earlier, making it bigger, bolder, and more opulent. He had been given free rein, and Clark spared no expense.

When Clark was asked why, at the end of a successful career with the I. M. Singer Company, he was investing his energy and considerable assets in as experimental a venture as a major apartment building, he replied that "it was to make money." Given the fact that the Dakota was in no way a speculative building, it was an odd answer. Hardenbergh's design and Clark's principles allowed few if any of the compromises that made other buildings profitable. The Dakota ranked with St. Patrick's Cathedral, the Plaza Hotel, and the Navarro as one of the most costly buildings in New York. It had been constructed like a fortress—its foundation was laid on solid rock; its walls tapered from twenty-eight inches thick on the first floor to sixteen inches thick above the sixth, for strength; its floors were laid three feet thick. All materials—including the cast-iron washbasins, porcelain bathroom fixtures, and solid-brass hardware—were of the highest quality. Four passenger elevators and four service elevators created a remarkable circulation system. Four thousand electric lights and three hundred electric bells were distributed through the building, with private wires running to the fire station, the Dakota stables, the telegraph and messenger offices, and the florist. In the basement, eight boilers supplied steam heat and 120-horsepower dynamos generated electricity—enough to supply the entire new neighborhood Clark hoped would spring to life between Central Park West and Columbus from 70th Street up to 74th.

In Clark's mind, nonetheless, the Dakota was a business venture. Historians point out that Clark applied the same principles of promotion to the project that he had used so successfully to create a large and gentrified new market for his sewing machines. "Like a sewing machine, the Dakota would offer convenience, a short-cut route to opulent living with none of the problems of upkeep, and at a fraction of the expense that went with owning a private house. Like a sewing machine, the Dakota would offer 'leisure for rest and refinement' and comfort . . . which could formerly be attained only by the wealthy few." Clark had perceived that there were new gradations of wealth in the maturing American society, that there were many rich and successful citizens, like himself, who were not among the anointed Four Hundred who filled Mrs. Astor's ballroom but who nonetheless shared their appetite for luxury. The Dakota was built to astound, to accommodate, and to reassure people of means like himself.

WALKING THROUGH the Dakota today, one can touch base with the mind of the 1880s. There are important elements in the building that not only fulfilled the desires of Old New York but even now make one yearn for the stability of a traditional style of architecture. Above all else the Dakota is the very image of a house—that is, a unified structure built with a single anthropocentric identity. It could be the palace of one very rich man, one local sovereign. Put in nineteenth-century perspective, it is a satisfactory reflection of a well-bred Victorian. Like a house, the Dakota defines its site and has a firm attitude toward the street. A low iron railing of gargoyles and a moat, which also allows light to enter the basement, separate the building from the sidewalk—a statement of propriety and privacy—yet they do not cut off a sense of the life within. The face of the building is symmetrical and open, directed toward and inclusive of 72nd Street and Central Park West. Its features are expressive and offer bits of artistry and individuality with which to identify and establish a sense of place and of home. However inflated its proportions, however grandiose its shape, the Dakota is scaled to human beings—it is familiar, romantic, and articulate.

Where the exterior of the building implies a certain image of home, the interior of the Dakota substantiates it. When one enters the building, exterior spaces diminish gradually into interior spaces and one is modulated into the scale of the building rather than submitted abruptly to its immensity. The generous arched entryway, guarded by sentry boxes, leads to the traditional space of a formal courtyard with fountains, which in turn leads to the elevators in the four corners. The elevator lobbies are small and intimate; the elevators themselves, leisurely and elegant, give direct access to an apartment, thus eliminating the possibility of unexpected public encounters.

Hardenbergh worked hard to obviate the communal and exaggerate the personal aspects of his building. He provided individual apartments with all the virtues of the finest town houses except verticality: walls so thick that apartments remained warm in winter and cool in summer, floors constructed to block city noises and neighbors' lives. Floor space was shaped into lavish versions of the traditional components of home: a typical plan had a vestibule or antechamber (12 feet square), parlor (15 by 27 feet), drawing room (18 by 20), dining room (12 by 20), bedrooms (14 by 22), bath, kitchen, butler's pantry, and servants' rooms. The larger suites, which held as many as nine bedrooms, were further extended to include a library, a ladies' boudoir, or a billiard room. All chambers were finished with painstaking attention to detail: mahogany paneling, elaborate gaslight fixtures and chandeliers, carved ceiling friezes, sliding glass doors, abundant and heavily ornamented fireplaces. (Clark's own suite had seventeen fireplaces.) The bearing posts in the drawing room were transformed into Corinthian columns—structural statuary that expressed the taste of the day and the artistic energy demanded of the situation.

The Dakota offered New Yorkers an apartment house that was a cross between a millionaire's mansion and a Parisian hotel. It was a communal palace, a new type of building in which every comfort of a great house was developed in multiple form. Not surprisingly, the building was fully rented by the time of its completion, although Clark had died, and the legacy of the building had fallen to his twelve-year-old grandson and namesake. Its first generation of tenants were prosperous New York businessmen; older people, without children; and those like Gustav Schirmer, the music publisher, Theodore Steinway, a piano merchant, or John Browning, an educator—people with an artistic or an intellectual bent. Schirmer, for example, the building's most active host, entertained a bohemian crowd that included European musical personalities like Peter Ilyich Tchaikovsky, and literary figures like William Dean Howells and the young novelist Stephen Crane. Neither Schirmer's cultural interests nor his radical ideas about respectable housing would have been approved in proper society downtown, where the very scent of something artistic was still suspicious. Not surprisingly, when the first *Social Register* appeared in 1887, no tenants from the Dakota were to be found in its pages. Those who would take up residence on the West Side in an apartment house inhabited a domain outside the dictates of form and fashion. It was smart and even a bit flashy to live in the Dakota, but it was not fashionable. As one of the original

tenants of the building explained, "Fashionable, to me, implies conformity, and the Dakota didn't conform to anything in the city at the
time."

The situation and the structure of the Dakota gave life within the
building a different character than life in a house downtown. To begin
with, its geographic isolation forced a well-serviced self-sufficiency on
its tenants. There were no shops, services, entertainments, or even
schools in the area, and Ladies' Mile, the commercial heart of the city
where everyone met, was a long journey away. The ride down to
Madison Square took nearly an hour by horsecar or horse-and-carriage,
and most ladies had to make a day of it, lunching at Purcell's across from
Lord and Taylor, or taking tea at A. T. Stewart's. It was an awkward
time to be dependent on public transportation for the process of social-
ization. Elsewhere in the city, society moved as pedestrians and took to
the streets for social purposes. It had grown too large to meet daily on
Fifth Avenue, but it still liked to promenade.

Until the telephone came into common use in the late 1890s, society
maintained its relationships by making and receiving personal calls. The
act of calling celebrated holidays, measured out courtships and friend-
ships, registered appreciation after dinner parties and balls. The ritual was
elaborate and time consuming, and provided the basic fabric of a day.
The flip side of delivering calling cards was receiving visitors and being
"at home." Being at home at the Dakota was distinctly different from
being at home on Fifth Avenue or Irving Place. Callers did come up to
West 72nd Street—bundled up with scarves, muffs, and lap robes as if
for an arctic expedition—but it was an excursion to come up far past the
effective end of town, particularly by coach, and a lady did not go calling
by the el. The Upper West Side was like an outlying territory, and the
Dakota an exotic outpost therein. It was apart from the bigger city, and
that apartness made it a great curiosity, both to sightseers who came on
weekends to gawk at its grandeur and to friends who had been invited
within.

The very architecture of the Dakota made it a dramatic place to
entertain friends. The great iron gates, the greeting from a uniformed
doorman, the grand march through the *cour d'honneur,* the stately rise
upstairs in a hydraulic elevator (powered by the rainwater collected on
the roof and radiator water collected in drip pans in each apartment)—
each introductory element made an aesthetic impression. Inside, an
apartment opened up with a spatial sweep that no respectable town

house could effect, and provided hospitality more impressive than the nicest corner of an ordinary parlor could deliver. Doorways draped with tasseled portieres opened into velvet-hung rooms that opened into other rooms, creating a palatial reception. The voluminousness of the suite made a visitor feel formal and grand. A trip to the roof garden, where the view expanded more than twenty miles in all directions, added a touch of theater.

To the tenants who lived there, the Dakota was a private village. The services it provided insulated it from the inadequacies of its neighborhood. The fine dining rooms with their elaborate menus stood in for restaurant life; the livery and boarding stables at 74th Street and Broadway provided horses and carriages to ease the transit to downtown New York. According to the custom of the time, hairdressers, manicurists, and dressmakers came to the house; the Irish cook or the German coachman worried about the marketing and groceries. There was at least as much room for servants in the Dakota as in a row house, given the extra rooms under the roof; three in service seemed to be the general rule for most ladies, although at least one tenant who was "not all that rich" kept a cook, laundress, chambermaid, governess, and coachman, and, from time to time, a valet. The building staff supplemented personal servants: a manager who oversaw general operations and screened prospective tenants; a janitor; and a fleet of chambermaids, hallboys, doormen, repairmen, and painters (the ones who had originally covered the interior walls with frescoes, friezes, and French tints). Central Park, which lay outside the door like a private preserve, provided recreation and populist diversions. From the Sheep Meadow or the lake, the Dakota looked even larger than it was, for it sat on one of the highest points of land in the city. Returning home after a walk or carriage ride, one couldn't but wonder at the very existence of the place.

In a single architectural gesture, the Dakota set the character of the West Side. Its grand style and scale invited imitation; its character encouraged company. As Clark had planned, it would determine the future development of the area, for it stood there with authority, as if to say, "This is the way the West Side is going to be." West 72nd Street, swooping directly out from the park drive and maintained with pride by the Parks Department, had the promise of an elegant new thoroughfare, the main street of a new residential quarter. It was by covenant a quiet street, for the city had restricted access to commercial trucks, and even delivery wagons made their calls before 9 a.m. It was broad enough to be a European-style boulevard and to hold apartment houses and apartment hotels. Clark and Hardenbergh had already built a row of twenty-seven private town houses on the north side of West 73rd Street and a small apartment house, like an anchor, on the corner of Columbus. This was Clark's vision of an urban neighborhood: a great apartment house set as a centerpiece amid a harmony of small houses and flats.

In response to the appearance of the Dakota, there was a sudden ground swell of activity on the Upper West Side, as the city rushed to grade streets and a first wave of speculators began to erect small colonies of row houses. Stands of modest houses—five or seven or ten structures banded together by similar design—appeared in the 60s, 70s, or 80s around the new el stations. Across the street from the Dakota, a picturesque group of brownstones imitated its prominent gables and chimneys.

Eagerly critics announced that the forces of change were in motion. The *New York Times* reported that outcroppings of rock usually crowned by shanties and goats were being blasted out of existence, and then predicted the rapid population of this long-neglected part of New York. The *Real Estate Record* said, "The future of the west side no longer admits of dispute. Its destiny is undeniably a great one . . . there is much to confirm the belief that the west side of the future will contain the residences of the great majority of our citizens of refinement and wealth."

Like missionaries, a handful of churches sprang up in the vanguard. Then a firehouse arrived, and a few decorative row houses on side streets. After several house ensembles had appeared on West End Avenue, critics, charmed by their dormers and stepped gables or corner turrets and bow windows, began to crow about the end of the tyranny of brownstones. Architects were blending styles and creating a more varied streetscape composed of houses that were more expressive and more individualized. There was talk of a "West Side" architecture.

By 1890, however, it was clear that the excitement was premature. If a block like 78th Street was dominated by expensive and artistic houses, the next one was filling with tenements, and the next one was

OPPOSITE TOP: Looking north from the roof of the Dakota, 1886, toward the Museum of Natural History, at center, and new rows of "artistic" houses beyond. Note the el on Columbus Avenue and the telephone lines on Central Park West, which were buried underground in the 1890s.
OPPOSITE BOTTOM: Looking south, the Central Park Apartments and the new Osborne appear at the far left of a ragged perspective.

leased for kitchen gardens, or simply left to the ways of squatters. In fact, in spite of all the promotional activity, most of the West Side remained undeveloped. Most of its roads were country lanes, roughly graded and rarely paved. Only one or two streets north of 72nd Street had both flagging and paving; property owners themselves had poured asphalt on short stretches of 73rd Street and West End. Between the Dakota and the Museum of Natural History, on Central Park West, there was only a long bare stretch of tumbleweed lots. North of 86th Street, especially toward the river, the contours of the land were still rural, rising and falling around farmhouses and sheds. According to a survey of 1885, more than three-fourths of the lots between 59th and 155th streets were vacant; an even greater percentage were empty north of 72nd Street. Only 245 lots out of 2,238 were developed between 86th and 96th streets, for example, and 390 out of 2,980 between 96th and 100th. Among the hundred-odd buildings in progress, very few were first-class developments. Looking out from the roof of the Dakota, the landscape was desultory.

The Dakota has been called the Dowager Queen Mother of luxury apartment buildings. It took many years, however, before there were enough offspring to see the parentage. Before the turn of the century, a number of decent and comfortable multiple dwellings cropped up on both the East Side and the West Side of town, but only one other building could qualify as a communal palace. This building, on 57th Street, the second apartment house to take the name Osborne, was proclaimed the second successful luxury apartment building in the city. Like the Dakota, it made a definite statement on the street; it turned people's heads and, to some degree, their minds.

Fifty-seventh Street was a broad street, more like a north-south avenue in amplitude and attitude than a crosstown lateral, and it invited a bolder, braver kind of architecture. From the first signs of uptown development, larger buildings had gravitated naturally to 57th Street, particularly to those corners where it met the equally generous widths of Seventh Avenue, Broadway, or Eighth Avenue. Since the brownstone fever had raged itself out, architects were beginning to recognize the opportunity to experiment for the purpose of effect and display. The first notable shape on 57th Street had been the gray stone Baptist church between Sixth and Seventh. Farther west stood a row of five pretty brick houses under one long mansard roof. Nearing Seventh Avenue there was Hubert and Pirsson's "well-behaved" studio building, the Rembrandt, then the new Grenoble apartment house on the southwest corner, and across the street, the Osborne, the highest and "the hugest" building in the city yet.

The Osborne, designed in 1879 by James E. Ware, was fashioned like a Renaissance palazzo. Constructed of a handsome, heavily rusticated deep-red stone, it had a simple boxlike shape and a rough fortified look that gave it an aura of romance that grew more powerful with age. Whatever else it was, however, the Osborne was most clearly a grand house inflated to fill six lots and eleven stories. What might be a one-story base and a one-story formal entrance was blown up to two stories, the crowning cornice normally at the roof line was placed under the top two stories to reduce the building's apparent height, and the middle seven floors were treated with such domestic features as balustrades and banks of bay windows to disguise their monotony and break up their mass.

Behind a plan that has been called "design by inflation" lay, in part, architects' inexperience with huge residential buildings. But the shape was also another literal version of home as a palace, and in that it was perfectly calibrated to the dreams of the day. It was Vanderbilt's vision answered. It was Villard's vision restructured and recast. It was also Queen Victoria's vision transposed, for Thomas Osborne, the stone contractor who had purchased the land and undertaken the construction of the building, had been enamored of the monarch's Osborne House on the Isle of Wight. It was rumored that he had sent his workmen to the premises so that they could reproduce its most opulent decorative motifs on West 57th Street. Osborne's extravagance soon forced him into bankruptcy, however, and like its near neighbor, the Navarro, the Osborne changed ownership before it was fully completed.

In the months before its opening, the Osborne was advertised in city newspapers—prominently, with emphatic boldface type—as "the most magnificently finished and decorated apartment house in the world." The building, all mass on the exterior, was all opulence inside. As if to announce its artistic intentions, an elaborate front porch and entry vestibule deposited a visitor in a lobby that had been designed to overwhelm, to transport. It was a richly architectural space, framed by arches and a pair of baronial staircases, and colored in jewel-like reds, blues, greens, and golds. With a carved Renaissance ceiling, an inlaid marble floor, and friezes and dadoes, it displayed a veritable museum of decorative effects—marbles, mother-of-pearl, iridescent glass, bas-relief sculpture,

The Osborne, 1885. The original design included a croquet court and garden on the roof. Note the delivery boy on the street.

The lobby of the Osborne at 205 West 57th Street had the opulence of the
Byzantine Revival churches of the era.

and foil-backed and trompe l'oeil mosaics. A Swiss-born sculptor and painter named Jacob Holzer had designed the space (proudly carving his name into his work several times) and the newly formed Tiffany and Company contributed the mosaics and stained glass.

The Osborne had a very different drama than the Dakota did. By power of suggestion, the Dakota seemed to have something open and adventuresome about its space, while the Osborne seemed effectively eastern—more ponderous, more cultured, more centered. It felt like a sanctuary. The richness of its decoration created a sense of well-being, of a beautiful Byzantine world closed in upon itself. The solidity of its construction, which provided fine insulation and soundproofing, guaranteed peace and quiet, a feature that would attract Carnegie Hall musicians into the building after the concert hall was raised across the street in 1891. It had its own florist shop, fancy dining room, and private billiard room, its own doctor and pharmacy; a year-round croquet court was planned for the roof, and it felt complete, like a small city. There were forty families in the building, arranged in four apartments on each floor except for the second, which also held the banquet room, and the eleventh, which was reserved for servants. Each was appointed with parquet floors, tile-framed fireplaces with elaborate firebacks, mahogany or oak wainscotting, and sliding doors, and was generously shaped into parlor, reception room, library, dining room, kitchen, and pantry up front, and two or more bedrooms in the back. By an ingenious arrangement reminiscent of Hunt's Studio Building and Hubert Home Clubs, the public rooms in the front had fifteen-foot ceilings, while the private rooms were stacked up eight feet tall to create a semi-duplex scheme joined by a half-flight of stairs.

The Osborne sat "on the highest ground below Fifty-ninth Street" as the advertisements read, and it was an imposing newcomer, even in a neighborhood that already seemed to have an unusually large congregation of "superior" apartment houses—the Albany, the Vancorlear, the Grenoble, the Bradley, the Navarro. Its very height gave it a special prominence because it was the last tall apartment house to appear in New York before June 1885, when the Daly Law passed the state legislature and limited such structures to five or six stories, which effectively confined them to the more modest category of French flats.

For the remainder of the nineteenth century, any apartment house with serious ambitions of height and mass had to masquerade as an "apartment hotel," upon which looser restrictions were imposed. Any architect with progressive ideas for the streetscape had to redirect his enthusiasms to the sort of commercial structures that were rising downtown. In structures like Hunt's Tribune Building of 1884, Bradford Gilbert's Tower Building the next year, in which the young architect had proposed "to stand a steel bridge structure on end" and George B. Post's World Building, the elevator would have its way, inducing "elevator architecture" that was first eleven, then thirteen and, in the World Building, a revolutionary fifteen stories high. New Yorkers were both fascinated and appalled at these spectacles; like ancient Romans, they gathered at their bases to discuss their certain doom. In 1895, when Bruce Price applied the principle by then called "steel cage construction" to a twenty-story tower, it seemed so farfetched it was called a "cloud presser," or "skyscraper"—the city's first. It stood on Broadway across the way from Trinity Church, once the icon of modern times.

If the Dakota set the character of the West Side, the Daly Law delayed character development for several decades. It is unlikely, however, that the rush to communal palaces would have been precipitous had a hiatus not been imposed. The West Side was a great enigma to planners. While by mere geographic extension of the mansions and fine buildings on and around Fifth Avenue, the Upper East Side was marked for a respectable future, the Upper West Side had no such projected character. Speculators had hoped to lure the wealthy up and across town, and in development schemes they made persistent allusions to the elegant Western sections of European capitals. But there were so few substantial structures in place on the street that it was difficult to anticipate the sort of building that would prove the most profitable or the most popular, or the class of people who would fill it.

The *Real Estate Record* had invested its heart and soul in promoting the West Side, but the new quarter was malingering. Broadway, called the Boulevard (or the Grand Boulevard or the Western Boulevard) until 1899, was an anomaly, a magnificent, landscaped thoroughfare holding a ragged assortment of saloons, coal yards, well-worn hotels, and a few flats with stores. West End Avenue, too, had not yet fulfilled its potential. Planned first to be commercial, long and straight as a die, it had emerged as an ideal residential street—quiet, breezy, panoramic, restricted by covenant to first-class private dwellings—but development had been sporadic and slow. Riverside Drive, winding above the Hudson from 72nd Street to 125th, was still rugged and wild, an escapee from the grid system and the most promising street in the city. With a dramatic configuration, and superb views, it seemed like a boon to architects and a natural home ground for the aristocracy. Yet at the end of the 1880s, Riverside was still barren and untamed. Cyrus Clark had commissioned a villa on the corner of 90th Street, but other streets had not even been cut through or graded. Some builders had talked of erecting French flats at the lower end of the drive, while others dreamed of filling its curves with magnificent mansions. Clarence True drew plans for elegant town-house ensembles. As Frederick Law Olmsted worked to complete the long picturesque park he was creating on the steep terrain at waterside, detractors predicated that this park, and the completion of Grant's Tomb at 125th Street, would make Riverside Drive a plebian pleasure ground, where people would come for food and drink, and family hotels would serve crowds of transients.

In the muddle of uncertainty about the West Side, the question of class was prominent, and had architectural underpinnings. Whether the West Side would be home to the fashionable rich, the respectable well-to-do, or the various shadings of the middle class depended on the extent to which it contained mansions, row houses, or apartment buildings. The choices were formulaic. More vividly than ever before, the shape of home reflected social status.

Architecture as an emblem had been implicit in the issue of the apartment house in America from the beginning. In 1892, Philip Hubert and James Pirsson, together with a new partner named August O. Hoddick, met the question head on with an essay in the *Architectural Record,* the new quarterly the *Real Estate Record* was publishing in response to the growing interest in architecture. Titled "New York Flats and French Flats," the essay compared a solid old courtyard flat in Paris with a small new apartment house in New York that was already in decline. After making a case for larger building lots and a better mode of construction (and decrying the Daly Law for impeding the progress of the city), the architects addressed themselves to "the intricate social questions" that had plagued the course of the apartment house in New York. Describing the French model as a happy hierarchy of social classes, where "all meet on the common stairs and the fine lady exchanges cheerful greetings with her poorest neighbors without a thought of presumption on their part or a condescension on her own," they noted that Americans seemed to resent all claims to social superiority, to regard the elevation of those above them as mere accidents of fortune that a day might reverse. On the other side of the Atlantic, the French enjoyed a freedom of intercourse between classes of society because the status of each individual was so clearly defined that it was not at stake. The French didn't live in apartment houses, they noted, but in small private dwellings, coincidentally built one on top of the other.

This was not the first such lecture delivered to intransigent New York house dwellers. In 1881, a small book titled *European Modes of Living or the Question of Apartment Houses* had been written by a self-appointed reformer named Sarah Gilman Young, who was residing in Paris. Mrs. Young had already addressed the subject of "making life a science instead of a daily battle for existence" in dozens of articles in *The Galaxy* magazine, a sophisticated literary monthly that had been founded to counteract the "provincialism" of *The Atlantic Monthly* (into which it was later incorporated after failing). "Architecture in America is in its infancy, and our houses, as far as artistic beauty is concerned, are not much better than wigwams," she said. Praising the virtues of its courtyards and gardens, light and air, big bedrooms and grand staircases, she concluded that "the French apartment is the product of another kind of civilization, which has conquered the first wants of life, and had the time to consider and wealth to lavish on the best mode . . . of constructing homes."

Like Hubert and Pirsson, Mrs. Young explained the American desire to live in a fine house as an obsession with rank. "There being no fixed caste in America, as in foreign states, we have established a certain style of living and expenditure, as a distinct mark of social position." She saw no objection to the apartment house except a prejudice born of youth, naiveté, and inexperience; she believed that eventually Americans would outgrow the ambitions that had led everyone to appear to be better than he was, and embrace the Continental mode of living.

These were lectures from abroad and from on high. Closer at hand, J. P. Putnam, a New York architect, dismissed traditional house dwelling, or "the old and barbarous custom of living perpendicularly in isolated towers," as a matter of habit. "In his savage state, the nature of (man's) existence necessitated the isolated hut," he explained. "As civilization advanced, however, the necessity for, and enormous advantages of cooperation became evident, but habits perpetuated the isolated dwelling long after the reasons for its existence had disappeared. . . ."

Putnam enjoyed apartment life himself, and had made precise calculations to demonstrate the comparable value of the new mode of housing. Some were economical (a given accommodation in a flat cost less than half the sum it would in an independent dwelling built on the same land), some structural (the only real difference was the lack of stairs), some practical (eighty independent Irish cooks gave way to a professional chef and half a dozen attachés), and all vividly exhorted change. He extolled the privacy, the freedom from housekeeping cares, the security against burglary and fire, and the beauty of the architectural arrangement of the rooms in an apartment, and he signed off with the euphoric "Add to these advantages the possibility for a greatly enlarged and delightful social intercourse and we have as near an approach to the ideal of a human habitat as has yet been devised."

Putnam's final tribute to the social life in an apartment house showed his true color, which was urban, Few people, however, were as eager as he to embrace the sort of sociality offered by, indeed imposed by, a multiple dwelling. A Victorian gentleman was not at ease in the café or in Whitman's colorful catchall society, but in the family, the private home, and the private club. These were the times Clarence Day illuminated in *Life with Father,* when the comforts of home life came first, and were not to be "set at naught." The contemporary New Yorker was not a boulevardier like his counterpart in Paris; he was a homebody, inexperienced with the world at large. Indeed, harangues against the apartment house always included the fear of the random encounters—a disreputable person on a staircase, an indecorous bit of conversation in the air—that were a boulevardier's staff of life. From this wariness it was clear that much of society still felt uneasy with urban life. It was difficult to know how to live in a city, and difficult to know how to live in apartments.

8

WILLIAM DEAN HOWELLS
IN NEW YORK

THERE WAS no escaping the fact that the city of the future was not going to look like the city of the past, that life in the city was not going to be conventional. Every year the population grew larger and more diverse as it absorbed arrivals from all over the world. Every day the newspapers announced a new shape in the landscape or a new scientific advancement. Inevitably one thing led to another—the elevator to taller buildings, the Bessemer process of making steel to the steel-framed building or the skeleton skyscraper. There was a complicity among new things that seemed to propel the city forward on its own. Since the end of the Civil War, an exuberant new technology had come into being. The telegraph, the telephone, the elevator, the electric light, the typewriter, the phonograph, and the camera had arrived and become accessories that altered the facts of daily life.

The signs that a new era impended were many. The landscape of the city was ragged, for it was breaking down and building up at the same time. The mind of the city was unsettled. On the surface, New Yorkers were alternately excited or anxious about the future. Underneath, the prospect of drastic changes in their daily lives made them self-conscious and introspective. It was brash to be too newfangled, and yet it was stodgy to be too literal about tradition. There were big questions to be answered about the relative values of the country against the city, religion against science, the hand against the machine. The architects, engineers, and builders of the city had to decide whether they welcomed the new technology or preferred to pretend it was not there. Ordinary citizens had to choose either to recognize or renounce the forms and forces of "the modern city." "The modern city" was a new phrase of the 1890s. It denoted a large city straining under the impact of industrialization and urbanization. By implication, it was the alter ego of the traditional city, the New New York to an Old New York. Increasingly, it was the subject of studies and stories of one kind or another. Suddenly, in the late 1880s and 1890s, essays, plays, short stories, and novels were written about a city that until Henry James wrote *Washington Square* in 1881 had inspired notably few works of literature. Three new humor magazines, the monosyllabic *Puck, Judge,* and *Life,* published lively portraits of the city and pointed out its contrasts. The illustrator Charles Dana Gibson used his "Gibson Girl" to study New York's social scene in *Life.* The playwrights Augustin Daly, Brander Matthews, and Bronson Howard treated New York and New Yorkers as if their manners and mores were worthy of attention. Plays like Howard's *Young Miss Winthrop* (1882) or *The Aristocracy* (1892) made society the subject on stage, and audiences flocked to the Lyceum on Fourth Avenue and 23rd Street to see comedies about the fatuities of the fashionable.

Whereas Henry James had effectively introduced the New York novel, he did not like the city after the Civil War when it was beginning to manifest its new shape, and he turned his back, literally and literarily, on the changing scene. Like a handful of similarly dispirited and disoriented intellectuals—Henry Adams, James Whistler, Ambrose Bierce, and to some extent Edith Wharton—he lived most of his adult life in Europe, grateful for its culture and the contemplative mood it promoted. In his fiction, which has been described as "indoor" fiction—it is concerned with character and manners, drawing-room-style, rather than exterior settings and social strivings, urban-style—he chose to describe the "established repose of an older New York," the small dusky homogeneous New York world of the mid-century. James could not identify with the "aimless ugliness and noisy irrelevance" of the emerging city. As he confessed to Edith Wharton, he had no ability to use the financial and industrial "material" of modern American life because it was "an impenetrable mystery" to him. Yet he did recognize that for other writers New York could be as rich in lore as Thackeray's London, for after reading one of Mrs. Wharton's stories in *Lippincott's Magazine,* he wrote to her, "I applaud, I mean I egg you on in your study of the American life that surrounds you. Let yourself go in it and at it—it's an untouched field really," and then, "DO NEW YORK! The first-hand account is precious." To one of her aunts, he admonished that "Edith must be tethered in native pastures, even if it reduces her to a backyard in New York."

As their eyes sharpened to the color, the texture, and the social interest of the developing urban scene, a new crop of New York writers found themselves tethered in native pastures too, observing the "multitudinous town" and then turning their true-to-life observations into fictional stories or satire. In a variety of styles and from differing points of view, Edgar Saltus, Brander Matthews, H. C. Bunner, Richard Harding Davis, and William Dean Howells all took upon themselves the task of picturing their age and their society, for suddenly it seemed important to capture the specifics. It was the very act of writing about New York and the truthful method in which it was undertaken that were the important facts.

That New York was a good subject for a novel or a play was in itself illuminating. Photographers delivered the same message, as amateurs and professionals alike trained new portable cameras (Eastman's new Kodak appeared in 1888) on houses, friends, ceremonies, or unposed scenes in the street. New York was a more important place and more impressive place than it had ever been—more populous, more prosperous, more cosmopolitan, more cultural. Sometime late in the 1880s, after Emerson died, everyone acknowledged that the intellectual center of the country had quietly shifted from Boston to New York. To those who had explored the city, New York was also more diverse, more dangerous, and more disturbing than any other city in America. It took a romantic or a reformer, however, to penetrate beneath the veneer of homogeneity and beyond the rule of manners to find the local color—the sinister alleys full of Chinese tramps, the anarchist meetings in bohemian cellars, the glovemakers on strike, the pushcart peddlers and sweatshop workers who were once scholars and concert violinists. Journalists invariably called this the "underbelly" of the city, its "lower depths." For years the reform-minded had been pointing out the harsher contrasts and contradictions in city life. With the development of plates for printing in the late 1880s and 1890s, magazines and newspapers had begun to use photographs to document and to polemicize. In 1890, Jacob Riis published his picture study of tenement life called *How the Other Half Lives*.

Technology was indirectly behind the realistic mode that photography induced in letters. Just as the camera began to raise awareness by exposing realities, so H. C. Bunner's sketches of street life opened a reader's mind to a larger view of the city. Bunner was the editor of *Puck* and "an ardent collector of slums" who described with Dickens-like feeling for the street all the "tragic oddities" and "queer fish" and "lonely souls astray from the village and the farm." Bunner's characters were remote from the ken of the privileged populations of New York. Those of Richard Harding Davis, and of Edgar Saltus, whose *Vanity Square* was subtitled *A Story of Fifth Avenue Life,* were familiar, thinly veiled versions of their social peers. There was a vision implicit in realism; its photographs or stories caught a subject as it was and illuminated it, made it accessible, familiar, and believable. Realism revealed, whereas the conventions of the preceding age had covered up and concealed.

William Dean Howells, the editor, novelist, short-story writer, poet, playwright, essayist, and critic who by 1895 was being recognized as the dean of American letters, called realism "nothing more and nothing less than the truthful treatment of material" and defined its proper subject as the common life of ordinary Americans, a group in which he placed himself squarely. Howells, who wrote more than two dozen novels that were serialized in magazines like *The Atlantic Monthly* and the *Century,* was, after Mark Twain, the most financially successful novelist of his time. He not only had a theory of the novel, but a vision of creating beauty out of the stuff of "poor Real Life." Almost religiously, he put his ideas to work in his own fiction, which steadfastly drew upon and chronicled his own life—his travels, his marriage, his moves, his ups and downs as an ambitious and idealistic late-nineteenth-century city dweller.

As a realist, with a quest to render the ordinary meaningful, Howells knew that he was breaking ground. To create fiction that was worthwhile, he had perceived that he "had to get into it from life the things that had not been got into fiction before," as he recalled in his memoirs. He was not interested in agreeable subjects or exotic intrigues or happy endings or redeeming virtues or any of the other conventions of the day, just as he did not wish to observe what he called "the heroic or occasional phases" of a man's life. One of his most steadfast characters was a genial, intelligent, moral man named Basil March, whose similarities to the author were considerable, and who is so good-hearted and unaffected that he becomes a sort of liberated upper-class Everyman. March first appears with his new wife in 1874 in Howells's first novel, *Their Wedding Journey,* and then resurfaces in 1890, as he is moving from Boston to New York, in *A Hazard of New Fortunes,* and lastly, in *Their Silver Wedding Journey* in 1899. Through the decades he bears witness to all he sees and feels without artifice or undue invention, like a good friend or traveling companion.

Howells's novels were like travel pieces, loose-limbed meanderings through the American scene, undertaken for the purpose of experience and enlightment. The early works took place in Europe and New England; then, after 1890, they opened up to include New York and Altruria or Utopia in their focus. Those were the parameters of Howells's own life, upon which he would dutifully comment. The son of a country newspaper editor, Howells had grown up in Ohio; spent several years as a consul in Venice; married Elinor Mead, a cousin of President Rutherford B. Hayes and the sister of the architect William S. Mead; established himself in Boston, where he became the editor of *The Atlantic Monthly;* and then, in 1888, moved from Boston to New York, to take over first the "Easy Chair" column at *Harper's,* and later, briefly, the editorship of *Cosmopolitan.* His instincts were sound and his steps were prophetic, some people would note, as fashionable readers shifted their loyalties to the "smarter" *Harper's* and then to the glossier, mass-produced *Cosmopolitan,* and New York succeeded Boston as the literary center of the country.

In New York, Howells encountered a whole new world of novelistic possibilities. In the early 1860s, when he had been a columnist for the young *Nation,* the city had overwhelmed him; now he strove to "catch onto the bigger life of the place." Like Walt Whitman, he loved to wander in New York, to ride the omnibuses up and down its axes, making cultural notes and taking impressions of all the smaller islands of activity that made up the island of Manhattan. Like Whitman, he studied the scene with devouring interest in the people, and sensed the vitality in the frantic panorama that spread from slum to high society and amused and touched him. Howells introduced a rich gallery of these indigenous characters in his first New York novel, *A Hazard of New Fortunes*—widows and painters and wild-eyed socialists and crusty millionaires—just as he had peopled his Boston novels, like *A Chance Acquaintance, A Modern Instance,* or *The Rise of Silas Lapham,* with proper Beacon Hill matrons, priggish moralists, and graceless new capitalists. For New England's evenhanded landscape of houses, he substituted a skyline that was up and down, "a delirium of lines and colors, a savage anarchy of shapes." "Boston seems to be of another planet," he noted in a letter of 1888.

Howells read New York well, an accomplishment that he claimed was a testament to the city's openness. "Her virtues, her vices, her luxuries and her misery, are in plain sight," he explained in *Impressions and Experiences,* a memoir that included sketches of the city from his first days of exploration. In these pages, without the distraction of novelistic responsibilities, he viewed the city straight on, fully engaged by its own inherent drama. He observed the unusual number of restaurants, hotels, clubs, and saloons ("the poor man's clubhouse") and noted "much eating and drinking going on constantly." He watched the parade of parvenus in the park, equipped with "all the apparatus of long-inherited riches" and wearing expressions of ennui. He saw hovels "where old people lived in a temporary respite from the building about them." He described a typical landscape as "jagged-toothed": "See a vacant lot, with its high board fence covered with painted signs, then a tall mass of apartment houses, then a stretch of ordinary New York dwellings of the old commonplace brownstone sort; then a stable and a wooden liquor saloon at the corner." He commented, "Inequality has [its] effect on the architecture."

Howells read buildings well too, allowing them both cultural and aesthetic dimensions, seeing them in relation to the people who created and inhabited them. Whatever intelligent sensibility he brought naturally to the subject was heightened by his wife's deep interest in architecture, not only as the sister of a partner in the increasingly eminent firm of McKim, Mead and White, but as an architect manqué herself. (By the 1890s, the Howellses' son, John Mead, was studying architecture at the Ecole des Beaux-Arts and would join his uncle's old firm.) In their five decades together, the Howellses lived in many houses and invested an unusual concern and effort in their specific styles and shapes. One of the major preoccupations of their marriage was house hunting, and its various fruits seemed to express their various postures of stability. The Howellses moved for a variety of reasons—illness, career, aesthetics, pragmatism, whim. In Boston they tried out an apartment and three different houses before they built Red Top, a Queen Anne cottage with a bright red roof, designed by William R. Mead. Eventually Elinor's poor health led them back to a boardinghouse in Cambridge, a rented house on Louisburg Square, and a purchased house on Beacon Street overlooking the Charles River basin. In New York, they lived for four months in 1866, with their first baby, in a wacky boardinghouse on Ninth Avenue they nicknamed "the Barichity-Barachity"; upon their return to the city in 1888, they occupied a fourteen-room flat in the Chelsea, a duplex apartment in a huge old house on Livingston Place, apartments on East 17th Street and Central Park South, and a big studio on West 57th Street. As the Howellses' personal life was a cultural allegory of modern life, so their houses were metaphors for security. The continual flitting from house to house was an expression of their continuing inability to feel completely at home in urban America. At a time when the rise of the city was transforming the fundamental quality of life, and the clash between country values and city values was troubling the minds of millions of their countrymen, they were not alone in their distress. Howells's novels showed his own fascination with the way people lived, and registered his own ambivalence about contemporary values, but he was effectively airing a national problem too. He was addressing the disorientation and the deracination of a society on the move.

In New York, the Howellses chose to live in apartment houses, although they were well-bred, tradition-loving people accustomed to and appreciative of private houses. Since they expressed themselves in their dwelling places even more conscientiously than other upper-class Americans, the choice of apartments indicated a rather radical shift in their self-image. Howells illuminated this transition in *A Hazard of New Fortunes* as he recounted the efforts of his alter ego, Basil March, to find a respectable home in New York, and drew upon the time, only a year earlier, when he and Elinor had looked at nearly a hundred flats and houses over the course of six days. The Marches, who, like the Howellses, left behind a comfortable town house in provincial Boston, investigate apartments evocatively named the Wigram, the Esmeralda, the Jacinty, the Helena, the Asteroid, and the Xenophon.

"We must not forget just what kind of flat we are going to look for," Isabel March begins optimistically, and then articulates her ideal.

> The sine qua nons are an elevator and steam-heat, not above the third floor, to begin with. Then we must each have a room, and you must have your study and I must have my parlours; and the two girls must each have a room. With the kitchen and dining room, how many does that make?

Ten.

I thought eight. Well, no matter. You can work in the par-
lours, and run into your bedroom when anyone comes; and I can
sit in mine, and the girls must put up with one, if it's large and
sunny, though I've always given them two at home. And the
kitchen must be sunny, so they can sit in it. And the rooms must
all have outside light.

Dozens of apartments down the road, the Marches deduce that the
New York ideal of a flat is a dreary seven rooms and bath, or, as they
describe it: "One or two rooms might be at the front, the rest crooked
and cornered backward through increasing and then decreasing darkness
till they reach a light bedroom or kitchen at the rear . . . any room with
a window giving into the open air of a court or shaft [being] counted
a light room." They conclude that apartments, the plain and the richly
decorated alike, are not compatible with either their tastes or their
values, and Mr. March sounds a gentleman's long lament.

Think of a baby in a flat! It's a contradiction in terms; the flat
is the negation of motherhood. The flat means society life; that is,
the pretence of social life. It's made to give artificial people a
society basis on a little money,—too much money, of course, for
what they get. So the cost of the building is put into marble halls
and idiotic decoration of all kinds. . . . It's confinement without
coziness; it's cluttered without being snug. You couldn't keep a
self-respecting cat in the flat; you couldn't go down to the cellar
to get cider. No; the Anglo-Saxon house is simply impossible in
the Franco-American flat, not because it's humble, but because
it's false.

There is no reason to think that the Marches' description of the New
York apartment situation is other than literal and accurate. They inspect
a variety of dwellings that typified the choices of the day: through a
house agent, they find a six-room housekeeping apartment with "all the
gimcracks" in a pretentious building, a furnished apartment without a
kitchen in a building with a general restaurant, and a furnished apartment in a divided house. From advertisements in the *Herald* and the
World, they unearth large "first-class" flats with "all improvements,"
bath, icebox, steam heat, and elevator; and huge elegant apartments with

ornate ceilings and bedrooms like closets. They poke fun at the excesses—at slippery inlaid floors and foolishly expensive finishes. They learn to distinguish the aesthetic line between shabbiness and gentility and to identify the "east-west line beyond which they could not go if they wished to keep their self-respect." All along, they suffer the physical and mental trials of trying to conjure up a home out of space that is defined by steaming radiators and dim halls and an echoing emptiness.

Most of the narrative elements in *A Hazard* are true to life and identifiable, including the great streetcar strike of 1886, which figures in the story. Specifically, the novel tells the story of March's editorship of *Every Other Week,* "a new departure in magazines," which he hopes to make a force in American letters—not unlike Howells's own fervent if short-lived wishes for *Cosmopolitan.* Through the magazine, the Marches find their way about the grid of Manhattan and encounter a host of characters so rich and varied that it brought Tolstoy to the mind of critics—newly rich midwestern natural gasmen, old and new southerners, a proto-feminist and an artist, an old German socialist, a highbrow fop, and dozens of the unnamed, unknown local people who make up the democratic panorama of the city. March feels complicity with the city and celebrates its foreignness. He discovers its painterliness, listens to its myriad voices, and delights in its ungainly human sprawl. Although his old-fashioned values make him wary too, gradually he and his wife open up to urban rhythms and ways, become tolerant and discerning, and relax. They settle into a furnished apartment in an old house downtown on Stuyvesant Square, "which had its good points, and after the first sensation of oppression in it they began to feel the convenience of its arrangement. . . . [The] children were pleased with its novelty; when this wore off for them, she had herself begun to find it much more easily manageable than a house." Several months later when they have to move to an apartment over the magazine's offices, where living will be "odd," Mrs. March comments only that "in New York you may do anything."

The Marches' domestic tribulations illuminate urgent late-nineteenth-century concerns. When Howells described huge apartment houses "chiefly distinguishable from tenement-houses by the absence of fire-escapes on their facades," he was seizing upon a detail to decode the whole urban experience of which he and his contemporaries were trying to make sense. When he explained why the poor did not care to live in a respectable quarter—"they would be bored to death"—he was suggesting that more vital life existed in the unconventional city than the conventional one. Howells made small things do great service, as Henry James commented about the novelist in a book review. James and Mark Twain were Howells's two closest friends of his age, a fact that said much about his breadth of interest and understanding, since neither of these eminences appreciated the other. It was the same breadth that lay behind Howells's ability to embrace a confusing city at a time when many in his society were struggling to find a place in it.

Howells contained multitudes, one of his biographers said. He believed in equality and fraternity and sympathized with socialism—he peopled his two utopian novels with a race of fair-minded aesthetics who build arcaded cities and live in communal apartment houses. He also admitted that "I wear a fur-lined overcoat, and live in all the luxury my money can buy." Howells described himself as a theoretical socialist and a practical aristocrat. For all his curiosity and compassion, he felt ambivalent about New York, and he saw and caught the ambivalence of all the other citizens who felt the lure of a great new city, with its technological progress, its democratic forces, and its vast array of new goods, but were still tied to the past, to its sound values, proper appearances, and predictable ways. To him, however, New York was a "life" and not a "spectacle."

In recognizing New York as a life, Howells probably did his most meaningful service to his readers, for he forecast a new urban consciousness. *A Hazard of New Fortunes* was billed as the first novel of the modern city. In fact it not only portrayed but also promoted the modern city—immigrants, labor strife, apartment houses, and all—as a genial democracy in which social differences could ultimately be bridged. It established an immense urban framework to which Howells would add depth with later novels like *The World of Chance* and *The Coast of Bohemia*. All of Howells's novels had an impact on the public mind; eagerly awaited, serialized in popular magazines, read aloud around the hearth in the evening, they offered intelligent, enriched versions of the world outside the door. If conventional ideas were born of the familiar, then, by making certain realities more familiar, his novels ultimately modified convention. They also influenced a band of young realists like Hamlin Garland, Frank Norris, Stephen Crane, Henry Blake Fuller, and Theodore Dreiser, who would write important stories of their own.

. . .

William Dean Howells in the study of his studio apartment at 130 West 57th Street, 1906.

WHILE LITERARY critics called it "The Age of Howells," Howells himself called his times "The Age of the Millionaire," the figure he had identified as the new American ideal. New Yorkers still had a weakness for heroes and heroines of decidedly unrealistic proportions, he noted, inserting a scene in *Their Silver Wedding Journey* in which everyone of fashion is reading a romance called *The Maiden Knight,* which was a direct reference to the fact that in 1899 everyone in New York was reading *When Knighthood Was in Flower.* In matters of taste, New Yorkers seemed to be acting out an extravagant historical romance, he observed as he watched a fantastic variety of equipages roll by the base of the newly implanted Cleopatra's Needle in the park (sometimes carrying only the servants sent out to exercise the horses), and asked if the Needle discerned any difference between their occupants and the occupants of the chariots that swept beneath it two thousand years before. "How far do the New Yorkers publicly carry their travesty of the European aristocratic life? . . . I should say that the imitation was quite within the bounds of good taste. The bad taste is in the wish to imitate Europe at all; but with the abundance of money, the imitation is simply inevitable. There is no American life for wealth; there is no native formula for the expression of social superiority."

During the 1890s, literary circles debated the relative merits of realism against romanticism. It was a small esoteric version of the larger debate raging about the merits of change, for realists found their sources in science, democracy, and the natural order, while romantics honored the traditional and classical past. It had its most dramatic counterpart in architecture, where the search for a style appropriate to a new age—and the effective answer—revealed the true temper of the times.

The search, of course, had been going on, at least in the minds of architects, since the end of the Civil War. The answer was formally unveiled in the spring of 1893, when the quatercentennial celebration of the discovery of the New World, called the World's Columbian Exposition, opened in Chicago. New York had been in contention for the event too, briefly, and had offered up a rolling plot of land that extended from 97th to 127th Street, and from Park Avenue to the Hudson, encompassing parts of Riverside, Morningside, and Central parks; Chicago's site was the forgotten and swampy Jackson Park, along the southern shores of Lake Michigan, which Frederick Law Olmsted and the consulting architects Daniel Burnham and John Wellborn Root transformed into a watery urban theater, and a congregation of the leading architects of the country filled with a stand of white classical buildings grouped around a lagoon. To many critics, the fair signaled "the arrival at full birth of that which may be called modern American architecture."

In 1893, Richard Morris Hunt, the grand master of American architecture, was sixty-six years old, hardly antiquated—for he had yet to design Cornelius Vanderbilt's cottage in Newport, called the Breakers, or the new wing for the Metropolitan Museum of Art—but nonetheless somewhat old-hat. The firm of McKim, Mead and White, whose classicism had a lighter touch than Hunt's, was in ascendance in New York. In Chicago, Louis Sullivan, age thirty-seven, was practicing a radical aesthetic in steel and glass with Dankmar Adler and a young draftsman named Frank Lloyd Wright in tow. These were the important forces in American architecture, shaped by different methods and beliefs. From among them, it was Hunt who was chosen to design the Administration Building, the most prominent of the fair's structures, and who domi-

By the time this picture of Richard Morris Hunt
was taken, he had designed many of the great houses
on Fifth Avenue.

nated all the architects summoned to Chicago like a luminary. Four
decades after introducing the Beaux-Arts to America, he was supervising
its final and ultimate ascent.

To those who were hoping to steer the public taste in a modern
direction, the fair was a disaster, for its message was anything but functional or progressive. The White City gleamed like an alabaster shrine,
and its buildings were opulent versions of the classical. They were
domed, columned, and decorated with heroic statuary, and they expressed in marble and limestone (or the polychromed plaster of Paris
verisimilitudes) dignity, wealth, discipline, permanence—all the traditional values. The best painters and sculptors in the country had contributed to the effort—John La Farge, Mary Cassatt, Kenyon Cox, Daniel
Chester French—"the greatest meeting of artists since the fifteenth-
century," Augustus Saint-Gaudens, their director, had called it. Few of

the hundreds of thousands of Americans who visited the fair had seen such a stand of "real architecture" before. As a spectacle, it was overwhelming and it was judged the culminating cultural event of the nineteenth century.

Like all the international fairs that had followed upon the founding example of London's Crystal Palace in 1851, the Columbian Exposition celebrated the material wealth of its age. It was a paean to progress, and it was significant that its most impressive and most important aspect was architectural. Inside Hunt's radiant gold-and-white-domed Administration Building, the allegorical statuary illustrated the evolution of man from barbarism to civilization, which was really the theme of the entire fair. Hunt himself, who saw the fine arts on splendid display, felt that his original mission had been accomplished. Here indeed was a small Beaux-Arts city, clean, white, and majestic. Even the profoundly skeptical Henry Adams, who wondered what the fair meant, observed that it was "the first expression of American thought as a unity."

The fair had its detractors, like Adams and Howells and other progressives who saw classicism as an imitative, derivative, and inappropriate style for a proud young democratic nation to adopt as its own. Some critics felt that the return to a style of the past had effectively destroyed the Chicago style burgeoning in the hands of architects like Sullivan. As it was, only Sullivan and William Le Baron Jenney presented nonclassical structures; the architects from the eastern seaboard, heavy with the French influence, dominated the design. Sullivan declared that the fair was a pathological aberration that swept him and his architecture before it; he predicted that the damage it wrought would last half a century from its date, if not longer. Virtually everyone, however, granted that the fair was beautiful. And virtually every professional recognized the importance of the fair, for until that moment, no American architect had had any practical experience with large-scale planning. In Chicago, government, business, architects, and artists had collaborated in the most ambitious endeavor in U.S. history—the creation of what was literally a small city. The unity of the design, the organization of the structures around broad spaces, and the harmonizing of architecture with the other arts had produced a vision that provided standards to give impetus to the future.

Whether or not a more dynamic modern style might have triumphed earlier in America without this blinding dose of classicism, American architects needed this lesson in city planning. They needed to understand and develop that sense of place the Beaux-Arts inculcated in students. In New York specifically, they needed to know how to create structures that would enable the growth of a great city, how to build a world capital like the one Napoleon had demanded of Haussmann. As Beaux-Arts–trained Ernest Flagg explained to his fellow architects in the *Architectural Record,* "With the same logical reasoning . . . and the same careful preparation that helps the Frenchmen to lead the world in the fine arts . . . America will enter upon a course which will make possible the evolution of a national style of our own, or perhaps enable us to set the fashion for the world."

The fervor with which city planners and city dwellers took up the Beaux-Arts example in the next twenty years brought to mind the rebuilding of Paris. The Columbian Exposition launched an age duly christened the American Renaissance, and a beautification movement that led to the creation of hundreds of public buildings and civic centers across the country. The message of the fair was that every city, given a coat of classical whitewash, could become City Beautiful, and, moreover, that such an architectural environment was *pro bono publico,* a just reflection of an important and successful citizenry. Within little more than a decade, ground was broken for important new public buildings in New York—the Metropolitan Museum, Columbia University, Penn Station, Grand Central Station, the Public Library—and the city began to acquire a proud imperial look.

The message was not exclusively municipal. Although the fair had made a grand public statement, the American Renaissance had been gathering momentum for more than a decade. Each of Hunt's houses, and McKim, Mead and White's houses, and the various collaborative artistic ventures in the decoration of houses like Villard's and Vanderbilt's, had exerted a Ruskinian influence on the aesthetics of the general populace. The middle classes as well as the upper classes had begun to react against architecture and decoration that was considered bourgeois. Art clubs and cultural societies burgeoned. Although a severe economic depression gripped the country in the years after the fair—closing hundreds of businesses and stalling much new construction—"art" continued to flourish, and "style," meaning rich formal style, was in great demand.

One of the voices raised in praise of advances in American taste belonged to a young writer named Edith Wharton. In 1897, she had published her first book, a serious and pragmatic text called *The Decora-*

tion of Houses. Written with a cultivated architect named Ogden Codman, Jr., who had recently remodeled Land's End, her house in Newport, the book was meant to educate the wealthy layman. Moving
learnedly from one feature of an upper-class residence to another—from
room to room and from window to ceiling to staircase—it explained and
illustrated the classical taste. Mrs. Wharton, who had traveled in Europe
since childhood and was a longtime devotee of *sèttecento* Italy, had spent
the last decade decorating her own houses—twin houses at 884 Park
Avenue as well as her summer cottage. Houses were important and
useful metaphorically to her, as the passion for detail in her novels would
illustrate so well—women wear veils as thick as curtains, room space
shrinks as a life dwindles, society is reflected in its architecture. In
Decoration, Mrs. Wharton used her childhood home on West 23rd Street
as a model of the cold, cluttered, uncomfortable house her book was
meant to oppose, thus indicting her whole narrow-minded background.
She used the ducal palaces of Italy and France as models of the appropriate. The aristocratic examples proved to be very attractive. *The Decoration of Houses* would be as important to a generation of upper-class
matrons as *Hints on Household Taste* had been to their mothers.

9

GREATER NEW YORK AT THE TURN OF THE CENTURY

B Y THE end of the nineteenth century, New York was too big and too diverse to be measured in traditional ways. It was impossible to cover its length in a walk, to keep up with the shops and the social events, to follow all the threads of its daily life. New York was many neighborhoods, many societies, many perspectives and points of view. Its heterogeneity was a physical and social fact, to which all the newspapers and magazines that illustrated and annotated the town bore witness. The scope of publications in New York had expanded dramatically from just 1880, with the addition of new monthlies like *McClure's, Munsey's,* the *Metropolitan* and *The Illustrated American* to the old ranks of *Harper's* and *The Nation,* as well as the revitalized *Cosmopolitan, Ladies' Home Journal* and *Scribner's* (which under the editorship of Richard Watson Gilder had become the *Century* magazine); with the hundreds of weeklies—the older *Harper's Weekly, Collier's Once-a-Week, Leslie's Weekly,* and the newer *Judge, Puck,* and *Life;* not to mention the many dozens of dailies, in an assortment of languages. These publications had been born of New York's heterogeneity, and they served to sustain it too, to explain the many worlds of New York and to create the atmosphere of shared experience that was once acquired over a backyard fence and through grapevine chatter.

At the end of the century, the architecture of New York also testified to the dramatic changes in the city's psyche. "No one who will study the development of the architecture of New York City in the last quarter century will fail to observe how completely it reflects the chief social facts of the time," the *Real Estate Record* declared in a special historical survey of 1898, referring to the increase in wealth, the explosion of commercial energy, the development of technology, and the show of public spirit, and thinking specifically of the neoclassic mansion, the skyscraper, the hotel, and the apartment house as illustrations. Pointing out how the "mental conditions" of the brownstone period had produced one sort of architecture ("The architect was virtually extinct. . . . We were still centered in the mother country. The hereditary instinct for the old home was not yet dead"), the *Real Estate Record* also noted how the new aesthetics and new social attitudes of a later day were producing another sort of architecture. Their conclusions waxed philosophic: "Social changes rarely come about consciously. Men do not plan for them. They are quietly imposed upon the individual whose methods and ideas are insidiously molded into conformity with the new order. The work is done, we may say, diplomatically, by minute conversions and perversions of the established order."

More conspicuously than ever before in America, architecture was a significant language, its message double-barreled. Just as the new buildings on the street were important social icons, the leading architectural critics of the day were important social commentators. Often they addressed social topics directly. In the new *Century,* a young literary woman named Marianna Griswold van Rensselaer wrote articles on the new homes of New York or the new classes of New York and treated her materials as if it were all one big subject, which it was. Her contemporary Montgomery Schuyler, who claimed architecture as only a hobby, was nonetheless one of the most penetrating urban critics of modern times. It was telling that Schuyler, who wrote for a variety of New York newspapers—the *World,* the *Sun* and the *Times*—and was the managing editor of *Harper's Weekly* for several years in the mid-1880s, published his most important oeuvre in the *Architectural Record,* where many of his wittiest and most scathing indictments of the contemporary scene appeared under the pseudonym Franz K. Winkler. Schuyler, who was erudite and indulged in obscure literary allusions, always seemed to retain both a sense of humanity and a sense of humor as he reviewed the streetscape of New York, pronouncing buildings appropriate or innocent or adventuresome or conformist, as if they were interesting characters or coded bits of behavior. He always seemed to sense where these buildings had come from, from the heart or the mind or the ego, born of ambition or pretension, nostalgia, or sheer mechanical ingenuity. His pronouncements applied as aptly to the citizens of the city as to their structures. As the new Fifth Avenue buildings were "amusing," so, in a way, were their pretentious owners. The older generation of houses, by contrast, were "primeval venerable things"—"dull" but innocent. As a critic, Schuyler was a behaviorist, and his perceptions cast buildings in their human context, and from this, a reader could draw sociological conclusions. When Schuyler noted how apartment house design on the West Side was straining for novelty, which he found "unflattering," it was suddenly clear how awkward and anxious both architects and tenants must have been feeling about the apartment. When he questioned why Fifth Avenue should automatically denote a gentleman and Central Park West a commoner, he was also pointing out that New York could not yet sustain more than one standard of respectability. Schuyler even criticized the tall new commercial buildings for being too tame, which was a reminder that the new technological advances were breeding certain expectations, encouraging invention and originality.

Schuyler's new editor at the *Architectural Record* was Herbert Croly, a young Harvard intellectual who in 1914 would found the magazine *The New Republic* as "the voice of the metropolitan intellect." Croly was another of the engaged young urbanists who understood architecture and used it as a metaphor. The early part of his career was devoted exclusively to architecture, but his subject was always public culture— the city as an agent for ideas and ideals. As he explained in the pages of the *Architectural Record,* Croly wanted New York to be an effective new "metropolis," to have a constructive social ideal, and to stand for more than the making and spending of money. He was thinking about the full meaning of *metropolis,* the mother city, as understood in its ancient Greek. Croly was a conspicuous spokesperson, but he was not alone in expressing his cultural concerns in the context and the language of architecture. In the wake of the world's fair and in the wings of a new century, other urban elites were beginning to believe that if New York was built like a grand and important city, it would function like one. Greater unity and coherence in the physical form of the city would enhance its public culture, they said; the right architectural forms would solve the problems of modern living. As if to underline the importance of this message, in 1902, under Croly, the quarterly and once recondite

Architectural Record became a monthly and declared its intention of becoming more popular ("in the best sense of that term") and more worldly.

IN 1895, two years after the Columbian Exposition, Richard Morris Hunt had died, leaving behind him a series of buildings that had reformed and revised the landscape. Hunt had been neither a social theorist nor a moral visionary, but his effect on the mind of the city had been revolutionary. His works reflected all the great social changes that had taken place in the previous forty years, Schuyler pointed out in a long and fervent tribute to the architect whom he eulogized as a case study of the national development in architecture.

That year, two other luminaries of a different and yet decidedly revolutionary bent had died too—Hunt's early client Mrs. Paran Stevens, whom Edith Wharton had satirized in *The Age of Innocence* as Mrs. Lemuel Struthers, the widow of the shoe polish king, and who, somewhat ironically, by 1893 was living in the same marble mansion at 57th Street that had belonged to Wharton's iconoclastic aunt. Also dead was erstwhile *arbiter elegantiarum* Ward McAllister, whose funeral drew only a bedraggled handful of the social elite. The newspapers pronounced Mrs. Stevens a woman of great courage and energy, and an abundance of fun; *Harper's Weekly* judged that her "indifference to the stiff and starched conventionalities of over-nice fashion, her brave, almost frantic opposition to what hinted of social cant, her disregard of 'form' made her in many ways the most notable figure in the fashionable world of this generation." The demise of these two figures seemed timely, for the society to which they had given direction was playing itself out in parody. McAllister was succeeded in his duties to an aged Mrs. Astor by a waspish man named Harry Lehr, who engineered a last cynical show of extravagance, notable for such social triumphs as a dinner party for dolls, where the guests spoke in baby talk, and a banquet for dogs, where the guest of honor wore a $115,000 diamond-studded collar. Lehr was Mrs. Astor's concession to social progress, it was said, created to arrest the dangerous blight of boredom attacking her world.

Already it seemed a long way back to the young cosmopolitan town Hunt had first adopted, to the first studio building, the first set of French flats, the first millionaire's mansion. As the century waned, it seemed possible that the city was preparing to enter the new world that the rollover of the numbers promised. There was daring in the air. The upper classes were eating and drinking and dancing high above the streets—roof gardens like the one atop the Majestic Hotel or the new Madison Square Garden were the rage, of which there were at least half a dozen examples. Down on the ground, they pedaled about the city like madmen on new bicycles, women too, hair and skirts flying in the wind, savoring the sharp turns in the park drive, the panorama on Riverside, the smooth new asphalt laid on Fifth Avenue in 1897, and the sheer spectacle of it all. Day and—by headlight—night, from May to November, bicycles offered a sense of release and a new kind of madcap mobility. They were also the latest objects of fashion, and subject to all those airs and indulgences. Diamond Jim Brady had a gold-plated bicycle with silvered spokes; his friend the celebrated Music Hall beauty Lillian Russell had a gold-plated model with jewel-encrusted spokes, and wore a white serge cycling costume when she rode in Central Park. The smart set organized chaperoned parties to ride up to dinner together at the old Claremont Inn, near the new Grant's Tomb; they formed cycling clubs, patronized bicycle schools, rode single and tandem wheels, the squat "safety" design or the taller "regular." The police department created a bicycle squad. The Lyceum Theatre checked bicycles for free during performances. Fifteen thousand people a day visited the Cycle Show held in Madison Square Garden in January 1896. Later that year the *Evening Telegram* awarded a prize for the best cycling costume and sponsored a bicycle parade up the Grand Boulevard. Late-nineteenth-century New Yorkers had long shown a weakness for stylish ritualized sports—for croquet, archery, tennis, and golf—but the craze for the bicycle was meaningful beyond its sportiness, emblematic of a new zeal for motion, for independent travel, for dispersal. A bicycle was an important and cherished new appurtenance, and the zeal was an early taste of what was in store with the horseless carriage, which made its first public appearance that year in a small private race at City Hall, arranged by the editor of *Cosmopolitan*.

It was quick-witted of the owners of a number of new apartment houses to advertise free bicycle storage along with the other special amenities like electrical elevators and filtered water and jewel safes in their buildings, as if to implicate apartments in the new mood of excitement. These entrepreneurs were becoming more sensitive to their potential tenants and more sophisticated in their efforts to "sell" their apartments, issuing brochures and prospectuses to the public to advertise their wares, explaining space equivalents and the servant situation and the unusual supplies and conveniences. Nonetheless, apart from the "add-ons," the new crop of apartment buildings was not particularly impressive, a fact that Montgomery Schuyler was quick to point out. Given the restrictions imposed by both the Daly Law and the depression of 1893, the luxury apartment house had not evolved since the mid-1880s. More than 90 percent of the buildings erected had been the work of speculators who generally paid more attention to the number of rooms that could be squeezed into a plot than the felicity of individual layouts or the grace of a cornice line. Most of the buildings had been sited on conventional 100-by-25-foot lots, inviting all the old problems born of the grid. Of the several dozen "superior" buildings in existence around the city, the majority were a decade old, and the best by far was judged to be the Dakota, a building that could not have been legally duplicated, even given a patron with a fat purse.

Ironically, perhaps, it was the working classes that were the object of the most intelligent, and in a conceptual sense, the richest work in turn-of-the-century housing. Architects like Ernest Flagg had been agitating for more thoughtful and more healthful designs for lower-class dwellings for many years: finally, as the grim realities of tenement life began to register on writers, photographers, and then on the general public, the city sponsored a series of model tenement-house competitions, beginning in 1896. The winning designs from architects like Flagg, James E. Ware, and Henry Atterbury Smith were simple—typically six-story walkups with few architectural effects—but they had big windows and central courtyards and showed visible concern with light and air. They illuminated the most crucial aspects of good apartment design, and they prompted the city into legislating better buildings. Since large, luminous courtyards meant larger lots, which in turn suggested higher elevations, height controls were revised upward; then in 1901, the New Law was enacted, which allowed a fireproof residential building to rise to ten or twelve stories. Model tenements had an impact on luxury housing, for they clarified concepts, and they spurred on improvements in form. After 1901, grandiloquent courtyard buildings followed on the heels of humble ones almost as a matter of course.

Model tenements were meaningful beyond the facts of their architecture, for they were the results of a new attitude in the city that was less isolationist, more democratic, and more engaged. A building like the Cherokee Flats, Smith's tenement on Cherokee Place between East 77th and 78th streets (which was also called Mrs. Vanderbilt's Sanitary Flats, in deference to Mrs. William K. Vanderbilt's gift of land), suggested that well-to-do New Yorkers were developing a conscience, opening up their minds to some of the ramifications of living in a city. At some time in the 1890s, the whole notion of the city as a collective entity—one that was useful socially, politically, historically, or architecturally—suddenly seemed to register on its citizens. Many reforms were kindled in the 1890s; many ideas of the decade became movements and isms.

Women, in particular, were conspicuous new revisionists. Finding voice as clubwomen, they founded the League for Political Education in 1894 to correct the ignorance that had defeated the constitutional amendment for suffrage. In 1896, they took on the dress code and formed the Rainy Day Club to promote a shorter skirt for the days when a long one was wet and oppressive. (The skirt itself was named after its first brave wearer, one Daisy Miller, and called the "Rainy Daisy.") The day of the clinging vine was over; dress was to be "as wings and not weights." One voice forecast that "as her life broadened from the four walls and the three d's—dresses, diseases and domestics—a woman would behold the urgent necessity of a better use for her strength than carrying about so much clothing and cloth." Another proclaimed that all classes of women could now look respectable in the rain, irrespective of access to a carriage. If this all sounded too big for the mere question of skirt length, the issue was in fact prophetic. Just as women were finding their old-fashioned clothes cumbersome, compromising, and socially coded, they would also find the shape of the old-fashioned home confining. Over the next twenty years, the raising of hemlines, rooflines, and consciousness would proceed in concert.

Even as the movement to apartments seemed to stall, other architectural events primed the city for its advancement. The rehabilitation of the Roman mode, as Lewis Mumford called the American Renaissance movement, provided a style, a scale, and a spirit that would suit the apartment house as soon as legislation allowed. Meanwhile, the proliferation of great service hotels and the wild popularity of hotel life boded well for communal living. The Savoy, the Netherlands, and a renovated Plaza now surrounded Cornelius Vanderbilt II's mansion on the plaza at 59th Street. When the economic depression lifted at the end of the decade, a veritable boom of even grander hotels followed. Large "family" hotels were filling out Central Park West, the Olcott and the Majestic on West 72nd Street, near the Dakota, and the San Remo and

Fifth Avenue, looking south from 37th Street, to the Waldorf-Astoria, 1895.

the Beresford nearby. They were effective stand-ins for the apartment.

The new Waldorf-Astoria outdid them all. It was the grandest and the most famous hotel in America. The Waldorf part was built in 1893 by William Waldorf Astor (as the story goes, to spite his august aunt, who lived in a house next door); the Astoria wing (on the site that *she* then ceded) was added by 1897. The whole splendid affair covered the block from 33rd to 34th Street on Fifth and stood seventeen stories tall. More than a mere hotel, it was a city in itself, an exuberant urban

experience. Three floors of luxurious public rooms were at the disposal
of the general public: galleries and lounges, a ballroom, a theater, a
barbershop, the Palm Court restaurant, where attire was white tie and
tails; the huge crystalline Palm Garden, where society ladies took high
tea; the Turkish salon, where a genuine Turk served coffee. The aura of
the hotel was exclusive, for the manners of the staff and the social
amenities suggested life with the Four Hundred, but the guests themselves—politicians, gamblers, gastronomes, divas, visiting dignitaries or

midwestern tourists—came from all ranks of society. "The poorest man living in or visiting New York, provided he is well dressed, may sit about these corridors night after night, spending never a cent, speaking to no one, and he will be allowed to stay," E. I. Zeisloft reported in his 1899 book, called *The New Metropolis*.

Compared with the quiet and genteel places of residence on Murray Hill, only a stone's throw away, the Waldorf-Astoria was a crassly commercial establishment. To most New Yorkers, however, it was glittering theater. It affirmed an almost Whitmanesque experience, for in its own way, it embraced all people; it brought exclusivity to the masses. The hotel was a microcosm of the urban good life at the end of the nineteenth century. Within its walls, it was clear that New York had entered a new stage of sociability.

The architect of the Waldorf was Henry J. Hardenbergh, whose reputation by then lay with hotels, to which the Dakota was an early footnote. With a frivolous mansard roofline, the hotel looked French, which suited a place that belonged to the Belle Epoque. It was high-spirited and huge, and it cast irreverent shadows over its low-lying neighbors. It lorded it over A. T. Stewart's mansion, which sat stolidly on the opposite corner, looking considerably diminished in its presence.

As a piece of historical architecture, the Waldorf-Astoria predated the American Renaissance. By the time of its opening, however, New York had begun to refashion itself as City Beautiful. McKim, Mead and White were the acknowledged chairmen of the movement, and they were working their will on the city. The firm seemed to be perfectly matched to the needs of New York. Their classicism—calm, sober, richly but discreetly ornamented—reflected the aristocratic aspirations of the day. Their concern for the architectural ensemble provided harmony and order at a time when the visual fabric of the city was fragmented and confusing. Most important, their enthusiastic urbanism took life in their buildings and established a positive view of city life out on the street. McKim, Mead and White created a series of monuments, from mercantile buildings for Tiffany's and the Gorham Company to Low Library at Columbia University; from the base for the statue of General Sherman on Grand Army Plaza to civic structures like Pennsylvania Station and Bellevue Hospital, which brought a swell of pride and a sense of power to the city. The way they built had its physical and metaphysical effects as well. They made large-scale use of marble, Indiana limestone, pale brick, and glazed terra-cotta, so that their buildings had a lighter, more elegant, and more permanent look than most earlier pieces of architecture in the city. They were exacting contractors so that their buildings were solidly constructed and meticulously handcrafted, reflecting both the economic conditions of the turn-of-the-century marketplace, which provided raw materials and highly skilled labor in abundance and at low cost, and the desire to endure. The architects were also exceptionally gifted spatially, so that they created places that were meaningful to be in, sometimes by using sheer volume or perspective well, sometimes by designing sequences of space that achieved both formality and informality at the same time. For the people who used them, such buildings offered important perceptual experiences; in intensifying the sense of place, they encouraged a sense of security and well-being. In the end, they personalized the act and fact of being *somewhere* in a tumultuous and often threatening city.

Behind McKim, Mead and White's classicism lay the desire to create a noble structure for urban life, to provide order and dignity and continuity for a city that was caught in the chaotic state of becoming. There were other ways to read the firm's work too, of course, for each building had something specific and pragmatic to say about contemporary life in New York. Each one had a purpose and a location as well as a shape and a style, and was tagged with social significance. The statue of General William T. Sherman, for example—its base designed by McKim (of an abolitionist family), its gilded horse and rider cast by White's frequent collaborator Saint-Gaudens—spoke of the importance of military heroes in an increasingly historical-minded and power-conscious young nation. Its siting at 59th and Fifth, at the door to Central Park, in the midst of Millionaire's Mile, and in full view of a semicircle of luxurious new hotels, established the vast and open Grand Army Plaza as a new social and spiritual center of the city. Likewise, the plan and buildings commissioned by Columbia University told of a new neighborhood coming into being on the highlands of Morningside Heights, shaped by the university and St. Luke's Hospital. It signaled, too, the fact that the neighborhoods from which these institutions had moved would be changing character, that large plots on Madison Avenue and Fifth Avenue were temporarily up for grabs.

As McKim, Mead and White built cultural institutions—the Morgan Library (1903), which opened up to the city one of the finest private collections of art treasures in the world; new wings for the Metropolitan Museum (1903–10); two neighborhood branches for the new New

York Public Library (1905)—it was a reminder that culture was becoming a public commodity. As they built clubhouse buildings—the Century Association (1891), the Harvard Club (1895), the Metropolitan
Club (1894), the University Club (1900), and the Colony Club (1904),
not to mention smaller clubs like the Players, the Brook Club, the
Harmonie Club, and the Lambs Club (the firm probably erected more
examples of the form than all other architects put together)—one was
reminded that at this point New Yorkers were great clubmen. They
were convivial and ceremonial, and they liked belonging. Belonging to
a club constituted a form of security and an act of definition. It was

Delmonico's new hotel on the northeast corner of Fifth Avenue and 44th Street, catercorner from the new McKim, Mead and White building for Sherry's, 1898. Like its eternal rival, Delmonico's had bachelor apartments on the top floor as well as an open-air restaurant on the roof.

essentially an extension of domestic life—going public in a limited, controlled sort of way.

McKim, Mead and White built very few apartment houses or hotels, for their type of client did not ask for them very often. They were horizontal architects at heart, with little interest in stacking up for efficiency's sake, and no passion for the abbreviated forms that suggested the future. Nonetheless, the firm designed a first-class apartment house that opened upper Park Avenue to multiple dwellings in 1890 (called the Yosemite, it continued the use of Wild West nomenclature to attract urban adventurers), and a sumptuously decorated ten-story hotel at 44th and Fifth for Louis Sherry, which included six floors of bachelor apartments to provide rental income. Most important, they shaped a new city in which the luxury apartment could find a natural place.

McKim, Mead and White's masterpiece was Pennsylvania Station, the vast train depot that was inspired by the Baths of Caracalla in Rome. It would crown a decade of achievement for both the firm and the city. By the time construction had begun in 1904, New York was already a different place. On January 1, 1898, it had become Greater New York, a city that numbered 3,388,834 people and 360 square miles. It had absorbed the city of Brooklyn, or Kings County, and Queens County on Long Island; the whole of Staten Island, or Richmond County; and the district of the Bronx. The idea for such a union, which was intended to be practical, had first been aired in 1833 when it would have been highly impractical given the lack of development; then in 1856, the legislature had discussed a proposal to fill in the East River in order to make Manhattan and Brooklyn one. Coming at the end of a period of rapid growth, renewed prosperity, and burgeoning civic pride, the so-called Consolidation of New York impelled the city out of one century and into another. It effectively annexed the future, for it created not only the largest city in the United States, but the second largest city in the world after London. Once and for all, it verified the passing of Old New York, and relegated the old ways and the old cityscape to the history books.

THE 1890s had prepared the city well for its new status as the national showpiece. It had been a decade of parades, which fortified the sense of New York as the capital city of America. Beginning in 1889 with the centennial celebration of Washington's inauguration, a series of commemorative occasions served as a barometer of the new civic energy. The anniversary of Columbus's landing in 1492; the Businessman's Parade in 1896, which protested the silver standard proposed by William Jennings Bryan; the dedication of Grant's Tomb in 1897; and the many military displays that annotated the war with Spain brought people into the streets of the city by the hundreds of thousands. In 1899, when New York was awarded the honor of welcoming home the victorious U.S. fleet, three million people were in attendance during the three-day tribute to Admiral Dewey. The spirit of triumphant nationalism seemed indivisible from the spirit of a glorious metropolitanism. New York was developing a very strong character. It was nurturing a sort of fame. It had the Brooklyn Bridge (which was already clogged with commuter traffic), the Statue of Liberty (which had been unveiled in thick fog in 1886), and skyscrapers that created a "sky-line," as the New York *Journal* coined in 1896, which was both unsettling and impressive.

Not surprisingly, the nineties produced many historical volumes about the city. They were studies of the origins and rise of New York. They celebrated its progress. They attempted to see it in an historical context and to put it in historical perspective. Like the interest in genealogy, the publication of these histories was part of a sudden rush to remember and record earlier times in New York, to document a way of life that was disappearing, to take stock before the future took over.

The most impressive testimonial was the fat, album-sized tome that appeared in official commemoration of the Consolidation of New York, edited by E. Idell Zeisloft and called *The New Metropolis or Events of Three Centuries, from the Island of Mana-hat-ta to Greater New York at the Close of the Nineteenth*. As its title suggested, it was a proud creation, sweeping in scope, specific in focus, and lavishly illustrated, comprising, as it noted, sixty-four subjects, three hundred thousand words, and one thousand engravings. Beginning at the city's beginnings, *The New Metropolis* offered a perspective in prose and pictures. Manhattan had been "the smiling land" of Henry Hudson, an emphatically rolling country of steep hills and deep valleys and innumerable brooks and ponds and watercourses. Where Broadway stood, a rocky ridge once ran diagonally up across the island like a sash. Where Canal Street cut west of Broadway, meadows were flooded by the evening tide. Where the Tombs prison had been built, the famous Tea Water Pump used to spill the finest water on the island. "Hardly the faintest hint to what the island of Mana-hattoes was can be found in the regularly arranged heaps of brick and stone that mark the Borough of Manhattan of 1898 and 1900," the chapter concluded, introducing as evidence engravings that showed off the new aerial views in the city and a night shot of the elevated-railroad curve at 110th Street that looked like the course of a roller coaster.

New York was sitting for its full-length turn-of-the-century portrait, and the eye of *The New Metropolis* was all-seeing. Broadway, Fifth Avenue, and Wall Street were explored, block by block, and sometimes building by building, in full chapters; all the other streets of Manhattan were described in a broader sweep that nonetheless included a full commentary on points of social and economic interest—an apartment building that was growing seedy, a lunch spot popular with downtown shoppers, the increased use of the parlor floor of brownstones for trade on Fifth Avenue in the 30s. Here was Eighth Avenue, for example: "the greater lower middle class highway of New York."

It is a famous highway for bicyclers, running as it does, with asphalt pavements, direct to Central Park from far downtown, which accounts for the large number of bicycle stores near the Park. Below Fifty-third Street it is made up almost entirely of flat houses (which rent for an average of twenty-five dollars a month) with stores on the ground floors. The corners are almost without exception occupied by saloons, the drug stores, which usually share them, being compelled to find space in the centers of the blocks. . . . Between Fifty-ninth and One Hundred and Tenth Streets Eighth Avenue is the western boundary of Central Park, where it is called Central Park West. Its character here totally alters. Only since 1890 has this land been built upon to any extent; it now shows costly churches and apartment hotels of much magnificence and elaborate architecture. There are, besides, some handsome residences in rows, all facing the Park. Above One Hundred and Tenth Street, the avenue resumes its old character; it becomes again a street of small shops; but these, on the whole, are purely local, and not of great interest.

Here, evoking more poetry, was Madison Square, still snug, resplendent, and respectable:

The uptown life of the city centralizes at the junction of Broadway and Fifth Avenue and Twenty-third Street, the latter a chief highway from the east and west, and a rival of both the former as a resort of fashionable shoppers. The broad asphalted plaza formed by the converging streets is full of life night and day. There is a constant mingling of human beings from the living streams of which this is the meeting place. When Madison Square is green and the weather bright, here is a radiant picture. Over the white asphalt the yellow cars draw swiftly back and forth along their electric tracks. The soft, almost musical rhythm of harness chains is heard with the approach of dashing equipages and well-appointed hansoms. Opposing currents of correctly dressed men and women throng all the sidewalks; the gray white of the Fifth Avenue Hotel, the dull yellow of the Garden's Moorish tower with its glittering gilded Diana, tempered by the gloomy spire of Dr. Parkhurst's church, dominate the plaza, and in the square there is the verdure of lawns, the sparkle of sunlit fountains, and the brillance of flowers.

As a document, *The New Metropolis* was vast. Its very vastness was a comment on New York in 1899. Zeisloft was gathering material to get to the essence of the city, but the sense of impossibly multitudinous detail about his task intimated that the city might already be too unwieldy to categorize properly. If one whole chapter could be devoted to news vendors (there were more than five thousand newsstands in Greater New York, many supported by "fabulous" incomes), and another to the many types of professional mendicants in the city, New York was no longer an old-fashioned town. Only society and society's attitude toward apartment houses seemed to belong to earlier times.

According to a chapter titled "Classes in New York and Their Ways of Living," New York society in 1899 still inhabited the traditional pyramid, which had suffered only a few bulges and cracks with the advent of modern times. From top to bottom, the Very Rich, the Rich, the Prosperous, the Well-to-Do Comfortable, the Well-to-Do Uncomfortable, the Comfortable or Contented Poor, and the Submerged or Uncomfortable Poor, as the classes were identified, lined up much as they always had, with the numbers swelling from ten thousand people in each of the top two classes to seven hundred thousand strong at the bottom.

At the top of the order, the Very Rich Man set an elaborate example, involving numerous residences, each one adapted to a season of the year (Thanksgiving until the New Year in a mansion in New York, spring on a farm on Long Island, summer in Newport, fall in the Berkshires, a winter interlude in Aiken, South Carolina) and each involving domestic machinery worthy of English nobility. This included a full cast of servants (butler, valet, cooks, chambermaids, ladies' maids, housekeeper, gardeners, coachmen, grooms, hostlers, stableboys, a Master of the Horse) and a full retinue of vehicles (from a trotting buggy to a full-closed coach, numbering eleven). Taste filtered down accordingly. The Rich Man lived in only two or three permanent homes; the Prosperous frequently didn't own either his New York town house, his summer house, or his carriage, and retained fewer servants. More industriously, the Well-to-Do Comfortable Man adjusted the facts of his existence, boarding in the country for the summer months, leasing a row house on a cross street of the city, as did the Well-to-Do Uncomfortable, who had "a certain fashion to maintain, but . . . not the means to do it with either comfort or decency."

City surveys estimated that by 1900 at least half of the middle class was living in apartments. *The New Metropolis* had taken its own census and found apartment dwellers among the Well-to-Do Comfortable and the Well-to-Do Uncomfortable, as well as among bachelors of taste and means. The Comfortable typically lived in ten-to-twelve-room apartments; the Uncomfortable in five-to-eight-room apartments or flats, which "in polite phrase are not called tenement houses (but are tenement houses all the same)." Bachelors, historically a lonely and uncomfortable race, were now "better housed than any other class of persons in the town"—enjoying three-to-five-room apartments with "attendance," or service. In addition, a few individuals from the Prosperous class had succumbed to gregarious living. Identified as doctors, lawyers, and mercantile figures who had not yet achieved millionaire status, and described as people of "good sense," "reason," and "industry," they lived in the highest-class buildings like the Navarro and the Osborne where they occupied two floors, with up-and-down stairs, and ten to twenty rooms, "most of which were well-lighted." Their accommodations were summed up as "suitable," affording them "perhaps, the least bother of all the classes."

On the eve of the twentieth century, apartment living was not a glamorous but a "sensible" modus vivendi. It was "to a certain extent fashionable," which meant that a small segment of society "countenanced" it and that "a brownstone was no longer indispensable to at least moderate social standing." This was a grudging recommendation, carrying with it the damnation of faint praise. Its message was lost in the social din of the day. The season of 1898–99 had been a particularly brilliant one, *The New Metropolis* reported with pride, describing in detail the best of its dinner cotillions and debutante balls, and noting how well it had shown off society's riches. It made a fitting finale for the most extravagant epoch in American history. Beneath all the splendid formal attire, society was unsettled, its leadership spent, its ranks diffusing. A new era was at hand. For a while, however, the glories of the old hung in the air like the last shower of fireworks.

THE NEW METROPOLIS

1900–1919

The Astor Court, by Charles Platt, under construction,
Broadway and 90th Street, 1915.

10

BUILDING THE UPPER
WEST SIDE: THE COURTYARD
BUILDING, THE STUDIOS

THE FIRST decade of the twentieth century was a time of visible, inexorable change in New York. By 1900, Trinity's steeple had been outstripped—"overtopped" was the word Henry James used—by a handful of buildings in the business district, and the changing skyline had unconsciously become a measure, if not a symbol, of the increasing power of the city. Downtown, the city had begun to "tower." Uptown, the shantytowns on the old northern frontiers at 72nd Street to the west and on Carnegie Hill to the east had yielded to fine residences. It was the good country air that had lured Andrew Carnegie to Fifth Avenue and 91st Street in 1901, but within several years of his arrival, wild game, wandering goats, and a clear blue horizon were things of the past. By the time the Great War stilled building activity, the grid of New York had been filled in out to its watery edges. The population had doubled since 1885, and as the whole country had grown apace and more than half of the citizens lived in cities, the census takers could report that the United States was an urban nation.

By 1910, New York was a different city. It had exploded, losing any sense of containment or shape and unleashing an amazing energy. Behind the energy was a sense of prosperity that was almost palpable. The recovery from the depression of the 1890s had been complete. When

Henry James returned to New York in 1904, he saw gold dust in the air. It haunted him as he toured the new museums and hotels and great houses, because it bespoke a national acquisitiveness and an affluence he found vulgar. James was struck, too, by a terrible aura of impermanence about the city. After an absence of twenty years, the eminent novelist was making a voyage of rediscovery to the place of his youth, and as he studied and reflected upon the teeming here and now of the city, he experienced a sense of astonishing loss. His birthplace on Washington Square harbored a shirt factory, his childhood home on 14th Street was gone, and the church across the way had been replaced by a faceless row of stores. Elsewhere his favorite buildings seemed lost at sea, deprived of their old dignity and visibility by a crude new dimension in the city. James's reaction was not purely Van Winklerian, for that same year, the New York writer Edgar Saltus spoke about "the gigantic upheaval that is transforming the whole city." New York looked like a boom town, he said, and surmised that the changes were mere tokens of those yet to come. Describing the twenty-story triangulated Fuller Building, which had just risen on a strange and stingy little pie-shaped piece of real estate pointed uptown at the southern end of Madison Square, Saltus pointed out, like a clairvoyant, that "its front is lifted to the future. On the past its back is turned."

The Fuller Building, which was dubbed the Flatiron Building for its unusual shape, caught New York's full attention. It was an outrageous piece of architecture on one hand and a very expressive one on the other. With its broad backside to the south and its aquiline nose to the north, it looked like an ocean liner. The angles of its prow at 23rd Street were so sharp that it seemed to be sailing uptown; real winds broke around its base like gales on the Atlantic, blowing women off course and sending their skirts swirling high. The feminine disarray was a physical manifestation of the psychological disorientation that was common in a city virtually under reconstruction. Saltus climbed to the top of the Flatiron to survey the many aspects of New York—the pockets of colonial squalor, the lingering streets of brownstone fronts, thoroughfares that were "nightmares in stone"—and realized that they were all transient, "like measles and mumps in a child." "They are not definite conditions," he explained, "nor is there, nor will there be anything definite here until, from the Battery to the Plaza, the buildings one and all are so huge that nothing huger is possible."

Indeed, from the turn of the century until World War I, New York experienced a building boom of unprecedented proportions. Like an architectural maelstrom, it left the city with a whole new landscape of skyscrapers, public buildings, luxury hotels, and luxury homes. They were in part the infrastructure of a great new city—a General Post Office, a Stock Exchange, municipal buildings, two immense new railroad terminals, a vast marble public library on the site of the reservoir where New Yorkers used to take their Sunday strolls. It was strange to live through such change, to watch this revised city take shape—unsettling but intoxicating too. The ethic of the Columbian Exposition was well in force, and the White City was taking form. Each building rose to be big and surprising. Each had presence and each had mass. Each seemed to represent such an important addition to the urban landscape that one wondered what kind of city New York could have been before, without them.

The two decades that surrounded the millennium constituted an era in New York history that has been named the Imperial Age, the Age of Confidence, and the Age of Stone. Of all the buildings that were erected in this era, none transformed the city more dramatically and more definitively than the new luxury apartment houses. Between 1902 and 1910, more than four thousand apartment houses were erected in Manhattan, and many hundreds of them were designed for the upper and upper-middle classes. Suddenly, it seemed, a host of factors had conspired to give what had been a gradual revision of home life such impetus that it had the momentum of a mass conversion. With the inflation of land values, speculators turned to apartment building for the better odds on profitability.

Technically speaking, it was the Tenement House Law of 1901, commonly called the New Law, that cleared the way for the apartmentalization of New York. Quite literally, it took the lid off the building industry and permitted the apartment house to take the large impressive form that made it a genre of its own. Specifically, the law, which had been revising its way to this resolution all through the 1890s, now allowed a residential fireproof building to rise twice the width of its street, which meant as high as 125 feet, or ten stories, on side streets and 150, or twelve stories, on north-south avenues and major crosstown streets. It encouraged large lot development, for a house more than one hundred feet tall now had to be forty feet wide, but held general land coverage to 70 percent. It dictated the minimum size of interior courts and required certain windows for light and ventilation. Plans began to improve immediately. Inside greater mass there was more room to play, to manipulate space into auspicious new attitudes and arrangements. With wider lots, the rule of the grid was countermanded, at last. In effect, this act of city government not only legitimized the modern luxury apartment building; it bestowed upon it a very specific blessing.

While the law allowed the apartment house to take new form, a new system of mass transportation paved the way for its proliferation. Right on time for the start of the twentieth century, the crews of the Inter-borough Rapid Transit Company began construction on an under-ground railroad, a project that had been discussed for decades. The new version was to run from City Hall up to 42nd Street, then veer west to Times Square to continue up Broadway to 145th Street. When the Broadway subway opened on October 27, 1904, a host of grand apart-ment houses was already in place or in prospectus along its route, for speculators had anticipated how the new mode of urban travel would open up the grid and unify the space of the city. The fact that the trip to Wall Street had been cut to twenty minutes meant that the Upper West Side was neither wilderness nor backwater, and that the days of sleepy, spotty, stop-and-start development were over. The subway served as an advance man for the apartment, and its advent was responsi-ble for a second intensive West Side building boom, which added many hundreds of luxury apartment buildings to its landscape and fulfilled long-held ambitions in a way the promoters of 1879 could not have imagined.

As the Upper West Side was making itself into a quarter of apartment dwellers, the Upper East Side was still consumed with the elaboration of its "billionaire district," as Schuyler now classified its northern reaches. Fifth Avenue, from McKim, Mead and White's neo-Italian Metropolitan Club at 60th Street to Carnegie's neo-Georgian home at the edge of town, was one long architectural extravaganza, with certain single facades offering such a rich show of styles they were "complete architectural meals," as Edith Wharton described in *The House of Mirth*. Eventually, the East Side would yield. Yet it wasn't the fact of conquest that was so interesting, for the topography of Manhattan made that a virtual inevitability. It was the process by which one landscape overtook another. In an uncanny way, the physical course of the city gave visible form to a new spirit and sociology. All the new buildings typified the peculiar conditions of New York's complex civilization. Watching them materialize was like seeing into the workings of the urban mind.

. . .

THE PHYSICAL transition from the nineteenth century to the twentieth century was one of the most vivid in New York history. As a whole section of the city like the Upper West Side changed its contours, it was like a great geological event—the collision of continents or the birth of mountain ranges. The territory literally erupted. Dynamite blasts rocked the neighborhood, shaking houses and scaring horses in the street. Broadway opened up like a fault. In almost every block of the grid, there were yawning pits in the bedrock, created by the vast excavations necessary for the foundations of the new, oversized buildings.

The Upper West Side had begun the century with a patchwork character. It was a series of scattered neighborhoods with distinct physical and social personalities, not unlike the many dispersed villages that described the area in the eighteenth and nineteenth centuries. There were the ivy and gables of West End Avenue; the churches, small stores, and family hotels of Broadway; the low-rent flats of Amsterdam. Central Park West was best described by the Dakota, the Majestic Hotel, and the Museum of Natural History; Columbus Avenue by the tenements and the ramparts of the el; Riverside Drive by its houses, often spreading mansions, with surrounding shrubbery like suburban homesteads. There were vacant lots everywhere, sometimes whole blocks of them, and occasionally, a truck farm or a farmhouse. There were working railroad tracks below Riverside, from which the smell of the cattle en route to market would rise with the eastern wind. There were barnyard animals and apple trees that bloomed in May at the corner of 79th and Broadway, on the farm on the Astor property. Lewis Mumford, whose childhood turf stretched north from 59th Street, remembers market gardens in the 90s; above 110th Street "a sort of no-man's land" that was neither city nor country and even less suburbia; and above 125th Street, agricultural tracts, interspersed with roadhouses and beer gardens, where Sunday cyclists downed schooners of beer for five cents.

Mumford, who was born in 1895, grew up in a brownstone on West 65th Street, a brown brick house off Central Park West on 93rd Street, and, after 1907, an apartment house on Columbus Avenue. His various neighborhoods were quiet, comfortable, colorful enclaves ruled by "a kind of bucolic innocence and neighborliness." Life, symbolized by the neighborhood grocery store, found its variety in little changes and little differences. Except for the strains of a piano, the rumble of the el, or the

The Ansonia Hotel, looking very French in the company of its neighbors.

clatter and clopping of horse-drawn cabs, "the human voice struck the dominant note" in the air. Mumford was "a child of the city," as he put it, and he watched the city grow up around him, the scale of its activity, amusement, and architecture changing before his eyes.

More pictures from a vanished era. A southern view from Sherman Square, at 72nd Street, taken in 1897, shows how lush and carefully tended the middle islands of Broadway are—the grass as thick and even as a lawn, the flowerbeds enclosed in ornate stone planters. Lined up on the street are the Sherman Square Hotel, flying an American flag from its roof, Christ Church, and the elegant Colonial Club, the first to admit ladies, albeit strictly as guests. "A Great City: Pure Air and Perfect Sanitary Conditions: Surrounded by Pleasure Grounds, Crossed by Fine Boulevards and Wide Streets, Lined with Artistic Buildings; Its Residents Live Long in Comfort and Happiness" is how the *New York Times* had summed up the West Side in a special section on the virtues of the area a few years before. A second photograph from this corner, taken a few years later, this time facing north, shows a new building beginning to loom above the roofline at 73rd Street, a giant street sculpture unresolved behind its scaffolding.

This new building, which would rise to seventeen stories and be crowned with fanciful turrets and carved filigree, was the Ansonia, the apartment hotel that opened a new chapter in the annals of luxury housing in New York. It effectively outdid every apartment building that had preceded it—most recently the New Century Apartments, at 79th Street and West End Avenue, a stylish nine-story building that had appeared punctually in 1900 and offered storage for automobiles in a two-story annex. Designed to be "the world's largest resort hotel" and designated "the most superbly equipped apartment house in the world," the

Ansonia had 2,500 rooms, 400 full baths and 600 additional toilets and sinks (providing the largest plumbing contract in history), a banquet hall, English Grill, and a main dining room to seat 550, a grand ballroom, cafés, tearooms, writing rooms, a lobby fountain with live seals, a palm court, a Turkish bath, and the world's largest indoor swimming pool. Its apartments, sized from one room with bath to eighteen rooms with three baths and four toilets, were furnished with

Persian carpets, ivy-patterned art-glass windows, domed chandeliers set with mosaics, and a remarkable selection of appliances. All this was enclosed within an architectural mass that became known as "The Wedding Cake."

The Ansonia was a Beaux-Arts confection, heavy with the ornament of nineteenth-century Paris—scrolls, brackets, medallions, and moldings. It was built in the shape of a fat H, with long recessed courts in front on Broadway as well as in back, and smaller courts cut out on 73rd and 74th streets. Its front corners were rounded like turrets, and its great looming bulk was interrupted by several horizontal bands of balconies before it closed, majestically, at a copper mansard roof. Like the Dakota, the Ansonia seemed to be summed up by its roofline, which was rich with windows and rose in the corners to cupolas capped with widow's walks and finials. Even without the lofty central tower that had appeared in preliminary drawings, the building was Belle Epoque in its highest spirits. An affectionate eye could find references to great French monuments like the Hôtel de Ville or Les Invalides on its facade, and those who saw Broadway, or the Boulevard, as a potential Champs-Elysées were gratified. The fact that the Ansonia bore more resemblance to an overgrown French resort than a proper *hôtel particulier* only made its presence more exotic.

William Earl Dodge Stokes, the builder and, with Paul E. M. Duboy, the architect of the Ansonia, had a propensity for architectural adventures. The heir to the fortunes of his father's Phelps Dodge Company and his grandfather's Ansonia Brass and Copper Company, he had speculated in West Side real estate and then built some forty row houses in the first boom years of the 1880s. In 1900, he built and then, after a divorce, never occupied his marble-fronted McKim, Mead and White dream house at 4 East 54th Street. The Ansonia was another personal dream house. From his brownstone home at 262 West 72nd Street, Stokes studied his lots at the bend of Broadway, and he made sketches of a building that would commandeer the auspicious site. He had been to France and inspected its buildings and their floor plans, and he had hired a French architect to draw up his ideas. He oversaw every detail of the construction of the building and supplied many of its materials and fixtures—terra-cotta, copper, elevators—from companies he owned. To a large extent, Stokes's eccentricities shaped the building's character: his mistrust of insurance companies resulted in the three-foot-thick terra-cotta partitions that created not only a fireproof building but also the best soundproofing in the city; his flamboyant sense of fun was responsible for the roof garden, where orchestras played through summer nights, and the roof farm where he raised his own breeds of goats, ducks, and chickens, which produced milk for making cheese and eggs he purveyed at half-price to tenants. His decision to create an apartment for himself and his young son on the seventeenth floor of the building had arrested its height, which was originally planned for twenty stories.

Inside and out, the Ansonia was a theatrical building, a Stokes extravaganza. Behind the curves and cornices were apartments with oval reception rooms or immense circular parlors, ellipsoidal living and dining rooms, a bedroom with an apse; on higher floors, there were apartments with panoramic views. All the apartments were heated and cooled by a unique method of air circulation, supplied with filtered hot, cold, and ice water, and equipped with the gadgets of the latest technology. Although a standard housekeeping suite provided a kitchen and accommodation for one or two live-in servants, half the apartments did not have kitchens, and maid service and room service were available, as well as a hotel-like inventory of towels, napkins, dishes, silver (polished once a month by the staff), light bulbs, soap, and stationery. To manage his vast domestic emporium, Stokes had hired Guernsey E. Webb away from the Plaza Hotel.

The Ansonia, which strictly speaking was an apartment-hotel, was hotel-like in many respects, but it was a residential establishment nonetheless. It was meant to be a home, even if it didn't look like the traditional place for peace and quiet and family unity, and most of its "guests," as they were first called, settled in to live there for years, and even for decades. They were a more exotic lot than the average middle- or upper-class homebodies, and they included a large number of musical and theatrical personalities who were attracted by the richness of the place as well as the soundproofing and the service—Florenz Ziegfeld and his wife, Anna Held (also his mistress and then his second wife, Billie Burke), stars of the opera world like Giulio Gatti-Casazza, Feodor Chaliapin, Arturo Toscanini, who moved in after he became conductor of the Metropolitan Opera in 1910, Igor Stravinsky, and the Menuhin family. These were not society people—in many instances they represented elements still considered alien or unsavory to old-fashioned society people—but they had worldliness and culture and fame that they in turn imparted to the building. They represented a breed of New Yorker who if not "proper" was lively, urbane, and professional, and if their lives were transient ones, then well-to-do New Yorkers in general were becoming more mobile and dividing their time between several abodes.

In the periphery of the Ansonia, hotels like the Majestic, the San Remo, the Beresford, and the Empire were flourishing. At Broadway and 66th, the Marie Antoinette, a hotel that was described as "a Palace of Good Taste" with private banquet halls "where actors and poets and soldiers met to discuss life" was being refurbished. The Belleclaire rose on Broadway at 77th, the Spencer Arms at 69th. Downtown, ever-grander examples of the form continued to arrive on the street—the Astor and the St. Regis, the Gotham, the Knickerbocker, and in 1907, a new Plaza, designed by Henry J. Hardenbergh. Hotel life in New York was so popular and so exuberant that Henry James wondered if it was an indication of a new stage of civilization. "One is verily tempted to ask if the hotel-spirit may not just be the American spirit most seeking and most finding itself," he said, adding a description of the Waldorf and "the hundreds and hundreds of people in circulation, the innumerable huge-hatted ladies in especial, with their air of finding in the gilded and storie'd labyrinth the very firesides and pathways of homes. . . ."

As Henry James identified hotels with the emergence of a new social attitude, Edith Wharton, too, observed that they illustrated many of "the modern tendencies" of New York. In *The Custom of the Country,* she used an apartment hotel on 72nd Street near Central Park West as a setting for a saga of social advancement. The "Stentorian" is a pretentious, gilded, excessive place, serviced by French maids, bellboys, and masseuses, and full of people like the Spraggs, new millionaires from Apex City, whose beautiful and ruthless daughter Undine, named after a hair-waving device her father has invented, covets a position in society. The Spraggs have moved to the Stentorian to be fashionable and because "they couldn't hope to 'get on' while they kept house." Old-fashioned society, like a Mrs. Fairford, maintain a house downtown, an unpretentious ungilded abode (in which a real fire burns instead of electric bulbs behind ruby glass in a polished grate), but they are "the Aborigines" of New York, doomed to rapid extinction.

Like the Stentorian, the Ansonia spoke in loud tones, and proclaimed a new taste. It stood alone in the neighborhood for less than a year. The Dorilton, just as massive and infinitely more confectionary, was completed at 71st and Broadway in 1903. Then came the Chatsworth (1904) on West 79th Street; the Clarendon (1906) on West 86th Street; the St.

Urban (1906), the Langham (1905), the Prasada (1907), and the Kenilworth (1908) on Central Park West; the Apthorp (1908) and the Belnord (1908) on Broadway. All were palatial and inspired by old-world taste. By 1910, several dozen outstanding apartment buildings, some built by financial giants, all painstakingly designed by good architects, made the West Side look like a Beaux-Arts nursery.

City Beautiful was a-building, and these were its new homes, monuments all, from the frivolous and bombastic Dorilton, dripping ornament like French pastry, to the graceful and composed Apthorp, appointed with finely wrought sculpture and cherubs. It was not surprising that important residential buildings would take the same grandiose form as new civic and commercial temples, and even hospitals did: their size invited such treatment, their mission such pretense, the aesthetics of the day such conspicuous display. As it turned out, the luxury apartment house was one of the great products of the American Renaissance. The millionaire had propelled the Age of Elegance into flowering, and it was his gilded taste that now shaped a new generation of apartment houses, which looked like mansions blown into ridiculous proportions.

EUROPEAN CITIES like Paris and Vienna had built Renaissance palaces in the seventeenth and eighteenth centuries and, then, in the nineteenth, converted them into buildings of flats. In New York, architects who now knew the classical vocabulary applied it to problems of the modern apartment house and, starting from scratch, came forth with a brand new generation of Beaux-Arts buildings. They bore little resemblance to buildings that had been erected in the 1890s, tedious, self-conscious six- or eight-story structures that Schuyler had described as "a panorama of platitude." Some were very elegant historical reproductions. Others merely had French trimming, as if a cartouche or a dab of floral frosting might impress tenants favorably. (Stokes's terra-cotta company in New Jersey made the sort of ornament that was often applied to unremarkable buildings to make them look remarkable.) Some were rethinkings of earlier ideas for the city. Others were directly inspired by the New Law. Few showed evidence of economic or aesthetic restraint. As they looked more elaborate and more expensive, they required more time and more money to construct. It was an increasingly complicated undertaking to build a fine apartment house. Once all the governing rules and statutes were mastered, there were the considerations of site, neighborhood, aesthetics, and of course cost and profit. And the whole project had to demonstrate those qualities of convenience and luxury that now seemed crucial to the success of an apartment building, that gave it an aristocratic bearing.

Of all the Beaux-Arts forms visited upon New York in this first modern wave of residential building, the most imperial was the court-yard building, a direct descendant of the Vancorlear and the Dakota, and a literal translation of the Italian Renaissance palazzo. William Waldorf Astor, whose family had bought up a large share of the old farmsteads between Broadway and the Hudson, was responsible for a pair of court-yard buildings. Graham Court—erected in 1901 at 116th and Seventh Avenue, farther uptown than fashion would tolerate for very long—was the prototype: an eight-story hollow square of brick and limestone, arranged around an open landscaped courtyard with a circular carriage drive and private entryways to the interior. In 1908, the Apthorp, which was designed by the same architects, Clinton and Russell, and filled the whole block between Broadway and West End from 78th to 79th streets, expanded and improved upon that model, for it was larger, taller, and richer in materials and ornamentation. A third, smaller Astor courtyard building, named the Astor Court, built by William's nephew Vincent Astor and designed by Charles Platt, arrived at 89th and Broadway in 1916.

William Waldorf Astor, who was called the landlord of New York despite the fact that he had lived in England since the 1890s, had been sitting on his properties for almost a generation, and his decision to build apartment houses on them now served to signal the world that the moment for development was nigh. Astor, like his forebears and other merchant millionaires who had invested heavily in New York real estate—August Belmont and the Vanderbilts and, on a smaller scale, men like Levi P. Morton and the Goelets—had a stake in the growth of the city and exerted a strong influence on its ultimate design. In turning over his lots on Broadway, which belonged to old-time New York and had not been "improved" since colonial days, he effectively deeded the past to the future. Where a pretty two-story stone-and-frame house had stood for a century and a half, the Apthorp Apartments rose now. Until conversion to a roadhouse and hotel in the late 1850s, the house had been the countryseat of Baron John Cornelius Van Den Heuvel, the son-in-law of the prominent lawyer Charles Ward Apthorpe, and sat at

The Van Den Heuvel house (top), built in the late eighteenth century with materials shipped from France and Holland, was one of the oldest in the city. Its land extended as far west as the Hudson River. The Astor family bought the place, and years later, in 1906, William Waldorf Astor began building the Apthorp (bottom).

the southern end of Apthorpe's rolling two-hundred-acre estate. Near the site on Bloomingdale Road where Apthorpe's own mansion had commanded a view to both the North and East rivers, the twelve-story Astor Court would eventually prevail.

Astor's endorsement of the Beaux-Arts courtyard building was early and expansive. Under his auspices, the form matured impressively in less than a decade. The Graham was eight stories tall and one hundred square feet wide, with a two-story Palladian entrance to its courtyard and a formal garden with a fountain; the Apthorp was twelve stories tall, slightly more than twice the width of the Graham, with a three-story porte cochere leading to a formal garden with two fountains. The Graham was grand; the Apthorp was triumphant. Astor of course could afford to make his investments sound by making his buildings superior if not extravagant. By the time he built the Apthorp, given his own belief in the future of the apartment house and the palpable excitement about apartments in the area, Astor felt justified in indulging himself in this creation. Money, of course, was no object, and Astor was not the frugal breed of millionaire. By then, his architects, Clinton and Russell, had acquired unusually rich experience with multiple dwellings: after completing the Graham, they had designed the colossal Hotel Astor on Broadway between 44th and 45th, and the elegant Langham on Central Park West. Astor focused his own personal attention on the Apthorp, offering ideas on its design gathered in his travels abroad, and then giving his architects and contractors carte blanche to build on a cost-plus basis.

Inside and out, the Apthorp was an exceptional building, and it showed off the new aesthetics to advantage. Its limestone exterior was a High Renaissance composition, beautifully carved and rusticated in the tradition of Florence's Pitti Palace. The entrances were framed with garlands and reclining goddesses and spanned by delicate wrought-iron gates. The sculpture, the statuary, and the overall architectural grace created a sense of place as explicit as the name spelled out in filigree in the front gates.

One hundred and four families lived in the Apthorp, which made it a vast holding, the largest of its kind in the world to date. Although its apartments were very private and richly elaborated—mosaic-tiled foyers, glass-paneled French doors, a Wedgwood-like frieze in the dining room, carved marble fireplaces in the salon—its sheer size gave it a public aspect. There were hundreds of house phones or ash bins or mail chutes in the building, for example. On the top floor, there were 150 porcelain tubs, 20 boiling tubs, and 20 steam dryers in the laundry rooms—and as many irons in the ironing room. As expressed in these numbers, communality was a daunting prospect.

The courtyard of the Apthorp changed the character of its communality, however, for it made of it something historical and stately. If the laundry rooms conjured up a working girls' home or a charitable institution, the fountain, the carriage turnabout, and the iron canopies over the entryways brought to mind royal residences and European squares. The courtyard was a ceremonial space, like the ones the Romans carved into their buildings to prevent a sense of overcrowding. It offered tenants room to breathe freely, to stroll idly, to see the sky, and it made them feel protected and privileged.

These virtues were even more pronounced in the Belnord Apartments, which broke the ground of another solid city block, seven blocks uptown, that same year. Its volume was greater, and its courtyard, which measured 231 feet by 94 feet, was almost twice the length and was bright with light. It accommodated three formally planted gardens and walkways that invited promenades and play. The Belnord, which was considered a spiritual twin to the Apthorp, although it was designed by H. Hobart Weekes and built by George Fuller, immediately usurped the Apthorp's place as the largest apartment house in the world. It contained 175 apartments, opening off six elevator halls, each with seven to eleven rooms. It was less grandiose than its kin, sparer with ornament and simpler in interior decoration, but its plan was at least as gracious— rooms were large and light, the public rooms were arranged en suite, and bedrooms enjoyed the quiet of the courtyard.

The single most spectacular feature of the Belnord was its courtyard; it gave the building its beauty, its stature, its identity. It was a surprising place, and one came into it dramatically through a porte cochere on 86th Street that was two stories high, deep like a tunnel, barrel-vaulted, and decorated with frescoes of figures from antiquity. It amounted to an architectural rite of passage. On one side was the city at large; on the other, the courtyard with its sudden open verticality, its formality, and quiet. It was like a stage set for somewhere else, a private world far removed from the urban circus. In the vast basement of the Belnord, which duplicated the space of the courtyard above and also had a circular drive accessible to service vehicles by a ramp from 87th Street, one could see just how large and how mechanical an entity the building was. A

The Belnord courtyard, circa 1908. A large goblet fountain was later installed at its center.

warren of spaces housed the dozens of repairmen, painters, polishers, and gardeners necessary to maintain the Belnord. The boiler room was as huge as a factory, with bridges and catwalks connecting its oversized parts. But above, with the fountain splashing and the six sets of uniformed doormen standing guard by urns of topiary, the Belnord could have been a new version of palace life in some newly formed principality.

THE COURTYARD building was an extravagant shape. Only a handful of other examples would be built before it would be deemed unrealistic to consecrate such valuable urban acreage to something as arcadian as a sense of privacy or peace of mind. The studio building, on the other hand, was a pragmatic one. It, too, was an earlier idea revisited upon an older and more adventuresome city, and could be traced back to Richard Hunt's Tenth Street Studios of 1857, a building many sources claimed was really the first multiple dwelling in the city, despite its paucity of bedrooms. That structure, which had evolved naturally from a popular clubhouse for the Hudson River School into a successful cooperative building, had been a fortuitous experiment and inspired a dozen-odd small studio buildings, like the Rembrandt or the Carnegie Hall Studios on West 57th Street, designed specifically for artists. From the beginning, artists had been willing and eager apartment dwellers, and their needs had shaped their buildings, sometimes quite directly and explicitly. The hand of A. A. Andersen, for example, a painter fresh from Paris, had guided architect Charles Rich's design of the Bryant Park Studios, which had cropped up before the small green on West 40th Street just as the Public Library was beginning its herculean task of dismantling the old Croton Reservoir. It was a particularly fine example of its kind, a ten-story Beaux-Arts building with conspicuously large windows in an elegant brick-and-limestone facade, and a particularly felicitous location facing north across open leafy lots. Inside, where residential suites unfolded around large, light-drenched double-height studios, it was at least as Parisian as without. Andersen's own apartment was hung with tapestries and Turkish drapery, which provided atmospheric background for his portraiture.

This was an artist carving out an appropriate space to activate his life, and it was not unlike the wealthy industrialist demanding chandeliered reception rooms and paneled libraries to achieve his own social ends. It

LEFT: The Bryant Park Studios, 1901. The glass penthouse on the roof offered amazing views across the city. The Sixth Avenue el bridge rises in the foreground, the Waldorf-Astoria in the distance.

BELOW: Henry Ward Ranger's studio at 25 West 67th Street, 1903.

was a sound urban idea and a particularly sane solution to a particularly exotic style of living—and it grew even more important when a group of ten well-known artists, led by the landscape painter Henry Ward Ranger and including Childe Hassam, banded together to finance a fourteen-story apartment house on West 67th Street. Their cooperative, or "joint venture," arrangement was one that had first been tried out by Hubert and Pirsson, whose success had been so marginal that this new effort represented the triumph of hope over experience, as a local critic expressed it. As reconceived by Ranger, the artists would occupy half the building—that is, ten large apartments with studios—and rent out the other half to pay expenses and produce a 23 percent return on their investment. The banks were wary, but a builder named William J. Taylor was intrigued, and, in the end, could share patrimony for a building type of which he constructed seven examples. Within several years of the success of that first Cooperative Studio Building at 25 West 67th Street, a second building at number 29–33, the Central Park Studios at number 11–15, and the Atelier Building at 37, all designed by various teams from the architectural firm Pollard and Steinam, had virtually colonized the park block of 67th Street.

The block quickly became known as a bohemian enclave. It conveyed its sense of fraternity physically, for a passerby was drawn in by the similarity of the facades on the front, the banks of double-height windows on the back. The harmony was rich, the sense of neighborhood strong. At heart, however, the studio building was a modest structure, quiet in appearance and functional in use. Each structure was what it said it was, a stacking up of spaces in which artists could work, live, and display. To maximize light and air and to minimize cost, the Cooperative Studios had been cleverly manipulated into an interlocking scheme of duplex apartments and smaller two- and three-room simplex apartments for rental. The duplexes ran front to back or south to north, with the eighteen-foot-high studios and a mezzanine balcony on the north, where a low horizon of private houses was guaranteed by covenant, and two tiers of smaller lower living quarters—study, dining room, kitchen, bedrooms—on the street. Inside, the interior design was straightforward and unpretentious, for the resident community was determined not to waste money on "useless or tawdry decoration." Marble and Lincrustra-Walton were conspicuous by their absence, a critic noted, adding that the mantelpieces in the studios were "architecturally correct" and "inoffensive." The entrance hall was decorated only with a frieze painted by tenant V. V. Sewall. The wood trim was stained oak. "Interesting" ceilings were created by simply plastering the arches of the floor above. All this pragmatism did not prevent the new studio building from having a very stylish air in spite of itself, however. Its ingenious use of space was appealing. In volume alone, its studios were sumptuous. And to a populace who had only recently been swept off its feet by the premiere of Puccini's *La Bohème,* its very raison d'être was romantic.

Anyone with an eye for fashion might have predicted that the studio apartment building could be popularized, for the world of art and artists had become more interesting to social people than it had been a decade earlier. Critics praised the sudden interest in these dwellings and expressed the hope that the trend would become a permanent one—"to enable people of taste to live more comfortably at half the cost of a house." They also hoped it would foster better design in apartment houses, which were still predominantly quick-rise speculative ventures and, in many minds, constituted the most objectionable variety of building erected in the country. By 1908, half a dozen more examples of studio buildings had been erected on the avenues or on wide side streets like 57th Street, where they could grow tall and fat and prosperous. Land on the more prominent streets was now at a premium, demanding larger subscriptions by cooperative shareholders, but that did not seem to deter the proliferation. Construction costs soared too, as new buildings modified the no-frills scheme of the working artists and added rooms for children and servants and multiple baths, features that did not conjure up typical atelier life.

In 1906, a new enterprise by William J. Taylor confirmed a distinct personality change in the studio building. The location was 131–35 East 66th Street, near Lexington Avenue, on the respectable East Side. The form was an eleven-story neo–Italian Renaissance palazzo, with three-story pedimented doorways, an interior courtyard, and full limestone sheathing. In a single architectural gesture, it elevated the status of the plainspoken studio building to patrician.

The founding tenants of the East 66th Street studio building represented the world of business and finance as well as the upper echelons of the world of art—they were men like Charles Merrill, the co-founder of a brokerage house, the painter and art critic Kenyon Cox, and Howard Ruskin, the President of the American Fine Arts Society. They had an ambitious vision of home, and they had chosen the aristocratic architect Charles A. Platt over Taylor's usual partners, Pollard and Steinam. Platt was one of the best-known landscape and country-house architects in America, and he was popular with society. He had designed many important large estates with formal gardens; he had also designed small summer cottages for himself and friends like Herbert Croly in the artists' colony of Cornish, New Hampshire.

Platt was an artist before he was an architect. He had spent his early twenties in Europe, etching and then landscape painting. His eye for garden design had developed from his observations of nature there, and his interest in architecture had sprung from his appreciation of Italian villas of the Renaissance. It was a natural progression for him, with each new expression built upon earlier experience. His paintings had always reflected an interest in buildings. His gardens were built into landscapes. By 1893, when he published a book called *Italian Gardens,* Platt was already dabbling in architecture. He served no apprenticeships, although he had hung around with Beaux-Arts architectural students in Paris. By 1901, when his commissions had progressed from gardens for houses to houses with gardens, he changed his professional shingle to read simply "Architect."

As a confirmed classicist in several media, Platt had a strong belief in integration, and his first Italian Renaissance villa accommodated itself well to the streets of New York. The eleven-story palazzo did not look like it was more than twice the height of its five-story neighbors, for its roofline was heavy and its facade was divided into five horizontal sections, separated by stringcourses. Decoratively, it was understated and called attention to itself only with its elegant doorways. Window boxes were filled with hanging greenery, and a delicate wrought-iron fence separated the building from the sidewalk. It looked like a large new white mansion.

As a style, Italian Renaissance provided a particularly appropriate model for Platt, and his appreciation of its villas, which Herbert Croly called "the first great residential style of modern times," enriched his plans. Behind the dignified facade at 130–37 East 66th Street, he created seven duplex apartments in each two-story expanse and grouped them in a U around a courtyard. In a typical suite, he carved out a library, a dark-paneled dining room with a massive fireplace, a kitchen and servants' rooms, and, at the top of a spindle-turned staircase, bedrooms as large as 15 feet square. At the heart of the design in all but the corner apartments, which had conventional living rooms, was an 18-foot-high studio, 24 feet wide, 28 feet long, with a carved fireplace, beamed and painted ceilings, and the gift of northern light. A critic described its effect as "exhilarating"—such amplitude, so much light and air. "It was so big and yet so intimate, so spacious and yet so economical . . . it gave one the sense of being in the country, not the city," he said. Nathalie Dana, who visited the Kenyon Coxes in the building, surmised that the studios had been provided to persuade people that apartments could be distinguished. "Studios of first-class artists or literary people had a certain cachet," she explained. "My father and most 'sound' businessmen considered the purchase of an apartment, which they called 'a hole in the air,' to be a gambling venture as unwise as playing the market. These beautiful interiors proved that however unsound they might be as investments, apartments could be attractive places in which to live."

The East 66th Street studio building was far more refined than any other example of its genre to date. Platt had given his full attention to architectural details like moldings and framings as well as the division of space. Critics showed unmistakable disdain when they tried to compare the new studios with their West Side antecedents, which they summed up as "adequate for an artist's family." If there was simplicity on East 66th Street, it was of the monumental type, as Platt's own studio-library, decorated with paneling, a king-size Renaissance mantelpiece, and antique tapestries, showed off so well. Platt, ever the Renaissance man, had also designed interiors for half a dozen friends in the building who did not know how to treat the unusual space. Studios were difficult to domesticate, as Dana had commented. They required outsized furnishings. For all their inherent drama, they were not familial spaces.

Despite its noble innovations, Platt's building did not inspire many immediate imitations on the East Side. Given its acclaim and popularity, that was surprising. In its wake, the duplex cooperative flourished, but the veritable studio building did not. It was, perhaps, too exotic a shape for everyday domestic life, even in its gentrified version. Even its cachet seemed uncertain, for when an elegant new building at 471 Park Avenue offered studios, they were called "salons" and faced west instead of north. When Platt's second apartment building, at 130 East 67th Street, went up in 1907, it was a mirror image of the first, joined to it across the back courtyard, but it contained large conventional duplexes and smaller suites for bachelors.

On the West Side of New York, where open spaces in the grid afforded a long perspective and the right light, a handful of working studio buildings continued to appear, and many artists were among their tenants. On West 57th Street, the team of Pollard and Steinam and William J. Taylor erected a new building a few doors down from the Rembrandt and Carnegie Hall Studios, in which William Dean Howells took up residence. It was large but unpretentious, cast in an earlier image. Most new buildings were much bolder and richer than their predecessors in the neighborhood, however, and they had forsaken any semblance of anonymity. The Gainsborough (1908), on Central Park South, announced itself with a bust of Sir Thomas himself, mounted high above the Ionic front portal. The Studio (1909), at 44 West 77th Street, by Harde and Short, was a Gothic fantasy, a facade of windows frosted with glazed terra-cotta gingerbread. In 1916, when the Hotel des Artistes appeared at the head of 67th Street with a folk gallery of muses on its facade and a restaurant, squash courts, swimming pool, theater, and ballroom as inner resources, it seemed to be the apotheosis of the form reinvented in the neighborhood. Only the most successful artists could afford to live there, but by then the vanguard had begun to perceive of the ideal atelier as a simple workshop in a neighborhood loft.

The West Side had been the proving ground for the studio building. It was, after all, the enterprising, unconventional side of town. When a housing idea was transplanted to the East Side, it was inevitably reinterpreted and refined. Fifth Avenue was still solidly private houses and continued to dictate taste. Duplex cooperatives became "private apartment houses" on Park Avenue and "clubhouse apartments" on Gramercy Park. It seemed as if the studio apartment had served mainly to remind well-to-do New Yorkers of the virtues of joint ownership and up-and-down living. Joint ownership allowed the selection of neighbors and fostered a privacy, an exclusivity, a certain control over the quality of life. "With the loss of her old private dwellings, New York was losing the loveliness of her homelife," a critic explained with sadness. Apartment houses had to offer more than mere "skins," for they had to "fill the social void between the isolated and unlovely life in a promiscuously populated flat and the highest standard of living known to mankind—a house all to oneself and his own in a choice quarter with old neighbors."

11

SELLING APARTMENTS

WITH ALL the different forms on the street, it was difficult to find a prototype luxury apartment house in New York. Even with the passion for classicism, there were few repeating patterns. Some buildings were French, some Italian, some heavily baroque. Besides palazzi, with and without courtyards, and studio buildings, plain and fancy, there were buildings that looked like villas, manors, and Belle Epoque resorts. Each one seemed to have a personality. Each one stood out on the street like a landmark.

Eventually, when New York was built and its population was settled, individual apartment buildings would not catch the attention like odd or flamboyant people. The eye would have grown nonchalant. The mind would be preoccupied. Apartment houses would be simply housing or real estate. For the moment, however, apartment houses were too dramatic and too intrusive to ignore. They broke up the uniformity of the old streetscape, literally and figuratively. After Henry James toured the Upper West Side in 1904, he described it as a "colossal hair-comb turned upward and so deprived of half its teeth that the others, at their uneven intervals, count doubly as sharp spikes." He thought the new apartment buildings looked vulgar—"crudely-extemporized." They were "the interrogative feelers of a society trying to build itself into some coherent sense of itself," he said. By 1902, the number of apartment houses in construction far surpassed the number of private houses being built. Only 120 new houses had appeared that year, compared with 835 a decade earlier. And while the numbers had shrunk by more than 75 percent, the average cost of a house had risen more than 600 percent.

The only class of private dwellings in construction was intended for the very rich.

Even the very rich could not shut their eyes to apartment houses, however. More than ever before, they had to keep watch on the street, to prevent developers from advancing into prime residential territory. The very rich did not wish to live in apartment houses, nor near apartment houses, and they did not like their effect on the city. Restrictive clauses were in effect on upper Fifth Avenue and on certain blocks below, limiting the height or the use of new buildings. In 1900, William K. Vanderbilt had taken it upon himself to protect the avenue and the family enclave by purchasing the sites of first the Hotel Langham, on the northeast corner of 52nd Street, and then the Roman Catholic Orphanage, on the block across the street, in order to prevent projected development and legislate their use for single family private dwellings. Buying up the street worked to preserve it for a while longer. Farther uptown, near 66th Street, the Astors bought the house next door to their mansion to safeguard its status, and leased it to a successful banker. When an apartment house was proposed for the site of an old house between 64th and 65th streets, the neighbors again engaged in defensive real estate by immediately buying the property for an undisclosed sum of money. Even talk of an apartment house in the vicinity threw the old guard into a panic.

The general public was less wary. Women in particular had begun to express their curiosity about apartment life, and popular magazines, with new "mass markets," ran their first thoughts on the subject. Tucked in among articles on "Correct Speech," "Indoor Fun for Rainy Evenings," or "The Young Ethel Barrymore" (who was "at home" in an apartment on West 47th Street), these reports expressed vague wonder at the prospects of a "modernized existence." "A lady needs only the telephone to order whatever she wants," a writer in *Harper's Weekly* marveled. "Aladdin and his wonderful lamp are not more astonishing than the possibilities of the apartment house today. . . ." In an article in *Cosmopolitan,* the intellectual Charlotte Perkins Gilman was less dreamy. "We think . . . that our national integrity and health and virtue are bound up in the Home, and that if it is taken from us we are lost," she began, voicing everyone's concern. "We see our homes lifted clean off the ground—yardless, collarless, stairless, even kitchenless—we protest that this is not a home." To take an apartment, she countered, was to open up to the great outside world. "It is right, quite right, that man, woman, and child all should demand something more than 'home life,' " she concluded. "The domestic period, so to speak, is long out-grown."

Vision like Gilman's was rare. Most New Yorkers were too inexperienced to hold authoritative views on the apartment house. Ambivalence was a more common response. Even forward-thinking critics had some reservations about apartment life. The *Brickbuilder* thought that the apartment was a good "economic" idea, the *Real Estate Record* made a causal connection between apartment buildings and small families, apartment buildings and divorce. When the *American Architect and Building News* devoted a whole issue to a discussion of the apartment, old-fashioned moral disapproval surfaced like a final warning: "Bring together in a single tenement-house a score of families enjoying equal incomes, each of which has hitherto lived in comfort and contentment in an isolated dwelling, and then add a family whose heads enjoy a better income, or, being of a more reckless nature, are willing to take all sorts of risk for the sake of cutting a dash, shortly thereafter, peace and comfort will vanish from most of the other twenty families, each of whom, disliking to be outshone, will also try to make a splurge and will sacrifice its children's rights to a 'plush rocker,' a piano, or a too expensive dress. That means debt, sooner or later, and debt too often means drink."

New Yorkers were "betwixt and between," seeking anchorage and finding none. The malaise was deeper and broader than the dilemma in housing, but housing was a valuable and appropriate metaphor. A 1911 lecture by the philosopher George Santayana elaborated on the point. America, he said, was a country with two mentalities, "one a survival of the beliefs and standards of the fathers, the other an expression of the instincts, practice, and discoveries of the younger generations. . . . This division may be found symbolized in American architecture: a neat reproduction of the colonial mansion—with some modern comforts introduced surreptitiously—stands beside the skyscraper. The American Will inhabits the skyscraper; the American Intellect inhabits the colonial mansion. . . . The one is all aggressive enterprise; the other is all genteel tradition."

THE APARTMENT house already had a history. The question of the apartment was therefore no longer *if* but *how* and *why*. Architects and builders had to sell a reality rather than a concept. There was no sure formula for success, however, because there was no consensus on what made a good apartment. For all the models on the street, there were as many different opinions. The duplex apartment represented the incarnation of the private house to one family, but was considered inefficient and regressive by another. While certain prominent families were choosing suites in apartment hotels like the Plaza or the Ansonia as their "permanent town residences," others saw these establishments as only glamorized versions of nineteenth-century boardinghouses. Oh, the waste of thirty different cooks in thirty kitchens, with thirty gas ranges preparing a multitude of dishes, and then thirty bouts of dishwashing, one reformer cried, promoting the central catering kitchen and the public dining room. Alas, the degeneracy of a home without a working hearth, sounded another.

Professional journals debated the technical issues. "Experience has shown that of two apartments similarly situated and having equal floor areas, tenants generally prefer that which has the handsomest entrance-hall, parlor, and dining room, . . . [and makes] the most agreeable impression on entering the apartments," the *American Architect* summed up in 1907. "When planning, mentally, the erection of a house for people of [the premier] class, one must in the first place arrange for the application of all technical improvements which have been devised up to date," a professor of architecture from Copenhagen advised, mentioning central vacuum cleaning and shoe-polishing machines.

With all the questions in the air, architects and builders were working very hard to make the apartment house attractive. Every new building amounted to a model home for one class or another. Its every fitting had significance. A living room with French doors, a dressing room with mirrors and a closet for millinery, call buttons for servants, a drying yard for laundry—every detail had almost totemic value, for it annotated and illuminated a new way of living.

Even the millionaire was not exempt from the most ambitious schemes to rehouse the city. In 1909, the Alwyn Court Apartments, at 58th Street and Seventh Avenue, and the Verona, at 64th Street and Madison Avenue, had addressed themselves specifically to the Rich and the Very Rich. They called themselves "City Homes for Those with Country Houses." Both buildings were great architectural piles designed to impress even the affluent and worldly-wise. The whole facade of the Alwyn was encrusted with terra-cotta ornament—cameos, urns, fleurs-de-lis, escutcheons, and Francis I's favorite motif, salamanders breathing

The Alwyn Court, designed by Harde and
Short, was built in 1909. Note the sign on the
side advertising available apartments, and (inset)
the ornate terra-cotta decoration.

fire—while the Verona looked like Florence's Strozzi Palace. Their interiors were comparably grand, and their rents were as patrician as the silken hangings and neoclassical moldings. The Alwyn proclaimed its costs openly, brandishing the idea that "swelldom" had its privileges and its price.

For all their grandeur, the Alwyn and the Verona were not substantially different from many other luxury buildings. It was their location in the fashionable district that made them particularly appealing, the critics said, for it was becoming difficult to find a private house to lease in the blocks around Fifth Avenue. In fact, few buildings had the space and the grace of the Alwyn and the Verona. Harde and Short, the architects of the Alwyn, were so pleased with their floor plans that they cautioned the industry against plagiarism under the threat of lawsuit. But many buildings had similar if less sumptuous accommodations. Browsing through one of the old apartment registries—the *World's Loose Leaf Album of Apartment Houses* or Hesselgren's *Apartment Houses of the Metropolis*—one sees other twelve-story palazzi with thirteen-room units and bedrooms with dressing rooms. Such virtues in fact seemed to be the common denominator among early-twentieth-century luxury apartment buildings.

Real estate people were as ambitious as the building industry in their efforts to promote apartment houses. The language used in advertisements was itself revealing, for it was full of excited hyperbole. Every building seemed to be of the very highest type, of the very best construction, have the latest conveniences, be blessed with the most exclusive neighborhood. Quite ordinary buildings were described as monuments or ornaments, their addresses as breeze-swept or panoramic, even if they happened to be set back in the middle of the island. A disproportionate number of buildings now seemed to have a long view on something. The six-story Bryn Mawr at 121st Street and Amsterdam Avenue had a perspective on Long Island Sound, a brochure promised somewhat improbably; a ten-story building on Broadway, an outlook on both the North and East rivers. There was romance in all the overblown prose, however, and it quickened the pulse. Behind all the promotional phrases about the healthy "altitude" of an apartment, or how "voluptuous" the Hudson River looked from an upper story, one could detect a budding appreciation of elements unique to apartments.

The message was that apartment houses promised a glorious new place in the world. This was most evident in the names assigned to them in the first decade of the twentieth century. These names had airs and ambitions. Some of them spoke of proximity to important monuments, real or projected—the Grant, the Cathedral Studios, the Central Park View, or the Stadium View, a western vista to a sports arena in New Jersey that was never built. Others invoked ancestral seats, predominantly Anglo-Saxon, or popular heroes from literature. Merely reading a list of apartment names was an incantation. The Sunnycrest and the Ogontz, the Veronique and the Hyperion; the Sandringham, the Bertha, the Marimpol Court; a block comprised of the Fanta, the Huldana, the Helena, and the Sigfried; the Nottingham, the Mannados, the King, the Zenobia, the Clifden, and the Dreadnaught—the list went on and on—a registry of new personalities in town, funny urban poetry.

All the vivid nomenclature was also a ruse, of course, a pretension and a conceit. The rule of thumb seemed to be the more modest the building, the more esoteric the name and claim. A discreetly elegant building like Platt's 66th Street studios, or the new cooperatives on Park, carried only the numbers of its address. The custom of assigning descriptive labels to domestic architecture was borrowed from the rural English, who named their manor houses and country estates to expedite the delivery of mail through uncharted countryside. In New York, no one used the Melba, the Sophomore, the Altoona, the Greylock, or the Pamlico as a mailing address. Nor did names necessarily have anything to do with physical realities: Les Chateaux was not castlelike; the courts of the Georgian Court, the Columbia Court, and the Chatham Court were aggrandized air shafts, and no one knew that the "arms" of the Washington Arms or the Clarendon Arms, among dozens of arms buildings, referred to a family coat of arms. They were used the way Beaux-Arts style was—to project an image of importance to the outside. Names, however preposterous, were yet another ornament, and tantalizing in that.

THE LUXURY apartment was houselike. That was its boast, and that was also its defense, for it served to quiet residual fears of multiple dwellings. The Alwyn called itself "A House of Select Residences," using the phrase like a validation, the way the Home Club used to do. Less self-important buildings simply carved out the message spatially. Anyone could detect in the blueprint of the average nine- to twelve-room luxury apartment of the day the old skeleton of a house. For the parlor floor, or piano nobile, substitute the public quarters, foyer or reception room, parlor, drawing room, and dining room; for the third and fourth floors, the private quarters, two to four bedrooms, or chambers, and two or three baths; for the basement and attic, the service quarters, kitchen, butler's pantry, and servants' rooms. Connective tissue, rather than a staircase, is a long hall. The layout sometimes meanders down corridors and around corners inefficiently, but efficiency doesn't count for much in the days of servants. Space is literal. However rudimentary the union, all the essential elements of home are there, extravagantly dressed, lined up for inspection.

The luxury apartment did not feel exactly like a house, however. It had the traditional parts, including the foyers and fireplaces, but in the sum of those parts, it was an entity conspicuously different from a cozy brownstone on East 71st Street or a pretty Tudor in one of the new suburbs of Westchester. It was a question of more than the verticality or common stairs or even the doorman and gilded lobby. The apartment had a different character. Almost in spite of itself, it had developed different virtues. It was social rather than domestic, pretentious rather than practical. More than a sequence of spaces programmed for family-oriented activities like reading or sewing or games playing, it seemed to have been conceived for more sophisticated, more courtly behavior. The majestic entryways, carriage turnabouts, and gilded lobbies set the tone. Inside an apartment, the most prominent spaces were designed for entertaining on a grand scale, almost like Fifth Avenue mansions. Rooms en suite that swept through fifty or sixty feet of elegant contiguous space and oversized windows that looked down on busy city streets put one in the mind of theater people, literary soirees, the cosmopolitan gatherings that were described in novels and newspaper columns.

The interior decoration of an apartment, too, conjured up a world of wealth and refinement. It was lavish but specific—parquet floors, marble or carved fireplaces, painted beams, plaster friezes, elaborate lighting fixtures—and it was intended to render rooms "artistic." The Langham, at 135 Central Park West between 73rd and 74th Street, offered tenants period rooms: a parlor with a carved ceiling and chandelier in the Adam style; a library with a fireplace and ceiling fixture in Modern French Renaissance; a drawing room with beams, fireplace, and chandelier, all colonial; a dark paneled dining room that was Elizabethan—each treatment unique. The designers of the Chatsworth on 72nd Street chose to express a room's character through the med-

LEFT: A view of the Apthorp's kitchen, with its hotel-capacity ten-burner Vulcan gas range and refrigerator in golden oak, 1907. BELOW: An engraver's rendering of a drawing room in the Langham, and (bottom) its subterranean carriage drive, 1908.

ium of wood, giving the parlor a veneer of white mahogany and the
library one of regular mahogany; the dining room was done in mission
oak. The specifics of the Dorilton were as carefully chosen as a lady's
wardrobe: mahogany, oak, white enamel, and bird's-eye maple trim
throughout; high wooden wainscotting carried under a Dutch shelf
molding for the dining room; five feet of marble wainscotting for the
kitchen; French plate glass above French tiles in the bath; glass doors
between major rooms. In most buildings, there were extra little touches
here and there like signposts of taste—a sculpture niche, a Wedgwood
frieze, a pair of silver wall sconces, a Delft-tiled fireplace.

These displays of elegance could be taken two ways, first as an
expression of the current taste, a taste that had filtered down from a
plutocracy that transported whole ballrooms, real Renaissance mantelpieces, marbles and mahoganies directly from Europe to dress their
houses, a taste that went with the classical architecture in vogue and that
fine craftsmen, still flourishing in great numbers, could readily articulate.
Secondly, it could be seen as a somewhat unconscious compensation for
the deprivations that came with an apartment. Few houses outside of
Fifth Avenue mansions had been subjected to the comprehensive interior treatment lavished upon certain apartment houses—built into their
structure like a certification of good taste itself. By making decoration
architectural, builders were creating a sense of security and permanence
that disarmed the fear that apartments were temporary habitats like
tenements or hotels. Edith Wharton had explained the history of this
attitude in *The Decoration of Houses.* "In the Middle Ages," she said,
"when warfare and brigandage shaped the conditions of life and men
camped in their castles much as they did in their tents, it was natural that
decoration should be portable. . . . When life became more secure
. . . portable hangings were in consequence replaced by architectural
ornament; in other words, the architecture of the room became its
decoration."

Prospective tenants were likely to be wooed out of their worries
about losing their individuality in an apartment by these refinements,
obviously the result of extraordinary endeavors. But stylish people were
also beginning to take the decoration of their homes less literally. In
1905, a woman named Elsie de Wolfe launched a career that would alter
the fundamental concept of what was appropriate in interior design. For
her first commission, she had dressed the new Colony Club with lat-
ticework in the formal dining room and flowered chintz on the furni-

ture, windows, and even walls of the drawing rooms. The scheme was symbolic—a statement of liberation from stuffy Victorian standards—and it suited the historic women's club, which conservatives denounced as a menace to the American home. Miss de Wolfe, who was America's first woman decorator, had a theatrical flair. She drew her inspiration from venerable eighteenth-century French, English, and American sources, but she also thought artificiality could be creative. She had a talent for color, and she appreciated light. In the late 1890s, she had painted her own brick house on Irving Place bright yellow, with shutters of deep bright green.

Miss de Wolfe liked to be in the vanguard and she enjoyed the twentieth century. She was full of invention and energy, and she was attracted to the big novelties of her age. She had been a fashionable actress before she turned to interior decoration. She was one of the first women to fly, ascending with Wilbur Wright from Le Mans in 1908, and one of the first to dance the foxtrot. She was a prominent suffragette. She was also in favor of apartments. Her principles—simplicity, convenience, and suitability—were their attributes. She decorated many apartments, and she devoted a chapter to their furnishing in her famous book, *The House in Good Taste,* which was assembled from her articles in *Good Housekeeping* and *The Delineator* in 1913. The book was different from other books on decoration, for it treated its subject as a branch of fashion rather than household management or architectural history. Unlike the aristocratic *Decoration of Houses,* it offered comfortable answers to the questions of home design, and it counseled its readers in the gentle art of making do.

Miss de Wolfe was moving, ever so stylishly, toward functionalism. She believed in the need for a simplified existence. She may have favored French antiques, hand-printed wallpaper, and open fires on the hearth, but she also welcomed mechanical contrivances and contraptions that eliminated the drudgery of keeping house. She championed the apartment for the myriad modern improvements that promised to streamline, even glamorize, a woman's work.

In fact, the era of apartment development had run parallel to an era of mechanical improvements for housekeeping, and their futures were coincidentally and conveniently linked. The telephone and the incandescent light bulb had been invented in time for use in the Dakota and the Osborne; the electric washing machine, the steam dryer, and the electric stove in time for the Ansonia and the Apthorp. As technology and the twentieth century progressed, apartment houses incorporated more and more amenities into their design for living. Simply following the advertisements for apartment houses through the early 1900s is enlightening, for they mapped out a colorful technological journey to the future. Every apartment in the Ansonia came equipped with an electric or gas cooking range and "a chamber in which carafes and bottles may be immersed and frozen." Pneumatic tubes delivered messages to and from the manager's office. Filtered hot and cold water, in addition to ice water, was provided, and filtered air was drawn from the subbasement, where large electric blowers forced it over coils that were steam-heated in winter and cooled by freezing brine in summer. The St. Urban, too, promised "artificial refrigeration" in its eleven-room apartments, as well as full-length mirrors in each of the three bathrooms. The Alwyn Court had plate-glass shelves in its millinery closets, and the Verona had the new "needle" showers. From the pages of apartment-house guides details sang out like a barker at the county fair: glass-lined refrigerators, elevators with safety devices and elevators with new gears for easy stops and starts, a patent clothes dryer "for use in stormy weather," crystal-clear long-distance telephones, vacuum cleaning systems, vegetable shredders, and vegetable coolers.

All this practical paraphernalia made apartment life sound contrived, even comical. But there was a great romance to this equipment then, even among conventional people. Inventions like the telephone and the light bulb, not to mention the elevator and the automobile, were wonderful toys before they became the stuff of everyday life. They were fanciful before they were familiar. They amazed and energized and stimulated new visions. Think of Stephen Crane's description of the sensation of riding in an elevator, written in 1899: "The little cage sank swiftly; floor after floor seemed to be rising with marvelous speed; the whole building was winging straight into the sky," he said. Think of Edith Wharton flying happily about the New England countryside at the wheel of her new motorcar. It was autumn of the year 1901, and she was heady with speed and motion. At her side, the newly arrived Henry James was tentative about the automobile and was experiencing it "from within," which he said was "the only way." Already, everyone seemed to be "hanging on the future," James noted, putting everything on modernity, on a great chance of a time to come.

Lewis Mumford explored the metaphysical effects of the new inventions in *The Brown Decades,* a book written about the era in which the telephone, the electric light, the phonograph, the improved camera, the gas engine, and the typewriter all had their inception if not their full development. "They had something of the profound fascination that the Leyden jar had in an earlier century; they were wonders of nature before they became utilities," he explained. "They had a power to stir the mind out of all proportion to any of their later effect." As utilities, they also had the power to change patterns of living; for housewives, the power to liberate from the routines of old-fashioned housekeeping. All the new devices for heating, cooling, washing, cooking, and communicating altered the physical realities of fuel to carry; wet laundry to churn, wring, and hang; stairs to climb; goods to produce by hand. "Why should we give our time and strength and enthusiasm to drudgery, when our housework were better and more economically done by machinery and co-operation," Elsie de Wolfe asked, for all women. "Why should we stultify our minds with doing the same things thousands of times over, when we might help ourselves and our friends to happiness by intelligent occupations and amusements?"

The machinery that came with an apartment was, for the moment, unique. Vacuum cleaning systems, refrigeration plants, and even laundry machines had been developed for large-scale commercial operations, and until small household-sized motors became available in the next decade, they were not adaptable to private use. An apartment was thus a rare laboratory in which a tenant might try out strange paraphernalia reserved for a modern life. Its gadgets and gimmicks and services distinguished it from the European counterparts, which had served as the models of design and urban behavior and had once been the source of all inspiration. In Paris or Vienna, apartments were still simple houses coincidentally built one on top of the other, as Hubert and Pirsson had phrased it twenty years earlier. Landlords sometimes provided an elevator and heat along with the service of a concierge now, but they gave little or no thought to the technology of convenience. It was not necessary, for apartments had long ago become social habits. Critics had always kept a watchful eye on apartments abroad, comparing the states of design and inferring social truths from the differences. It seemed to be a measure of urbanity that the French or the Viennese accepted the cooperation and conviviality of apartments, while Americans added conveniences and comforts to make them attractive. In one respect, Americans were like children in their new homes, served and serviced, playing croquet on rooftops, playing house in the rooms below. But in another respect, they were expressing energy, enthusiasm, and enterprise peculiar to the national character. In New York, the Beaux-Arts style prevailed on the exterior of buildings, but other aspirations were stirring inside.

12

THE CONVERSION OF THE RICH: FIFTH AVENUE AND PARK AVENUE

THE WATERSHED year in apartment history on the Upper East Side was 1910, the year that an apartment house began to take shape at 81st Street and Fifth Avenue, in the midst of Millionaire's Row, nearly in line with the cascade of steps from the new entrance to the Metropolitan Museum of Art. Number 998 Fifth Avenue caught and held the public's attention, for its every aspect was announced and appraised. The first plans of the building were published. The awarding of contracts was aired. Details of construction down to the soffits and gutters were broadcast. After completion in 1912, the formal portraits appeared, then a long sequence of reviews and evaluations. There was a sense of amazement that a multiple dwelling could claim a place among the mansions that had been the sole proprietors of the Avenue. Fifth Avenue was hallowed ground. Restraining covenants regulated the use of certain lots and certain blocks. The Fifth Avenue Association had been formed to keep guard against the "chaos" of indiscriminate building that threatened other parts of the city.

The opulence on upper Fifth Avenue was little more than a decade old. Surprisingly, the street had remained largely vacant and unfashionable until the late 1890s, a spare dusty stretch of building sites filled in only with a few brownstone residences, and, at 85th Street, an example of French flats identified as "The Fifth Avenue" on the front. The early residents of the area had been middle-class merchants and professionals,

Germans, Jewish, Irish who had ventured uptown after the extension of the Second and Third Avenue els. When the Astors moved into their new Richard Morris Hunt home on 65th Street in 1896, there were few stylish houses above 59th Street. Fifteen years later, their house was but one colossus amid an assembly that stretched a mile and a half from Eldridge T. Gerry's residence at 61st Street to Andrew Carnegie's at 91st. Here and there, tucked in between Beaux-Arts showpieces, a few odd fellows lingered on from the old days before the aesthetic of the Columbian Exposition had taken hold, before the neighborhood had become so exclusive.

The high pitch of building activity remained constant as new houses continued to fill in the gaps in the grid. Some were unusually fine town houses built by seasoned speculators like Jeremy Lyons or the Farley brothers; others were distinguished mansions built by some of the city's most important architects for some of its most important citizenry—Henry Cook, Payne Whitney, Felix Warburg, James Duke, the Woolworth family. Away from Fifth, as the streetscape grew less uniform and more relaxed, an occasional apartment house or apartment hotel had cropped up amid a broad spectrum of private houses. Andrew Carnegie's settling on Carnegie Hill had encouraged a variety of building ventures on the periphery. His own block on 91st Street had quickly filled in with private residences, but around the corner on Madison, the early apartment house at 89th Street had been joined by a pretty seven-story Beaux-Arts dwelling at 90th. On side streets, a few elegant seven- or eight-story apartment houses looked like larger versions of town houses.

The aggregate streetscape, a comfortable pacing of houses, schools, stables, churches, and an occasional institutional office, was not seriously disrupted by a handful of apartments poking up like exotic weeds, for they did not intrude or alarm. Private houses still dominated the neighborhood, and the clang and clatter of carpenters and steam shovels came more from the reconstruction of single residences than the construction of multiple ones. Face-lifts were a widespread phenomenon, especially near the Avenue, where twenty- and thirty-year-old brownstone facades were being altered from the Italianate, neo-Grec, or Queen Anne to the newly popular Beaux-Arts and neo-Renaissance styles. The colors of the neighborhood lightened as limestone replaced brownstone; its posture straightened when front entrances were foreshortened, and steps and stoops disappeared. "The process of reconstruction is covering ground with the utmost rapidity," Herbert Croly reported as early as

1903, explaining that a few cases involved only the destruction of the stoop and the placing of the entrance on the ground floor, "but for the most part people demand that the old houses shall be either utterly destroyed or subjected to such a drastic process of purging that every trace of the brownstone is removed." Henry James had made similar observations that same year, declaring the destruction of these recent nineteenth-century residences comparable to sending young men to the guillotine.

Such were the demands of fashion. On 80th Street, the Boehms, who had built themselves a pretty Queen Anne at number 5 in 1892, had revised it in limestone eight years later. At number 11, Hiram Bloomingdale tore down a brownstone in 1909 and commissioned a five-story limestone affair from Schwartz and Gross. On the south side of 81st Street, a row of four-story brownstones changed character when half of them were remodeled with new facing, new window treatments, new moldings, brackets, and balconies. On the north side, brownstones that the Arnold and Constable families had built for investment back in 1878 (when they were the first structures on the block) were given City Beautiful facades. These buildings and this activity created the context in which 998 proceeded to take its place, touted and trumpeted as the very newest issue of twentieth-century architectural fashion.

The architects of 998 were McKim, Mead and White. They were a reassuring choice to design a big new building in sacrosanct territory. They were intimately linked with the aristocracy that held the ground, for they had built their houses, their clubs, and their memorials. They had in fact taught the aristocracy all they knew about the Renaissance style; they were responsible for the cultivation of their taste. They were doubtless the busiest, the most fashionable, the most eminent architects in America at that moment—the high priests of classicism and the standard bearers of the City Beautiful. Pennsylvania Station, eight years in the making, eight acres of New York real estate, had been dedicated in the summer of 1910. Outside of New York, they had been chosen to reorganize the Mall and the parks of the nation's capital and to restore the White House to its former splendor. The firm stood at the pinnacle of its success.

McKim, Mead and White was nonetheless not the same firm it had been only a few years earlier. It had aged as irrevocably as longtime patrons like the Goelets or the Louis Sherrys, who were now coming in to commission their mausoleums. The high-living and multitalented

Stanford White was gone, shot to death in the roof theater of the Madison Square Garden in 1906 by a jealous and deranged young man named Harry K. Thaw. The press capitalized on all the unseemly circumstances of the case, and the scandalmongering seemed to accelerate the decline of the proper and perfectionist McKim, who died three years later. The end of the original partnership had not impeded the continuum of the firm, for it was a "perpetual organization," conceived to be larger than its founders, and Mead remained a kind of senior advisor until 1919, but it tipped its taste in the direction of the future. There had been radical changes in scale in the city during the lifetime of the firm, and the twentieth century was becoming decidedly vertical. Of the great trio only Stanford White had been interested in this new dimension, and welcomed its challenge. McKim had seen but "bigness" in the new city; he thought its skyline was growing daily more hideous. It was the younger partners who designed 998, just as they sponsored the skyscraper Municipal Building a few years later.

Known as "The Millionaires' Apartments," 998 Fifth was a full-scale neo–Italian Renaissance palazzo of exquisite refinement. It was cast in the mode that McKim, Mead and White had introduced to New York with the Villard Houses. One saw flashes of the firm's old character in it—the subtlety of proportions, the carefully wrought ornament, the sheer artistic élan. Its most striking feature was a strong roof cornice with medallions and bold dentils that contained the building like a heavy lid. It had two band courses with balustrades that divided the building into three stages and stressed the horizontal rather than the vertical. These details by themselves were just exponents of the palazzo form, but their effect was to mold a twelve-story mass into a shape that could keep company with five-story Beaux-Arts neighbors.

Number 998 sat on land that had been owned by August Belmont II, who had been planning to build himself a private residence on the lot until he sold it to two enterprising young lawyers named Fleischmann and Lee. Like Belmont, whose hand was orchestrating many of the big changes in the city, they were savvy about the future. (Belmont, a large Upper West Side landowner, had built the subway, and Lee had bought property along its proposed route.) As the Century Holding Company, Fleischmann and Lee had given their architects carte blanche to build an apartment house fine enough to lure the wealthy out of their houses. The result was something *Architect and Builder* described as "a building containing seventeen private dwellings." In every detail, it validated its

Number 998 Fifth Avenue rising in
a neighborhood of houses, 1911.

Fifth Avenue status. Its facade was limestone and marble. Its entrance
was grand—"appropriate to a large city mansion, amplified slightly to
meet the requirements," a critic explicated. The courtyard was faced
with rusticated stone, rather than common brick, for the sheer pleasure
of the tenants. The lobby was lined in Italian marble; the halls were
floored in durable Tennessee marble (like Grand Central Terminal), and
the elevators were paneled in French walnut. Some doors throughout all
apartments were framed in marble, and each front door was fireproofed
with a sheet of galvanized steel that was painted to simulate fine wood.
Ceilings measured ten and a half feet high, except on the fifth floor,
where they were a foot higher.

The interior design of 998 provided three apartments for every two
stories, which added up to six duplexes, located in the advantaged
southern corner, and eleven seventeen-room simplexes. In either
schema an apartment was as large as a neighbor's town house and
finished with every appropriate refinement. In a typical simplex, the
reception room, which was copied from the Long Gallery in Hadden
Hall, England, and included a powder room, measured 14 by 36 feet and
was paneled in English oak; it led, on the right, to a living room with
a wood-burning fireplace, a hexagonal salon, a dining room with a
fireplace, a kitchen (with a refrigerator chilled from a central plant and
a large gas range with hood), an oversized pantry, a servants' hall, and

a bank of six maid's rooms. Leading left from the foyer, a private hall enclosed four large bedrooms with ample closets, a dressing room, fireplace, and three baths.

Even before its completion, 998 evoked a barrage of superlatives from the public. Its construction was "of the highest type known." It was "the most expensive and the most exclusive multi-family house in the city." It offered "a most intriguing scheme for modern living," a critic pronounced, recounting the delicately carved moldings, cut-crystal doorknobs, nine coats of paint, the three wall safes with combination locks, the adjustable steam heat, and the individual laundries, wine cellars, and cold storage rooms reserved for each family in the basement. The conclusion was, "998 can be called without exaggeration the most highly specialized apartment that is now in existence."

Despite the hyperbole, 998 was not an extravagant apartment house, such as extravagance had been defined on the West Side of New York. With all its costs and comforts, there was nothing overblown about 998 except, perhaps, its esteemed location. The difference between a building like the Dorilton and 998 was the difference between opulence and grace; 998 was formal, grand, imposing—the great iron-and-glass canopy was even a little intimidating—but it was also serene and understated. It had the air of an arrivé, rather than a nouveau arrivé. Andrew Carnegie had once described his mansion at 91st Street as the most

The marquise and entrance to 998: solemn statements of impeccable good taste.

modest, plainest, and most roomy house in New York. His statement was wry, of course; his house was the talk of New York, modest only in that it was not a château reproduction. But Carnegie, at his station in life, had no need to impress others. There was the same sense of confidence and propriety in his remark that there was in 998; it said that a newcomer, however well endowed, did not brag, or speak in a loud voice, or wear gaudy clothes. In fact, the building at 998 was no more modest than Carnegie's home, for it brought its occupants the luxury and space that a Fifth Avenue address had promised, but it was not showy and overbearing like its West Side antecedents. It was solid, refined, and roomy, and relatively well designed.

As the city had grown, several factors had sapped the ardor of resistance to apartments: the rising costs of maintaining private houses with servants; the trend toward country houses which, with their lawns, gardens, animals, and space, became alternate family centers; and the new civic enthusiasm, which drew people away from the confines of their houses into public places for entertainment. The fact remained, however, that high society was still conservative on the issue of sharing a roof. Then, much as A. T. Stewart had pioneered the geographic extension of nineteenth-century New York, Elihu Root came forth to set another example for his peers. Root, not many years earlier, had made upper Park Avenue respectable by building a house at 71st Street. Now, according to real estate stories, Senator Root walked through 998 with the young broker Douglas Elliman, who pointed out the thick walls and fine pantry and real fireplaces, and then offered him a cut rate to give up his brick town house on Park and sign a lease. Root agreed. A Vanderbilt, a Guggenheim, and a Morton followed, and the tide turned without further ado to apartment living.

It is always curious to see how a few men crop up to become storytellers for their generation, how their comings and goings substantiate the movements of a whole society so that, looking back from some future point, the small stuff of their lives has symbolic value. Elihu Root was one of these characters; Levi P. Morton was another; and the fact that Morton too moved from a new private house to a new apartment house at the moment he did was meaningful beyond the bare fact. Morton's migrations up Fifth Avenue had always seemed to forge the way for the city's elite—from 17th Street to 42nd Street in 1891 (where he provided the setting in which Edith Wharton could come out more discreetly than at Delmonico's); from there to 55th Street in 1894 (when he converted his "noisy" 42nd Street property to French flats; now from 55th Street to 81st Street, where he forsook the genteel tradition of houses altogether. Morton, the former governor of New York, vice president of the United States, and active fellow of the city's pre-eminent cultural institutions, was a public figure who wielded many kinds of power. It shocked New York profoundly when he moved into an apartment and proceeded to tear down his seventeen-year-old McKim, Mead and White house at 681 Fifth to erect a thirteen-story commercial structure on the site. Drastic decisions like Morton's set radical new precedents.

The conversion of the rich had begun. Whereas the tide did not turn overnight to apartment living, it turned, methodically, over the next decade, with each good apartment house that appeared—three on Park, two on Fifth, another on Park—building up a new landscape that after the First World War suddenly looked like the real Upper East Side. At such a point, most of society would be living in apartments with style and without hindsight. "It was thus," Archer reflected at the end of *The Age of Innocence,* "that New York managed its transitions, conspiring to ignore them till they were well over, and then, in all good faith, imagining that they had taken place in a preceding age. There was always a traitor in the citadel; and after he (or generally she) had surrendered the keys, what was the use of pretending that it was impregnable." The success of 998, coming as it did on the heels of the success of the Alwyn and Verona, suggested that the Four Hundred, who now numbered many thousands, were part of the potential market. It said that a fine building with a fine address might wean the wealthy from their preju-dices, and at the same time produce an attractive investment for builders, the costs offset by high rent, which was, anachronistically, a drawing point, a measure of superiority. If the floor-through on Park Avenue produced more income than the four units per floor on West 55th Street, there was no real economic reason not to cater to the wealthiest class in New York.

The requirements of society as deciphered by architects during the next few years were substantial. They began with the selection of a respectable site, followed with the faithful rendering of house space, and ended with attention to small pragmatics—the placement of clothes closets, for example. As for the finishing touches, it was no longer a question of piling on more ornament and service but of addressing a higher aesthetic. In 998 some of the celebrated founding tenants had dictated the specifics of that aesthetic directly to the architects. In the case of Murray Guggenheim, it was twenty-four rooms and nine baths, a backlighted stained-glass ceiling in the conservatory, and hardware custom-gold-plated by Tiffany's to prevent tarnish. In most cases, however, simplicity and dignity, introduced where there had been ostentatious "special architecture," disposed of major prejudices. In 998, and in three subsequent buildings on Park by a new architect named James Edwin Ruthven Carpenter, certain aesthetic choices—the restrained use of hardwoods in entrance halls, the simple treatment of white woodwork and cornices in other rooms, the plain mantels with working fireplaces—came as a great vindication to those who anticipated the offending gingerbread of most existing upper-class apartments. The East Side version of luxury was more subtle, and perhaps more evolved, than the West Side's—less frivolous, less self-conscious, less determined to *épater les bourgeois*.

J. E. R. Carpenter had a lot to do with revising apartment standards upward. Critics who were taking longer and longer looks at the apartment said that he was a real apartment architect, a new breed, and society endorsed his architectural interpretation of their needs. Carpenter, in contrast to McKim, Mead and White, for example, whose reputation was won with great public buildings, designed apartment houses almost exclusively, and in contrast to the often nameless architects some speculative builders commissioned to elaborate on "plan factory" methods, he liked innovation. In 1912, at 635 Park, on the site of an earlier apartment house built by Hardenbergh, he manipulated the thirteen-room four-bath floor-through into a state of grace by arranging the salon, drawing room, and dining room of the public quarters about a circular foyer, by insulating the extensive family quarters well, and by then placing service areas so that they were convenient to both. He paid particular attention to the proportions of rooms; he held hallways—those long somber processions of doorframes—to a minimum. The resulting efficiency and fluidity were a prodigious improvement of the form. The shape of the whole made sense in itself, not just as the sum of its parts.

Carpenter verified his ideas at 960 Park, which was also built in 1912, and four years later he elaborated upon them at 907 Fifth, a building many critics consider *the* typical Carpenter building. Number 907 established a new paradigm, for behind its quiet exterior were apartments of magnitudinous space. The largest of them measured twenty-eight rooms, which short-circuited once and for all the idea that apartments were standardized. (Servants' rooms in 907 numbered anywhere from four to twelve or more, counting the spare rooms tucked under the roof.) Retaining his basic tripartite layout and his careful aesthetics, Carpenter further articulated the domestic scheme of the upper classes by adding a small conservatory or glassed-in breakfast room between the dining room and the reception room, several dressing rooms, and either a private sitting room, a boudoir, or a study within the bedroom area. He added little that could be called extraneous or overbearing. Critics noted that he made no effort to supply "glazed rooms," which were sleeping porches or sun parlors, for the simple reason that "to the wealthy New Yorker, his townhouse or apartment is merely his winter residence and so used."

Number 907 was a revolutionary building in a more significant respect. It was the first apartment house to replace a mansion on Fifth Avenue. Dramatically, it raised a new flag of dominion on the south side of 72nd Street, on the choicest corner of an area that was graced with some of New York's most famous private houses—Tiffany's fortress, the Gertrude Rhinelander Waldo extravaganza at Madison, the Pulitzer mansion at 11 East 73rd Street, and Henry Clay Frick's palatial mansion and art gallery on Fifth between 70th and 71st streets. The lots occupied by 907 had once been a parcel of James Lenox's farmland. In recent years, they had held a baseball field and a fine 1890s house that belonged to the Burden family, who had been trying unsuccessfully to rent it. At the first rumor that the Burden house might be replaced by a twelve-story apartment house, local homeowners had objected to the project and fought it in court, but the block was not restricted, and even the daunting presence of the Frick home had not seemed to deter ambitions. As a lawyer for the real estate speculators had explained, "If the Strozzi Palace, or any of the other seignorial houses of Florence or Rome . . . were to be exactly repeated with the most beautiful part of Central Park as a background, the only possible modern adaptation of them would be to divide them—as they are today divided—into splendid apartments." When 907 appeared, it signaled that revisionist thinking was in play in uptown real estate. As confirmation, a fourteen-story palazzo arrived the next year at 925 Fifth Avenue, and it, too, took the place of a late-nineteenth-century homestead. Within the next decade, Carpenter designed fifteen more Renaissance apartment houses for the Avenue, most of them on the sites of once glorious private houses.

Once it had been the tall and ungainly new apartment house that was a self-conscious presence in the urban landscape. Now it was the old brownstone manse that was beginning to look awkward and isolated, like a survivor—brave, vulnerable, and no longer indomitable. All over town, where there were standoffs between the old and the new, between houses and commercial structures or between houses and apartments, the new seemed to triumph. After a long battle, the old Langham Hotel property at the northeast corner of Fifth and 52nd Street had been sold to commercial interests, which meant that even the Vanderbilts, who controlled the neighborhood, had not been able to stave off the advance of commerce. The Morton house at 53rd Street and the Webb house at 54th had ceded their ground on Fifth to businesses. By 1916, ironhanded Vanderbilt, desperate and resigned, had lifted his own restriction on a property at 52nd Street and agreed to lease the house to the Cartier jewelry firm.

The fashionable East Side was a hive of building activity. Between 40th Street and 96th Street, from Fifth Avenue to Park Avenue, fifty-nine new buildings had been begun in 1915; fifty-three buildings had been completed, and fifty-four buildings were still in progress. This made the area the busiest construction site in the city. The volume of new apartment houses was "phenomenal," even for New York City, which was to say "entirely impossible" elsewhere. Everywhere, it seemed, tall new facades were obscured by giant billboards that read "eight rooms with three baths," "ten rooms with four baths." A sign at 903 Park at 79th Street announced "ABSOLUTELY FIREPROOF, INCLUDING WOODWORK AND FLOORS" in big block letters and, in lowercase, "seventeen rooms, five baths, one apartment on a floor." Popular magazines were saying that the apartment was the most striking feature of modern American life. Photographs showed smart street scenes with automobiles, a storefront labeled "Ocean Travel," strollers in straw hats nodding to doormen in long coats. There was mobility and adventure in the air. New York was beginning to savor its distinction as the birthplace of the apartment house, the scene of its proliferation and success. Even on Fifth Avenue, the apartment was not deemed an invader, but merely an indication of the spirit and demand of the times in which one lived.

ABOVE 59TH Street, the old Park Avenue was growing taller as apartment houses joined fine private houses in areas that were being called "the Mayfair of New York" or "the New Murray Hill." Below 59th Street,

Park Avenue, looking south from 56th Street, 1905. The Steinway factory, the large building on the east side beyond the pedestrian bridge, will give its site to the area's first apartment house, the Montana.

a new Park Avenue was taking shape on what until 1903 had been the New York Central Railroad yards—a sooty, steamy, industrial district containing a piano factory, slaughterhouses, and breweries. Early in the century, after smoke and steam caused a tragic accident in the tunnel under Park Avenue, William J. Wilgus, the railroad's chief engineer, had conceived the idea of electrifying the tracks and sinking them below ground level. This introduced the notion of "air rights," which led to

a scheme to develop the space above the yards to offset the cost of conversion. Terminal City, as the whole area surrounding the new Grand Central Terminal was to be called, was planned to embrace modern apartment houses and hotels, clubs and restaurants, department stores, exhibition halls, and even a new Metropolitan Opera House—all the latest in urban culture. Terminal City as a name did not catch on, but Park Avenue, the area's grand boulevard, was carved up into big

block-sized lots, and gardenesque islands were sketched out in paint along the middle of the wide roadway. The Biltmore Hotel at 43rd, the Ritz-Carlton at 47th, and small downtown specialty stores called Brooks Brothers and Abercrombie and Fitch appeared in the wings on Madison and opened for business.

Grand Central had always affected its surroundings dramatically. Its early versions, in the nineteenth century, had brought shops, hotels,

Park Avenue, looking north from 46th Street, 1913. The railroad tracks have been covered over, and building lots prepared for development. The Montana has risen to the north of the F & S Schaefer Brewery, between 50th and 52nd streets on the east, which by 1919 will be replaced by St. Bartholomew's Church and the Hotel Ambassador.

eateries, and saloons to an underdeveloped 42nd Street and transformed a northerly outpost of the city into a busy crossroads. By February 1, 1913, opening day of the twentieth-century terminal, plans had been filed on half of the new lots on Park Avenue, and there was talk of "the greatest civic development in the country." The first apartment house, called the Montana, arrived at 375 Park later that year and filled the site of the old Steinway factory, on the east side of the avenue between 52nd and 53rd streets, with twelve stories of elegant classical limestone-and-brick mass. Within a few years, classical buildings were rising on the west side of the avenue too, all but one designed by Warren and Wetmore, the architects, with Reed and Stem, of Grand Central Terminal. By 1917, when the din of building abruptly stopped and America entered World War I, almost a dozen new apartment houses had given the avenue new height and bulk. The neighborhood was far from finished, however, and it still had an idle, expectant look. Above 50th Street, parcels of the old Park Avenue lingered on—a stand of early row houses, their faces long since darkened by flying cinders and smoke; a grocery store; the four-story bow-fronted South Kensington Apartments, built in the 1880s. Below 50th Street, no building had yet risen on the blockbuster lots that had been preassembled for structures of monumental size. They sat empty and challenging, bulldozed flat, squares of air carved out above the tracks.

When Warren and Wetmore's Marguery appeared at 270 Park in 1921, it was everyone's vision of the colossus that belonged on one of those squares. It was elegant and oversized, and it settled before the terminal like a conquering hero, filling the block between 47th and 48th streets all the way to Madison Avenue and swallowing up Vanderbilt Avenue in its volume. Seventeen stories of Beaux-Arts majesty, it aggrandized the scale and elevated the tone of the avenue dramatically. It had a vast arcaded courtyard with gardens, which spanned Vanderbilt Avenue with twin arches. Looking inside, a passerby saw sculpted shrubs, braid-festooned doormen, and tables decked out for alfresco dining. It was a world of privilege, like a European duchy.

Warren and Wetmore had already been instrumental in articulating the shape of a would-be Terminal City. In addition to their earlier apartment houses, they had designed commercial structures and an array of grand hotels in the area, including the Ritz-Carlton, whose smart style had immediately given rise to the expressions "ritzy" and "the ritz." Whitney Warren, who had studied architecture at the Ecole des Beaux-Arts in Paris, and Charles Wetmore, who had studied law at Harvard, had caught the public eye in 1899 with their first commission together, the New York Yacht Club, a fanciful and exuberant Beaux-Arts design that looked like a Roman warship at rest on West 44th Street. Warren was a cousin of Cornelius Vanderbilt's, and some people said that the decision to put Warren and Wetmore in charge of the actual design of the terminal was nepotistical, since Reed and Stem, who were subsequently relegated to its engineering, had in fact won the original competition. (Among their rivals was McKim, Mead and White, who submitted a proposal for a fourteen-story building with a sixty-story tower that was to be crowned by a jet of steam driven three hundred feet in the air and illuminated red at night.) Vanderbilt's New York Central owned much of the land in the neighborhood—forty-eight acres en-compassing some thirty city blocks—and Warren and Wetmore's com-missions were many. They designed the Biltmore Hotel, which had its own arrival room in the basement; the Commodore Hotel at 42nd Street; the Ambassador Hotel between 51st and 52nd; in the end, they would also design more than a dozen apartment houses on Park below 59th Street. Warren and Wetmore had established their fine facility with apartment houses in 1912 with 903 Park, at 79th Street, a building some critics thought was at least as "truly upper class" as 998 Fifth. The architects were comfortable with the restrained classicism in vogue; they were lavish in their treatment of interior space; and by the 1920s, it was clear that they had developed a highly successful formula for large residential palaces.

The Marguery set a grandiose pattern for postwar development. Other new buildings followed in quick succession: large limestone masses lit by courtyards and graced at rooflines with garlands or rosettes or Grecian urns. On the west, numbers 280, 290, and 300 Park created a solid front of Warren and Wetmore right up to McKim, Mead and White's new Racquet Club. Across the street, the Ambassador and the Park Lane hotels, and McKim, Mead and White's 277 Park, called the Heckscher Apartments, were cast in the same image. They were all "modern multiple mansions," and their solemn exteriors belied the luxury of the appointments within. Even critics could not hide their happy incredulity at the space and services now readily available to the well-to-do: seventeen or eighteen rooms, separate entrances and indi-vidual elevators, wood-burning fireplaces, jewelry safes and wine cellars, professional decoration.

The Marguery had simplexes and duplexes with many baths, many closets, and the promise of light and air, for all its rooms except the galleries and foyers were lined up on outside walls; it also had a fine restaurant, café, and lounge managed by its backyard neighbor, the Ritz. In size and cost, this building exceeded anything ever attempted of its kind. Over a total floor area of more than 20 acres, its 108 apartments had 1,536 living rooms, 1,476 closets, 100 kitchens, 100 sculleries, and

2,000 windows fronting on the street, a reporter announced, this great mass having been achieved by way of 10,000 tons of structural steel, 500,000 pounds of architectural iron, 7,500,000 bricks, 600,000 feet of terra-cotta, 65 carloads of limestone, 50,000 barrels of cement, and 824 miles of flooring.

While the Marguery was "the largest of apartment houses," 300 Park Avenue was "the very apotheosis of the American apartment house." "It looks plain," a reviewer explained, speaking of "the exquisite simplicity of the repressed Italian Renaissance," and "it makes its greatest appeal inside," referring to a new two-story Louis Sherry restaurant that offered tenants a splendid restaurant, meal service, and "individual servants of every type and to meet every need." This was "Housekeeping De-luxe"—"Comfort and Magnificence in Living Equalled Nowhere Else in this Wide Wide World"—to which a Dupont, a Taylor, a Wilson, and a Rockefeller subscribed before the building was completed.

The popular response to the new Park Avenue was as zealous as the critical word. Will Irwin, who wrote a guidebook to New York in 1937, described the early enthusiasm for the new avenue and remembered how, returning from war in 1919, he first heard the name of Park as a synonym for wealth, and beheld "this grandiose conception" in the process of building. "Only the newly-rich, I thought to myself; the seasoned families will never live on apartment-house terms, like larvae in a honey-comb. And yet—every month some member of 'the exclusive set' was giving up his mansion on Fifth Avenue or the near East 70's and 'buying a duplex' in a Park Avenue apartment." On closer inspection, the "strange luxury" of these apartment houses impressed him too. "Faintly forbidding though these habitations be on the outside, within they have individuality and warmth. Sometimes all the owners of a cooperative apartment belong to the same social layer. . . . Each apartment has its separate and private elevator; often, its separate and private entrance. If the lobby be cooperative, the proper retinue of liveried servants open the door, bow you in. Always in the background of this lobby stands a quiet man in quiet clothes; he is the detective, guarding the house against jewel-robbers. From the elevator doors of the richer and more expansive apartment you step into a hall like that of any grand house; you must look out of the window to realize you are dwelling with the eagle."

As early as 1921, Park Avenue was hailed as the new Fifth Avenue. Magazines called it a Cinderella story, this magical transformation of a bleak industrial town into an affluent residential oasis, for despite its years a-building, it seemed to be a sudden phenomenon. Other apartment buildings, the Ritz Tower and the new Waldorf-Astoria Hotel, were still to come, and yet even with conspicuous gaps in its grid, the avenue had an imperial look that came from its classical order, a unity that came from its purpose. Its buildings looked like they belonged there; they had a rightness of scale and place. In 1918, when the city celebrated the end of World War I, and again in 1923, when it commemorated its first twenty-five years as Greater New York, Park Avenue, even as incomplete as it still was, provided the appropriate setting for displays of national pride and civic ardor.

Park Avenue achieved its full integrity in 1929, when Warren and Wetmore's New York Central Building took its place bridging the avenue at 46th Street like the marshal at a great parade. It was a distinctive silhouette, twenty-two stories high, slender, gold-domed, taller and more romantic than its stolid neighbors, and with this one important flourish, the whole avenue made sense. The apartment buildings, which were tied to one another by style and by roughly even cornice lines, had a focus now. They looked like a court, and they seemed to march right down from 59th Street to pay respects to the building that stood for the prosperous railroad. The treatment of a whole area, residential buildings interacting with a great symbolic monument at their center, was not unlike Napoleon's plan for Paris. It was comprehensive urban design, and it was the most stunning aftereffect of the Columbian Exposition to date.

Years later, when the erstwhile Terminal City was well established as Midtown Manhattan, a new urban center, critics would speculate on just how the exclusive residential enclave of Park Avenue happened to take root and flourish in the commercial heart of the city. More than anything else, it seemed to be the physical fact of Grand Central Terminal that was responsible for creating this elegant backwater, as if the monument itself had deterred the northern flow of commerce just as it deflected the flow of traffic around its Beaux-Arts girth. The 1920s grew more frantic with speculation, and 42nd Street became crowded with skyscrapers (forty-six of them were built on the street between 1921 and 1931), but for a while Park Avenue was insulated against the ruder aspects of city life. Its park malls, landscaped with undulating walkways to suggest a leisurely stroll, looked like trim little European gardens, and photographs of the time showed nursemaids with prams resting there in

the sun as a lazy stream of motorcars meandered by on the street. Heavy commercial traffic was banned, but the iceman and the milkman continued their rounds. Water troughs were placed along the way for the horses, which wore little straw hats in the warm weather. A squadron of men in white uniforms kept the pavement clean. And special bronze signals that looked like mechanical gendarmes were designed to regulate traffic. They disappeared in 1927, when the avenue was widened and the islands narrowed and replanted to provide room for the increasing number of cars in circulation. The sounds of traffic, however, were barely audible inside the great residential palaces.

Park Avenue quickly became the most prestigious residential address in the city. It was the "new quarter of the very rich, new goal for the supremely ambitious American business man, new bonanza, Golconda, El Dorado," as Irwin's guidebook explained it—the most amazing development in the city in fifteen years, the critics said. Park was a showcase, and it was startling to realize that brownstones and mansions had no place in its scheme, that they would not have suited the scale or the style of the street. One had only to imagine how insignificant and eccentric even the Villard Houses might have looked on this wide and panoramic avenue to understand how irrelevant the fine old forms had become. Park Avenue offered a new and revised version of well-to-do urbanity; it spelled out how the modern aristocracy intended to live now: lavishly, privately, but also cooperatively and efficiently, well served and well serviced, "near 'business' (and yet not actually, in their homes, on a business street)." From a Park Avenue address, it was walking distance to the new "Little Wall Street" of Madison Avenue, to the theaters and clubs of the West 40s, to Grand Central and points north and west. The city encircled, but it did not encroach.

Irwin called Park Avenue "the melting pot of the rich" and studied it for the insights it offered on postwar society, which he suggested was "vaporizing" in the heated activity of the time, becoming less rigid, more diffused, and more diverse. He saw the singular success of the avenue as a function of the economic and the cultural trends of his times

OPPOSITE TOP: Park Avenue, looking south from 56th Street, 1927. Twenty-odd years after the electrification of the railroad, only a handful of houses remain from the nineteenth century. OPPOSITE BOTTOM: Park Avenue, looking south from 54th Street, 1928. A year and a half later, the wide park malls have been narrowed, and the New York Central Building nears completion.

too. The year 1913, when Grand Central opened, had also brought the first federal income tax, which affected the rich almost exclusively, and accelerated new thinking about household management. Separate houses and large staffs of hand servants suddenly seemed wasteful, indulgent, and hopelessly old-fashioned when they were measured against the smart new pragmatism of luxury apartments. By 1916, the *Real Estate Record* had gathered data to show that dramatic increases in the number of apartments built for and occupied by the well-to-do came in the first years of taxation. Given the magnificence of apartments like those on Park, however, it could not really be declared a conversion from houses, but rather what the *American Architect and Building News* called "a consolidation for the sake of convenience." Society seemed to be restless, jumping from New York to Paris or the Riviera or Palm Beach, establishing a country house as the family seat, expressing, according to Irwin, "the unquiet spirit of our times—or is it the enterprising joy of our times?" William Dean Howells, nearing eighty, had just written a short story called "The Daughter of the Storage," which told of the marriage of a young couple in a storage warehouse where their first meeting and courtship had taken place. Their respective aristocratic families were perpetually either "going into storage" or coming out, and they served to allegorize the times well.

Nineteen thirteen was also the year of the tumultuous Armory Show, which introduced New York to postimpressionism and cubism and futurism and, as historians would claim, changed its taste forever. It was a mass event—some 4,000 people a day passed through the Sixty-ninth Regiment Armory at Lexington Avenue and 26th Street to view the 1,600 pieces of sculpture, paintings, drawings, and prints that had been assembled there—and public response reverberated through the press for months. Dancing nudes by Matisse, dislocated bodies by Picasso, abstractions by Kandinsky, Léger, and Braque, works like Marcel Duchamp's *Nude Descending a Staircase* bewildered, shocked, and scandalized New York sensibilities and destroyed once and for all any sense of complacency about the times. From that point forward, it was not possible to disregard the evidence that "The New Spirit," as the exhibition was called, was in fact bubbling up all over the city. It was in the Colony Club, at which society women had installed a bar where they could smoke and drink; it was downtown at 291 Fifth, where the photographer Alfred Stieglitz promoted modern aesthetics; or at number 25, in Mabel Dodge's living room, where Emma Goldman, John Reed, and Sigmund Freud might be found, where "Evenings" were dedicated to experiment and change. In Greenwich Village, a stone's throw from patrician Washington Square, young intellectuals discussed everything from Isadora Duncan and Harlem jazz to syndicalism, socialism, and feminism, searching for a richer sense of culture than their parents had to offer. Greenwich Village was a kind of sanctuary for rebels, but it was also "not merely a neighborhood. It was also a state of mind." New theatrical groups like the Provincetown Players and new magazines like *The New Republic, The New Masses, The Dial, Seven Arts,* and an avalanche of important and ephemeral little avant-garde magazines expressed that state of mind. Skyscrapers, railroad towers, and apartment houses did too.

Skyscrapers made the boldest statements, for they showed change to be explicit and visible. Perhaps the most dramatic event of the year 1913 was the completion of Cass Gilbert's Woolworth Building on lower Broadway, which was heralded to the world when President Wilson pressed a button in the White House and illuminated its eighty thousand brilliant lights. It was an elegant, graduated fifty-story tower, crowned with light Gothic lace, and it eclipsed Ernest Flagg's forty-seven-story mansarded Singer Tower as the greatest new achievement in architecture. Both buildings stood for more than their dimensions or even their architecture, however, and they exerted a powerful influence on the city's psyche. Both buildings had taken historic styles, stretched them into slender towers, and imposed them on larger bases. The buildings, as they rose from the street wall, became lighter, more fanciful, as if liberated by sheer air space. They seemed to grow up, and their crowns seemed barely able to contain their energy. The effect was both lyrical and exhilarating. It set imaginations soaring. Despite its capitalistic underpinings, the Woolworth Building evoked praises that sounded like poetry or religious fervor. The Singer Tower was the central figure in "King's Dream of New York," a drawing of the imagined future that appeared in the 1908 publication *King's Views of New York.* Around it, lower Broadway has been transformed into a stepped range of tall buildings, linked here and there by aerial walkways and finished off with small pantheons, cupolas, statuary, or flags. Dirigibles are casting off from lofty mooring masts (according to their labels, bound for Japan, Europe, the Panama Canal, the North Pole); several unidentifiable flying structures veer about like strange mechanical birds. The upper atmosphere teems with activity; it is not mere space but a realm of great potential drama, and it appears to be almost within arm's reach, for the hypothetical viewer is perched aloft, thirty or forty stories above the street.

"King's Dream" must have seemed a little fantastic to prewar New Yorkers and yet, with the possibilities opened up by technological advances, not at all improbable. With electricity, the telephone, the automobile, the first moving pictures, with old landmarks coming down to make room for taller and taller structures, the city of the future seemed close at hand. The metropolis seemed to be growing at random, in unpremeditated shapes, as if propelled by an independent, irresistible force. There was a pungent sense of what Max Eastman of *The New Masses* called "the just-before-dawn of a new day." The Singer building had remained the tallest structure in the world for only eighteen months. The rocketlike skyscraper cathedrals that were the shape of the future as it existed in people's heads were proliferating on the street. With reality only steps behind the vision, it is no wonder that New York got caught up in the future, became obsessed with height, and by the twenties was, in Ada Louise Huxtable's phrase, "hitched to the machine and the stars."

The Singer Tower and the Woolworth Building made an impact on the Housing Commission too, for in 1916 New York City adopted a zoning resolution requiring that, above the street wall, each new building be set back one foot for each four feet of added height. This was an early attempt to control the bulk of buildings in order to maintain good light and fresh air for adjacent properties and streets—in effect, to prevent the city from becoming a cloister of shadowy canyons and oppressive towers. But this "setback law" also testified to an official and fundamental change in man's way of looking at the city. It said that New York was vertical, and that builders had to think of this new dimension in new ways. It said that New York had changed, and that circumstances seemed to compel further change. It effectively legislated into being buildings that looked like utopian schemes or abstract paintings.

Almost a decade would pass before an apartment building took the shape of the future. The ornamental classical lay heavily on buildings that were held together by skeletons of utilitarian steel. This style continued to fulfill the desire for an image, and the need for tradition. But the very existence of apartment houses had been prompting progressive thinking and encouraging revolutionary behavior. While old-fashioned moralists were appalled at the apparent obsolescence of the old-fashioned home, women, the tenders of those homes, were showing signs of independence. They were shortening their skirts, smoking cigarettes in public, learning the foxtrot and the tango, and talking about careers, divorce, family planning; in the new phase they were "leading their own lives." In 1912, Mrs. August Belmont, who was the former Alva Vanderbilt, led a suffragette parade down Fifth Avenue. The same year, *Harper's Bazaar* ran an article linking the apartment with the emancipation of women. It said that the flat was "the city girl's best friend"; that it answered the new social needs: "that women's brains, strength, and ability be used efficiently . . . in every business, trade, and profession from law to shoe-making"; that "they be freed from as much squaw-like drudgery as possible." To those who pitied the apartment dweller, it argued that a home was not an end in itself but an instrument of social progress. "Hardly four generations ago, the Patriarchal Age died, and each budding family began wanting its own home instead of a place beneath the ancestral roof; yet today, when the race is swarming again, and many families are getting back under one roof, dear ladies who are a little less then one hundred years old cry out that the flat is destroying the home!! . . . Why should the domestic virtues flourish in a cubic container standing on end, and pine and die when the same space is turned on its side?" Elsie de Wolfe, soon to be the aristocratic Lady Mendl, had her say too: "This is the age of the apartment. . . . Modern women demand simplified living, and the apartment reduces the mechanical business of living to its lowest terms. A decade ago, the apartment was considered a sorry makeshift in America. . . . We Americans have been accustomed to so much space about us that it seemed a curtailment of family dignity to give up our gardens, our piazzas and halls, our cellars and attics, our front and rear entrances. Now we are wiser."

Not that the voices of enlightenment were either constant or pure. Wisdom notwithstanding, Elsie de Wolfe lived in a remodeled brownstone on fashionable new Sutton Place and in an eighteenth-century house in Versailles. Preceding the bright exhortation in *Harper's Bazaar* was a story titled "How Love Passed Me By: Confessions of a Business Woman" and an illustrated article on "The Perfect Nose." Fashions for the month featured a summer hat dripping morning glories and long, tight-waisted taffeta dresses with high collars. As a bemused male explained in his own paean to the city apartment, "For family life there is still, I know, a lingering feeling against a flat because it is flat, or on the ground that it is not on the ground."

Nonetheless, tradition was visibly cracking. The raising of hemlines and consciousness and rooflines all showed people beginning to think of themselves as "modern." "Modern" was energetic, visionary, and inevitably anticonventional. It was more than a "trend." The old symbols of gentility—the private house, the proper dress—which were once as reliable a gauge of social and moral fiber as a certain seat at the opera house, were as shaky as the social pyramid. New York was too big, and its population too diverse, to be codified. Traditionalists asked how you could tell a respectable woman from one who wasn't. By what standard of respectability did one judge a Fifth Avenue apartment house if it numbered among its tenants both society matrons and underworld kingpins? An apartment house, like the city, contained multitudes. Its society was a hodgepodge. "Con men, clergymen; heiresses, actresses," a critic enumerated, "fast people, slow people; good people, bad people; people you know, people you'd like to know, and people you don't want to know—but all of them interesting to look at, to think about." At the end of *The Age of Innocence,* the now elderly protagonist reflects, "People nowadays were too busy—too busy with reforms, and 'movements,' with fads and fetishes and frivolities—to bother much about their neighbors. . . . [The new generation], they feel equal to things—they know their way about."

The Age of Innocence, which was written in 1920, had less rancor than Mrs. Wharton's other novels, for its plot was set safely back in time, rendering her pen more benign. It was her valedictory, Edmund Wilson has suggested, and it had a largesse that could even have been mistaken for nostalgia. "The compact world of my youth has receded into a past from which it can only be dug up in bits by the assiduous relic-hunter," the author explained, "and its smallest fragments begin to be worth collecting and putting together before the last of those who knew the live structure are swept away with it."

The Manhattan Skyline

1920–1930

Hugh Ferriss's vision of twentieth-century New York,
Skyscraper Hangar in a Metropolis, 1929.

13

APARTMENT–HOUSE ARCHITECTS

HE 1920s formed a self-contained age in New York. F. Scott Fitzgerald named it the Jazz Age, because from the beginning it had its own feverish rhythms. It opened, a little prematurely, when the troops came home from World War I and filled the streets of the great metropolis with energy and joy. "New York had all the iridescence of the beginning of the world," Fitzgerald remembered from his own arrival in 1919. "We felt like small children in a bright unexplored barn." "New York in 1919! The city never wore a brighter look than it did that year," Lewis Mumford said about the days when he, too, was first finding his voice and authority. Five years older than the century, he had set up housekeeping on the top floor of a rear apartment on West 4th Street in Greenwich Village, and begun to write about buildings. He was interested in the exploration and documentation of cities, and he valued architecture and engineering as fresh aesthetic expressions of modern culture. "Mind takes form in the city" was his credo.

The mind of the 1920s could be seen very clearly in its buildings. The drama of New York was now urban, and it was set in urban places—skyscrapers, apartment buildings, hotels, theaters, movie palaces. Skyscrapers represented the triumph of many things—technology, ambition, fantasy, an American style of architecture. Luxury apartment buildings, taller and more elegant than ever, represented domestic and moral reform, the shrugging off of Puritanism, the loosening of tradition, the conversion to convenience and efficiency. Watching the number of these skyscrapers increase, it was possible to witness the consolidation of the community. As the big formal buildings settled and grew together into new street walls, they signaled security and stability. Standing amidst skyscrapers, the shapes that had looked ungainly and self-conscious were conservative and tasteful now. Rooflines were beginning to stir with expression—not merely with garnishes of ornament, but with loggias and penthouses. It was not until mid-decade, however, when apartment hotels first broke the classical mold and headed skyward, that the shape of residential architecture caught the excitement in the streets. And it was not until 1929, when the party was effectively over, that an apartment house appeared to match the times in style, structure, and spirit, to crystallize the terms of its culture.

Until it ended abruptly with the stock market crash of 1929, the decade of the twenties saw the biggest building boom in New York history. According to Valentine's guide for 1920, the population of the city was almost 6 million people, or 96,000 per square mile—six times the density of any other American city and five times that of Paris or London—and 350 new citizens arrived each day. New buildings appeared every fifty-one minutes. Old buildings came down at an equally dramatic rate. The city could be described as steel skeletons against the sky and piles of rubble under foot. Luxury apartment buildings rose up, and French flats, family brownstones, and historic mansions were carted off in pieces to the dump.

Henry James would have mourned this spectacle. Long before, he had concluded that New Yorkers had little respect for the past. The metropolitan spirit was grounded in the present. The promise of the city lay with its future. Visionaries like the French architect Le Corbusier expressed impatience with New York. After he visited the city in 1920, Le Corbusier wrote, "Between the present skyscrapers there are masses of large and small buildings. Most of them are small. What are these small buildings doing in dramatic Manhattan? I haven't the faintest idea. It is incomprehensible. It is a fact, nothing more, as a debris after the earthquake or bombardment is a fact." He visited New York again in 1926 and 1928. "New York is not a finished city," he continued. "It gushes up. On my next trip it will be different."

Le Corbusier was a revolutionary theorist who designed modern villas that were "machines to live in" and ideal cities that were built around huge apartment buildings set vast distances apart in great parks. He loved New York, the vertical city that was barely twenty years old.

He liked to climb to the roof of a friend's apartment house at night and let "the Manhattan of vehement silhouettes" sweep over him. "If you have not seen it, you cannot know or imagine what it is like," he said. He wrote a book, *When the Cathedrals Were White,* about New York. When the cathedrals were white, men had built with fresh vision. New York could be a white city in the sky. "New York has such courage and enthusiasm that everything can be begun again, sent back to the building yard and made into something greater, something mastered."

An American architect named Hugh Ferriss had a similar vision, which emerged in the drawings he made in his leisure time during the fifteen or so years he worked as illustrator or consulting designer on buildings that architects were erecting in the city. Seen through fog or eerie shades of light, his towers, inspired in shape by the setback law, were mystical, surreal, compelling, like powerful hallucinations. They were romantic portraits, infused by washes of black and white with strength and gloom and an almost extraterrestrial force. To accompany a watery panoramic sketch titled *The City at Dawn,* Ferriss wrote lines that conveyed the wonder of the city. "Literally, there is nothing to be seen but mist; not a tower has yet been revealed below, and except for the immediate parapet rail (dark and wet as an ocean liner's) there is not a suggestion of either locality or solidity for the coming scene. To an imaginative spectator, it might seem that he is perched in some elevated stage box to witness some gigantic spectacle, some cyclopean drama of forms; and that the curtain has not yet risen. . . . As mysteriously as though being created, a Metropolis appears."

The drawings of Hugh Ferriss were symbolic. His mind caught the spirit of the twenties and translated it into architectural forms that were vehicles of the energy, idealism, and mystery of this particular moment. The setback law of 1916 had touched off his imagination. For him, it freed form; it took the lid off classicism. Convinced that it would encourage a sublime and spacious new city and "a new architecture for civilization," he explored the effects of the ordinance, and designed exhibits on the future city. He was a dreamer, but also something of a magic realist, embroidering the shape of the present with the chiaroscuro of his imagination, and his drawings exerted a strong influence on all those who saw them. Ferriss was in a company of progressive architects who were looking to the twentieth century for form and materials and ideology, and regarded classicism as decadent—a sham, a lie, a pompous affectation. He was part of the broadening modernist movement, and his new aesthetic shared with cubists, fauvists, futurists, postimpressionists, and even socialites in flapper dresses and bobbed hair a spirit of liberation and reform. Architecture, however, took more time than fashion or painting to integrate into the structure of the community. Ferriss's assessment of trends was right, but his vision of the city was not fully substantiated in residential architecture until 1929, the year 55 Central Park West went up, and the year his collection of drawings, *The Metropolis of Tomorrow,* was published in book form.

Ferriss said something else relevant to changing attitudes: "It is an indubitable fact that the character of architectural forms and space which all people habitually encounter are powerful agencies in determining the nature of their thoughts, their emotions, and their actions, however unconscious of this they may be." By his theory, people living with apartments and living in apartments, continually glancing up at the rising masses of residential buildings, or glancing out at a strange new geometry, were quietly revising their psyches. One can further imagine people within apartments setting up their households with a sense of up-to-dateness, accepting, even enjoying, a complicity with neighbors, beginning to realize the advantages of height. If an apartment seemed less permanent than a private house in principle, well, little in the landscape seemed certifiably permanent, particularly since the war, and society itself was more migratory than ever, moving about the country and to and from Europe. The war had shrunk the world, tempered absolutes and ideals, diminished expectations. After World War I, the age had taken as its motto "Be Modern," the critic Henry Hope Reed said. Women had the vote, and a generation born with the century had grown up with a taste for the future. As the old matriarchs of society died out, they were being supplanted by a bolder sort who accepted bohemians and café society and enjoyed the movement and diversity of the city. To them, the carefully structured order of Old New York was a memory or a grandmother's tale.

The popular culture seemed to reside in apartment buildings. The Ansonia was in its golden years; night and day it bustled with the comings and goings of Babe Ruth and his Yankee teammates, famous actors, and a firmament of opera stars. The tall palaces on Central Park West or Fifth Avenue provided the perfect settings for the parties of the decade that bubbled on despite Prohibition. Even the doormen on the scene, long-coated or top-hatted, bowing and winking beside topiary clipped into curves, looked like true twenties characters. When *The New*

Yorker magazine was founded in 1925, expressly for "caviar sophisticates," it put "New Apartments" on its beat, along with theater, music, golf, tennis, polo, and books, and offered a regular column, signed either "Duplex" or "Penthouse," which reported in depth on the best new buildings in town. An apartment was not only a stylish way to live in New York; it had become a symbol of the stylish life—tranquillity and grace in the midst of activity and noise.

The apartment architect was the man of the hour, the mind of the decade. While the limelight was new, the special interest had existed since the early days when it was more of an eccentricity than a professional calling. Back in 1878, when a man named Eugene Hoffman built an unusual apartment building called the Hoffman Arms, he was a pioneer with a single passionate idea. Ernest Flagg and James Ware were driven by social conscience to their interest in multiple dwellings, and in particular to model tenements. Beaux-Arts graduates like Hunt and Hardenbergh had been formally taught to appreciate urban institutions.

By 1920, the apartment-house architect was a breed unto himself, and his ranks were crowded. Both American architecture and the American apartment house had entered their fifth decade. A second generation of Beaux-Arts men had grown to maturity, among them Lawrence G. White and John Mead Howells. Architecture was still considered gentlemen's work, but its highest orders now included men like Rosario Candela and Emory Roth, both first-generation immigrants, and versatile hard-driving teams like Schwartz and Gross, who were caught up as fervently in the business of building as in its aesthetics and ideas. Commercially minded architects reflected the animus of the twenties, which was increasingly materialistic and pleasure-seeking. "Buy, Enjoy" was the byword. Many apartment architects worked with real estate firms who now developed and promoted properties as well as sold them; many worked in partnership with builders, and many had financial investments in the success of their ideas. Such relationships were not new, of course—even a utopian like Hubert had an economic stake in his crusade—but they were more calculated, more purely capitalistic. While the idea of living at the top of a twelve- or fifteen-story apartment house was romantic, the idea of selling that apartment house was pure business.

Apartment architects put the finishing touches on residential New York, closing the circle on an extraordinary era in architectural history. A few of them had very special talents that made lasting impressions on the city, talents as particular to the moment as to the men. Of an earlier decade, one remembered how Hubert had made his reputation with co-ops, Harde and Short with studios, Platt with his impeccable taste. Now J. E. R. Carpenter was famous for his plans, Rosario Candela for his detail, Emory Roth for his romantic skylines, and Simon I. Schwartz and Arthur Gross for a sense of composition and an occasional surprise. These simple facts summed up the present. These firms, four among many, dominated the last extravagant decade of apartment building in Manhattan. Both Carpenter and Candela were essentially twenties men, and their careers flourished and peaked within its parameters. Roth and Schwartz and Gross had a wider span, for their first apartments dated from early in the century, and their last pointed the way to another age.

CARPENTER WAS the man who set the twenties in motion. He was a Fifth Avenue architect, and he launched the decade with an apartment house that rose up above the Astor mansion at 66th Street like the ultimate challenge. For one last time, the neighbors, together with the Fifth Avenue Association, the City Club, and the Real Estate Board, responded with old-fashioned alarm, and for one last time, the city responded with restrictive legislation, which reduced the maximum building height on the park blocks between 60th Street and 96th Street from 150 feet to 75. It was a brief release from the tide of the times. By 1923, Carpenter had brought a successful test case to judgment, which overcame the ruling and opened Fifth Avenue to apartment-house construction. The next year, the Astor place itself fell, and it was suddenly clear that the great family mansion—indeed the family house of any description—was going the way of the farms and shanties of earlier times. A well-known developer named Benjamin Winter, the son of poor Polish immigrants, had purchased the property, which served to bring the social revolution full circle.

Houses now disappeared in bunches, in the pairs and triplets needed to free an apartment-house space, and architectural eminences named Fish, Blair, Roosevelt, Cutting, Hutton, or Phipps passed on into rubble and dust. A few blocks on Fifth were still protected by covenants, and

OPPOSITE TOP: The Fifth Avenue, on 84th Street and Fifth Avenue, built in 1883, was the only apartment house on the Avenue above 59th Street for thirty years. This photograph dates from 1924. OPPOSITE BOTTOM: The same street several years later, now with two fifteen-story buildings (1030 and 1035 Fifth) designed by J. E. R. Carpenter.

side streets, ruled by different zoning laws, remained a backwater of
private houses for a while longer. But Millionaire's Row was doomed
to disappear. Under the banner "Upper Fifth to House the 4000," the
New York Times predicted that one-third of the avenue would be converted to apartments within three years. "The die is cast, a new day is
here, and its terms must be accepted," they said with apparent calm. In
1926, when Senator Clark's $7-million fantasy in stone and gold leaf was
judged a white elephant, and sold for less than its land value, they
attributed the loss to the "modern mood." "The city is too large and
busy, the nation too occupied with realities, to tolerate the old make-
believe," they said. The rude disassembling of the Clark mansion made
a strange and poignant spectacle the next summer, for its sumptuous
interiors were exposed to the elements, and its most intimate accessories
were revealed willy-nilly to the public gaze. Two years later, when the
Vanderbilt mansion at Grand Army Plaza and Hunt's landmark creation
at 52nd Street were demolished too, no one seemed to take notice.

J. E. R. Carpenter, who designed at least a third of the new buildings
on Fifth Avenue, was instrumental in effecting "the passing of the old
Fifth Avenue and all that it stood for," as the *Times* put it. Carpenter
believed in the aesthetic as well as the material value of the tall modern
apartment house. He had become a successful developer and a professional eminence, with whom other architects collaborated and to whom
builders and developers submitted their plans for review. Such was his
authority that it is impossible to know exactly how many buildings in the
city he influenced significantly—more than five hundred, authorities
suggest. On Fifth Avenue, besides 907 and 845, he was the sole architect
for ten buildings below 96th Street, classical palaces of a variety of widths
and depths. His hand lay heavy on Park Avenue too. There he had
pioneered its uptown development and shepherded the apartment house
to acceptance in the area. Carpenter, with his large, carefully planned
foyer-centered apartments, was the one responsible for overcoming
upper-class resistance to apartments. He knew all about luxury, and he
laid it out carefully in his spaces. His successor, Rosario Candela, took
those spaces and refined them even further.

To MANY architectural historians, Candela stands as the pre-eminent
designer of luxury apartments in America. His buildings, it is said, were
the grandest in the decade that was itself the greatest. Candela, the son

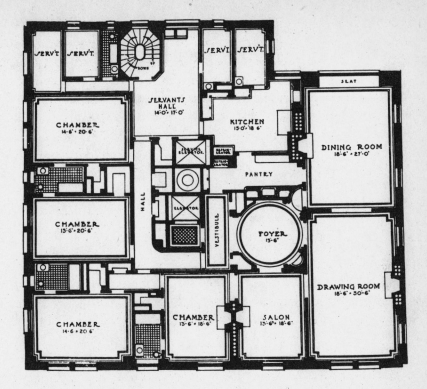

A Carpenter floor plan, from 635 Park Avenue, which replaced an earlier apartment house by Henry Hardenbergh.

of a plasterer, who was born in Sicily and entered Columbia University at nineteen with only a scant knowledge of English, was perhaps an unlikely candidate to add the final grace notes to this elegant age. Yet from his very first luxury building, the gently baroque Clayton Arms on Broadway at 92nd Street, built in 1922, to his last ones, the gracefully modernist courtyard apartment that replaced the Tiffany mansion on 72nd Street in 1936, for example, his touch was confident and true. Working closely with a band of successful Italian-born builders and developers—Gaetano Ajello, Anthony Campagna, and his rival, Michael Paterno—Candela moved progressively eastward in the city, from Riverside Drive and West End to Fifth Avenue and Park, much as the luxury-apartment movement had done. By 1927, he had twenty-five buildings to his credit. The best of these was 775 Park, also known as 101 East 72nd Street, a thirteen-story limestone-and-brick palazzo built in 1926. On the outside it was unassertive, although it occupied the full eastern front of the avenue, but inside, its simplexes, duplexes,

In 1901, the view south from Fifth Avenue and 78th Street (above) showed only houses. At 77th Street, a new home (right) was in construction for Senator William A. Clark of Montana.

By 1929, the view had been revised, with number 969 Fifth (left) claiming the very narrow lot on the corner, and 960 Fifth (below), designed by Candela and Warren and Wetmore, replacing copper king Clark's famous extravagance.

maisonette apartments with private street entrances, penthouses and roof garden apartments (including a triplex with fifteen rooms and an elevator direct to its door) fulfilled anyone's dreams of an urban home.

Until the late twenties, Candela's buildings were known for their quiet exteriors. They were classical limestone boxes with flat tops— bland characters, tall and thin or tall and stocky. On Fifth Avenue, they rose from the rubble of famous and faded old houses—Frank W. Woolworth's at 81st Street or Senator Clark's at 77th—their huge steel columns and girders swinging into place for the second growth of aristocratic homes, as they became part of the tall new street wall facing Central Park.

In 1929, however, when a new law allowed setback apartment houses to rise even higher, Candela's buildings began to fly and to suggest on the outside some of the extravagant behavior inside. The first to appear was 770 Park, on the southwest corner of 73rd Street, which rose to twelve stories and then broke up into tiers of setbacks that were topped with a lanternlike penthouse tower. A year later, 778 created a similar silhouette on the northwest corner, and together, the pair framed the street like important monuments. The rooflines could be seen from far away, and they expressed the essence of these buildings elegantly, for they looked like clusters of houses or small European villages.

Critics often referred to Candela's apartments as houses. The *Times* described 960 Fifth, which replaced Clark's colossus, as a pile-up of mansions. With its eleven- to eighteen-room suites, it rivaled 998 in its accommodations. Developers of 770 Park called their offerings "country houses." Candela's special ways with apartments were relevant to houses. He had a respect for privacy and an eye for significant detail. He was a complete thinker. He added duplicate water connections to street mains and multiple switches for ceiling lights as well as beautifully turned staircases and separate wine cellars. Most significantly, he designed buildings from the inside out. He placed windows where they received light, balanced a room, or allowed a graceful arrangement of furniture. Unpredictable patterns of windows, of course, created problems in a case where a collaborating architect had to fit Candela's plans to a symmetrical classical envelope. Most architects designed their facades before their interior fittings. Nevertheless, irregular fenestration animated the facade of a building like 770 Park, adding rhythms that suggested the life within. Candela also invested unusual energy in the entry hall. In a typical apartment, he made it a full-sized room with rich views into the interior because he thought it was important to greet a visitor with a full sense of a home.

By 1929, a mystique had grown up around Candela's apartments, as if he had a hegemony on luxury. He designed dozens of buildings on Fifth and Park and another dozen about town. They needed no promotion, for they sold themselves. His pride was 740 Park, which appeared in 1929 on land relinquished when the Presbyterian Hospital moved uptown to Washington Heights. It represented all that Park Avenue stood for on the eve of the Depression—solidity, security, and the height of luxury—and it represented Candela well too, for it was Park Avenue style he was dispensing around town. As he designed tall new apartment buildings for Sutton Place, Gracie Square, and East 57th Street, he was literally building the leading edge. In 1927, One Sutton Place showed the rich how to live on the waterfront; its porte cochere led to a private garden on the banks of the East River where a yacht landing facilitated the weekend trip to the country.

Like Carpenter, Candela was business-minded and received work from developers and speculative builders as well as private parties— sometimes a whole building, sometimes its plan. He worked instinctively, out of an innate ability to inhabit as well as articulate a space, and he was often called in to fix other architect's buildings or to solve specific problems, like Carpenter's awkward entrance at 825 Fifth. Candela liked puzzles. During the Depression, he took up cryptography, and during World War II, he broke the Japanese code.

LONG BEFORE either Carpenter or Candela had begun the practice of architecture, Emory Roth had already put important buildings on the street. The Belleclaire Hotel at 77th and Broadway in 1903, 570 Park at 61st Street in 1915, 417 Park at 55th Street in 1916—they had all been pioneers in their neighborhoods and pushed the course of development forward. Roth's monograph was a version of the era in shorthand. Over three decades of designing, his buildings had grown bigger and more composed, and his career had progressed accordingly, so that by the postwar years, when apartment living was not only popular but booming, Roth was established as a leading architect.

Roth had believed in the apartment house from the beginning; he thought it had a future. He had no formal architectural training, but events, instincts, and experience had conspired to give him vision and skills that would make him a specialist. His education was almost circumstantial, but the happenstance jobs and coincidental encounters enriched his work almost as directly as classical training. Roth had come to America from Hungary at the age of thirteen to be apprenticed to a cabinetmaker; he had moved to Chicago to become a draftsman at the World's Columbian Exposition; he had worked in Hunt's office there and in New York; he had done some interiors with Ogden Codman at the Breakers in Newport. The fair was his "beneficent Alma Mater," he said, where he found his lasting style. The Breakers was his finishing school, where he came to understand the housing requirements of the wealthy.

Roth was a new breed of architect, and he had a peculiarly American kind of energy born of optimism, pragmatism, and dreams. In an age when his confreres were gentlemen, and got their commissions through family, clubs, and social connections, he was a businessman. He formed an early association with the brothers Leo and Alexander Bing, who had launched a firm that sold plots to speculative builders. Quick to grasp the principles of building costs and operating expenses, Roth established himself as an expert in real estate. He was not an aesthete or an ideologue, but an activist in the affairs of his day.

Roth felt strongly about classicism, however, and he believed in masonry buildings covered with Renaissance detailing. He also had specific ideas about apartment houses, although when he began, he had no experience with the form. Where other architects put all their energy into a rich main facade and treated side and rear walls as leftovers, Roth wanted to design a complete building, with homogeneous sides. As early as 1905, he was committed to foyer-based plans instead of rooms strung rangily along corridors. He also espoused the idea of elaborate enclosures for the water tanks and elevator bulkheads that made rooftops look like industrial cities, structures that were later called "Roth's towers." Roth's concern with the aesthetics of the roof was precocious, and his towers would evolve, in time, into high-fashion penthouse apartments. In the first decade of the twentieth century, however, only architects and artists seemed to want to live at the top of buildings.

Roth put his ideas about apartment houses into practice early. Bing and Bing, which quickly became one of the most distinguished and active builders of apartment houses in the city, gave him virtually all of its projects to design, and other builders followed suit. It was only in the 1920s, however, as buildings and spirits began to soar, that Roth could begin to express his intuitive attraction to height and let classicism bend to contemporary yearnings. Then, with a single building, the Ritz Tower on 57th Street and Park, he changed the direction of residential architecture.

The appearance of the Ritz in 1925 seemed like a symbolic event. It expressed what was in people's imagination, caught the Jazz Age in stone, announced the beginning, at last, of the modern age. At forty-one stories, it was the first residential skyscraper in the city and the tallest such structure in the world. It looked like sheer verticality as it narrowed, like a telescope, up through its setbacks, to a tower in the clouds. It was a "sky-puncture," "a flare," the critics said, quite overcome, noting that "even the 'professional' New Yorker, who has ceased to [be] awed by the wonders of the present age, stops to view and contemplate the actual arrival of the home five hundred feet high."

The Ritz Tower was a residential hotel, managed by the Ritz Carlton Hotel Company, for the building code still restricted the height of even a setback apartment house. Yet the Ritz was as full-blown a response to the 1916 zoning law as Ferriss might have orchestrated. Its verticality was insistent, exaggerated by corner ornament that drew the eye up from setback to setback to a finial on the roof, and there was active life up on the terraces and balconies and behind the tall windows of the towers. Arthur Brisbane, the popular Hearst editor and real estate developer who had commissioned the building from Roth, lived in baronial splendor in an eighteen-room duplex with a solarium and garden on the nineteenth and twentieth floors. He and all his vertical neighbors had unbroken views for twenty-five miles in four directions.

The Ritz Tower invited attention, for it was strategically placed at the intersection of New York's most fashionable cross street and its premier residential boulevard. It dominated the skyline with its image and its ideas. It inspired a new generation of hotels and apartment hotels, and it effected a new attitude toward an aerial city and an aerial home. Architects came to see it and to study it, for it established a precedent in high-rise construction. Penthouse and terrace apartments became fashionable and proliferated; style-conscious tenants staged parties on terraces and planted gardens in the air. Artists, too, sought out the roofline for the perspectives it offered on the burgeoning city. Alfred Stieglitz and Georgia O'Keeffe took a top-floor apartment at the thirty-four-story Shelton Hotel and sketched the sights from their window. O'Keeffe painted the tall buildings like mountains, with natural

The Ritz Tower, on the northeast corner of 57th Street, 1925. In its shadow,
the South Kensington Apartments and a handful of row houses are reminders
of earlier working-class Park.

dignity, and Stieglitz photographed them straight-on, like historic events.

By now, Roth's practice was one of the largest in New York; his work was transforming the city. On Fifth and on Park, he joined Candela and Carpenter in filling in the avenues with the last classically inspired luxury apartments ever built. On Central Park West, he designed the Beresford at 81st and the San Remo at 74th and changed a forgotten street into a majestic skyline.

The construction of the Beresford in 1928–29 and the San Remo in 1930 came just as a swaggering age teetered and then collapsed. Their multitowered edifices were symbols of the glamour and materialism that ended in the Crash. The Beresford looked like a sumptuous urban villa, a fat, buff-brick, twenty-two-story classical pile with three domed cupola towers. The San Remo was an elegant, more ethereal building, which rose up subtly through setbacks to twin towers with circular pantheon tops. The towers changed the building, for shaped as they were, with prominently defined sides, they seemed to lift the building into an almost vertical mode. The city had just revised its last restraints on height, and the San Remo was Roth's response to an open sky.

Roth's ultimate gift to New York was the so-called Italian skyscraper, of which the San Remo was his premier example. All of his enthusiasms and values came to bear in this building: his desire to create an architectural entity rather than a facade, his affection for rooflines, his Newport-trained notion of luxury, his fidelity to his times. Roth designed a building that combined prewar ideas with high-density urbanism. He was not a modernist, however, for his feelings about classicism ran too strong. "It took years for me to forsake my early love and to forget Renaissance palaces and Greek and Roman temples," he stated in his autobiography, yet according to the Beresford and the San Remo, he was still in love. Their massive facades were modified with Italianate details, and when they reached the sky, they broke out into Renaissance lyrics—finialed Roman temples atop the San Remo, modeled on the Choragic Monument of Lysicrates in Athens, and three baroque crowns on the Beresford. Roth's genius was his ability to adapt the details of classicism to modern building forms; he made elegant compositions of the new size and the old spirit. If he was modern, it was because he liked the city, its gregariousness and its drama. His buildings showed his urbanity and broadcast the romance of cohabiting height for miles around.

The San Remo, which set the example of twin towers on Central Park West,
1930.

By 1931, three new twin-towered edifices had joined the Beresford and the San Remo on Central Park West; one, the Eldorado at 90th Street, was designed by Roth. The avenue was effectively finished. It had been in disarray since 1925, when the construction of the first line of the new Independent subway system had fired a building boom on the Upper West Side. Above the subterranean excavations, the street had been widened, its streetcar tracks excised, and outdated buildings removed from the path of progress. Family hotels named the Beresford and the San Remo had been among the fallen. They dated from post-Dakota days when the avenue was the place for adventurers. Now, almost fifty years later, it was an apartment street on the grandest scale. The hotel owners were compensated for their losses with large duplex suites in the namesake buildings.

ACCORDING TO his sons who carried on the firm, Emory Roth probably designed more apartment houses than any other person in the world—more than five hundred they say, although even half that number would be significant. In a city that supported dozens of apartment-house architects, only the firm of Schwartz and Gross was as prolific, and its work was often distinguished more by its ability to maximize rentable space than by any other notable characteristic. The ranks of Schwartz and Gross were those of Gaetan Ajello, Neville and Bagge, Pennington, Lewis & Miller, Rouse and Goldstone—firms whose medium was the speculative apartment house and whose muse was necessarily the marketplace. The sheer volume of their work, however, made Schwartz and Gross both typical and noteworthy, for their buildings appeared on block after block of the city and, in the end, determined street character more widely than landmarks ever could. The architects' range was wide, sweeping from the West Side to the East, uptown and downtown, and embracing hotels, studios, courtyard buildings, and setback towers. Their style was sophisticated, and once in a while so well articulated that it caught everyone's attention.

Schwartz and Gross had both endurance and panache. The firm's career progressed apace with the apartment-house movement, beginning modestly in the first decade of the twentieth century with buildings for the middle and upper-middle classes on the Upper West Side. These buildings had names like the Arizona and the Tennessee, on West 114th Street, or the Paterno and the Colosseum, on Riverside Drive, and they took a variety of shapes. They were all questing ventures, for the apartment was still a queer thing, and its social status was unclear.

By 1920, Schwartz and Gross had developed a prototype apartment house that brought the respectability of the American Renaissance to a variety of popular neighborhoods. Their standard parti was the familiar classical cake, twelve to fifteen stories high, with a two- or three-story limestone base, stringcourses, and a lightly ornamented roofline. With only the modest variations necessary to give a building a suggestion of individuality, this design appeared on avenues and side streets around town, its shape creating a pattern and a texture in the grid by its very repetition. It had a dozen examples on West End Avenue, elevating and stabilizing a street that was being updated to apartment living. It had a dozen more on Park from the 30s to the 90s, including one example at 470 in the erstwhile Terminal City. Schwartz and Gross designed more and more buildings for the well-to-do as the pace of the age accelerated, and the last objections to apartment living were lost in the sounds of what Fitzgerald called "the gaudy spree." While other architects were edging toward the relaxed Georgian style or the liberated modern, Schwartz and Gross were reluctant to abandon the classical convention. Their last Beaux-Arts buildings were among their most enlightened. Number 1185 Park Avenue, for example, erected in 1929 between 93rd and 94th streets, was an engaging version of the old-fashioned courtyard building, with a fully planted garden. It was the last large apartment house ever to be built in New York in the form of a hollow square. An eleven-story Tudor building at 14 East 75th Street, with magnificent double-height living rooms designed like lofts, was the last studio building to be erected, at least before the term *studio* was revised to mean a single room.

The hand of Schwartz and Gross had grown lighter and less predictable with age. Their last buildings were their most expressive, which was a fitting climax to their long careers and to the era that had sustained them. On Central Park West, they effectively closed that era by opening a new one. Here, with their designs for three new buildings at numbers 55, 241, and 336, the firm broke once and for all with tradition. These buildings, erected in late 1929 and 1930, were tall, machine-inspired Art Deco towers, colored subtly in earth tones and decorated with sunbursts, bold flutes, or vertical sprouts. They were romantic technological creations, and, joined together with Roth's landmark buildings, they framed the most memorable skyline in the city. Schwartz and Gross had always read the time accurately, which together with consistent quality, accounted for their success. They had begun, tentatively, with one of the first generations of apartment dwellers, and they had ended, flamboyantly, with urban sophisticates.

LOOKING BACK over the twenties, critics settled on 1927 as the year of triumph for the apartment house. That year, for the first time in a century, the Building Department did not receive a single application for permission to build a private house for six months. That year, three Vanderbilt houses came tumbling down. From that point on, the few remaining great houses on the avenue began to look like relics, and the limestone apartment houses began to look as if they had always been there and always would. Not that there weren't still pockets of resistance—bankers who persisted in the quest for the colonial good life and erected, or reconstructed, Georgian and Federal town houses on the side streets of the Upper East Side, or the social elite who simply transferred their domestic seats from Fifth Avenue to Sutton Place, the way Mrs. William K. Vanderbilt I had done. Not that there weren't visible signs of longing for the way the city used to be—the construction or reconstruction of quaint and old-fashioned blocks like MacDougal Alley or Pomander Walk, the conversion of groups of houses into intimate enclaves of apartments, and the critics who continued to complain that the apartment was not homelike or did not have atmosphere, which were different ways of saying the same thing.

Even at this last stage of transition, apartment architects were mindful of the recalcitrant. They sought to individualize apartment space to the extent the multiple form allowed. They designed duplex and triplex suites; they staggered floor levels and stacked up rooms, and, whenever possible, they catered explicitly to a residual taste for extravagance. In a few instances, they designed whole buildings around the specifications of the shareholders, who had purchased blocks of unshaped space.

Some of the most extravagant spaces ever carved out within multiple dwellings resulted from these last efforts to sweep the parties of resistance into the apartment movement. The triumph was only nominal, of course, for incorporating the literal facts of an old mansion into a new colossus was hardly forging out any new architectural identity. When Mrs. E. F. Hutton, for example, was reluctant to sell her town-house property at 1107 Fifth, the builder contracted Rouse and Goldstone to re-create her fifty-four-room mansion atop the apartment structure. To ensure her autonomy, they cut a private porte cochere into the side of the building, which gave entrance to a private elevator that ascended directly to a three-story suite that filled its crown. In appearance, that crown might have been a grand house, planted like a dizzy fiefdom on a huge pedestal. The heavy band course above the lower floors might have been a garden wall. Like a great portal, a Palladian window at the center of the twelfth floor opened into a main foyer, with separate men's and women's coatrooms. From there, the apartment, decorated in the manner of a Newport estate, spread through a drawing room, a library, dining room, breakfast room, kitchen, and a servants' wing up to the bedrooms, sitting rooms, workrooms, sun porches, and on the roof, a laundry, children's bedrooms, a playroom, and gardens that changed with the seasons. It included a self-contained guest suite with maid's rooms and a private elevator, a silver room, cold-storage rooms for flowers and furs, and valets' workrooms. Its appointments—ten fireplaces, gown closets, cedar closets, bedroom balconies—showed the extent to which architects were still willing and able economically to gratify individual demands under the guise of changing styles.

This was true not just for Mrs. Hutton, although her apartment has gone on record as the largest and most elaborate in New York history. There were others who turned to apartment living on their own terms: Mrs. William K. Vanderbilt II, who had a separate address for her seven-bedroom triplex maisonette at 660 Park; Vincent Astor, who built 120 East End Avenue and reserved the entire thirty-five-room seventeenth floor for himself. These tenants were public figures of untold wealth, and their apartments were one-of-a-kind dwellings, but they were also no more than extreme examples of the luxury of the time. The cooperative plan had made it possible for many people to have mansions within apartment houses. Given the proper investment of time and money, no two apartments needed to look alike, and any apartment could be shaped to replicate home. Mrs. Hutton's apartment was a faithful rendition of her house—marble mantelpieces were moved to identical positions in identical rooms, custom-made rugs were transferred from the parlor floor to the thirteenth floor. Other tenants reproduced conservatories for their statuary, cinquecento dining rooms for their tapestries, or other epic or eccentric spaces for which money might have cultivated a taste. Architects were particularly accommodating to the first generation of tenants, and landlords made frequent concessions.

Many tenants refused to close a deal until they were assured that the library paneling or the carved doorframes could be moved from their house to their new apartment.

Early in the century, William Randolph Hearst had set an important example for this consummate style of luxury apartment living. In 1907, he had taken the top three floors of the new Clarendon Apartments at Riverside Drive and 86th Street to house his young family and a growing collection of art objects that, besides paintings and statuary, included tapestries, suits of armor, mummies, figurines, bronzes, and bibelots. The apartment measured three-quarters of an acre of living space, excluding the roof garden, to which Hearst soon added two more floors, eventually purchasing the entire building. Within these walls, he fashioned a Georgian dining room, an Empire bedroom, a three-story galleria modeled on a vaulted Gothic cathedral, a two-story display room for his collection of silver salvers, and an office suite; he continued to redecorate, adding carved ceilings, choir stalls, stained glass from French cathedrals, redesigning to incorporate new possessions from his warehouse full of art treasures, until he left New York for his castle at San Simeon.

On a grandly inflated scale, Hearst's apartment suggested many New York apartments. Hearst, like other apartment dwellers, was engaging in a bit of make-believe, creating the illusion that he was living elsewhere than in a large new apartment house. With his scores of rooms and his compulsion to buy and to build, Hearst articulated his taste more literally than did tenants who had to modify reality with furniture, wallpaper, and paint. Yet a legion of interior decorators, inspired by Elsie de Wolfe, was now available to transform impersonal dwelling units into anything a client might desire, a Victorian retreat, a surrogate country house, a silver-and-chrome salon. They in effect closed the gap between the apartment house and the private house with a bridge of style.

Curiously, in the twenties, an age that was celebrating the lightness of being, the medieval was still popular, and many of the social elite abandoned their town houses for the twelfth floor of an apartment house, only to expend great effort in the elaboration of vaulted vestibules, stone arches, and Gothic stairways. They were still seeking the reassurance of the heavy and permanent, albeit encased in the steel skeleton of a fifteen-story skyscraper. Given the insistent variety of the age, however, the most stylish New Yorkers displayed eclecticism in their furnishings, which expressed their readiness for change. They

William Randolph Hearst's vaulted galleria (left) with a few of his many suits of armor, and his double-height reception room (below), designed to display a collection of silver salvers.

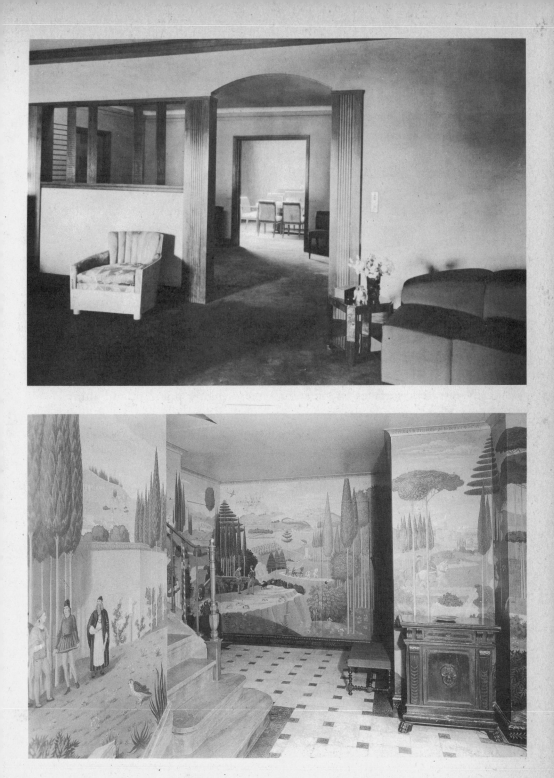

Art Deco in the Beresford (top) and intimations of the medieval on Upper Fifth Avenue, both in the 1930s.

favored modern living rooms, Jacobean libraries, Chinese Chippendale dining rooms, Early American bedrooms, and Italian Directoire bathrooms. Decorative trends came and went quickly. The Victorian was revived even before it had been properly buried. For a while, large bathrooms and then small efficiency-minded kitchens made news. There was an irresistible chic to the gadgetry of convenience—kitchenettes and dinettes, fold-down ironing boards, Murphy beds and Murphy tables— even among the advantaged. Styles came now from unpredictable sources. Style was a manifestation of an attitude toward life, and New Yorkers were increasingly free-wheeling.

The most important source of style in the late twenties was the Exposition Internationale des Arts Décoratifs et Industriels Modernes in Paris in 1925, which introduced New Yorkers to a modern version of classicism. The French ideas were interpretative ones, taking traditional elements and stylizing them, but they conveyed a sense of newness that seemed almost revolutionary. Columns were sleek or fluted and shorn of their capitals, forms were cutout or sculpted, ornament was geometrically inspired, surfaces and materials were highly polished and shiny. New York, primed for change and flush with its boom economy, responded with passion to the spectacle in Paris. Almost overnight, architects and decorators took up the new kind of modern. Department stores mounted their own exhibitions of the new furnishings and fabrics. Specialty stores redesigned their premises to make themselves living showcases of the French style. Apartment houses incorporated the new materials and motifs into their lobbies and living rooms.

Modern classicism, or Art Deco, as the French ornamental style was later renamed, was particularly well suited to apartment houses. Its glossy, stripped-down, man-made quality expressed contemporary urban life in the same way that apartments did. Art Deco was an evolutionary style that did not break with but modified tradition. Some of its appropriateness lay in the abstraction and abbreviation of forms that had always been expressed literally; some came from the rich machine imagery. Art Deco was favored by transatlantic steamships and nightclubs as well as apartment houses. It looked fast, sinuous, exact, and racy, quite like the modern age.

14

A New Beginning

THE NORTH-SOUTH streets of Manhattan had acquired, again, a uniformity as ruled and as rhythmic as the old brownstone pattern had been. The scale was bigger and the lines bolder, for the basic components were more voluminous. As one drove down Riverside Drive from the northern end of the city, the sweep of apartment buildings looked like a range of mountains, powerful, theatrical, and quite overwhelming. Walking down Park Avenue was like walking along the bed of a canyon. Above, to the left and right, carved into the sheer walls like aeries were the homes of contemporary cliff dwellers, stacked up behind anonymous windows. On Fifth, the classical street wall was now as symbolic of society's character as the lineup of frivolous houses had once been. Fifth Avenue mansions had been the material manifestation of the top of a social pyramid that had crumbled and been absorbed into a larger society. The old configuration was deeded and republican; the new was strictly democratic. The very sameness of apartment houses was revealing. Apartment houses had leveled society and, with respect to appearances, had established a basic equity.

The whole era of the luxury apartment had been one of transition. The task had been to ease a new generation out of the quarters built by its ancestors. With the vast majority of Manhattanites already living in apartments, this was essentially a fait accompli. The social and moral implications of that fact were enormous. Yet architects had not created anything revolutionary, any form that, ipso facto, could properly be termed *modern*. They had persisted in maintaining the pretense that the apartment house was the same thing as a four- or a five-story palazzo, only bigger. The stereotypes of traditional architecture had been reassuring, but they were borrowed, and had little to do with the methods and materials and ideas of twentieth-century America. "We do not glue feathers on the wings of airplanes because men have always associated. flight with the forms of birds; and there is no reason why, to pay respects to traditional notions of domesticity, we should resort to similar practices in the building of houses—as if what the architect had now to offer the housewife were not something infinitely more attractive to her than slate roofs and roughly smeared stucco walls," Lewis Mumford said in *The Culture of Cities,* urging architects to turn to fresh forms for the new urban order.

Moreover, the concept of the luxury apartment had not really changed since the Dakota. Although apartment living was considered ultramodern, little in the planning of the apartment showed any heed to all the new thoughts about honesty and simplicity and economy that characterized the increasingly vigorous modern movement, or even to the popular excitement about height, light, and view. There was all manner of mechanical contrivances in kitchens and in maintenance basements. There were chrome chairs and unframed fireplaces in living rooms. There were terraces and penthouses for the chosen few at the top of many buildings, but windows were essentially the same shape they had been in brownstones. The garnishes had little to do with the fundamental concept of home. In that, the apartment was basically an amalgam of nineteenth-century elements—a marriage of convenience between a house and a hotel. It was not planned as much as it was contrived. It was not sui generis, least of all in its most luxurious examples.

As far back as Viollet-le-Duc, who was lecturing at the Sorbonne during Hunt's student days, or Louis Sullivan, who had laughed at Hunt's first mansion on Fifth, architects had been decrying the dependency on ancient historical styles. By 1929, most architects in New York were seeking to express modernity in original ways, either in a progressive manner, like the modern classicists and the Art Deco movement, or in a radical manner, like the modernists, most of whom embraced the so-called International Style. The modernist credo was "Form follows function." The very spareness of the phrase suggested its aesthetic, which found inspiration in engineering rather than nature and eschewed all embroidery or ornamentation. "Less is more" was one of its corollaries, as was "Nothing for show and nothing that can't be shown." This meant stripping off the heavy coats of stone and statuary, building with a minimum of structure, and celebrating the technology of the times— steel frames and glass skins, simple planes, and pure geometric shapes. The movement found immediate expression in words like *honesty, morality,* and *truth*.

It would be several decades before the movement of modernism really achieved ascendancy in New York (and then with commercial skyscrapers), but in 1929, a building went up at 55 Central Park West that looked like a new beginning. Critics called it "innovational," but to a lay person, who sees a building not as a matter of design choices but as whatever he wishes—an image, a person, a sculpture, a metaphor—and who can free-associate without the constraints of professional discipline, the building was the note of honest fantasy that the mind of the age desired. It romanticized modern imagery so unabashedly that it might have been drawn by Hugh Ferriss. Everything about it—the stepped tower form, the facade overlaid with a pattern of vertical bands, the stylized fluting, like vestigial wings on the top stories— focused upward. The structure seemed to celebrate the height it achieved; this impression was reinforced even by the coloring of the brickwork, shaded in tones from red at the base to pale tan at the top—forty different hues of earth colors, Lewis Mumford reported— done, it was said, to create the illusion that the sun was always shining on the building.

The architects of 55 Central Park West were Schwartz and Gross, who achieved here, at the end of their careers, one of their most spectacular successes. After years of producing safe and proven forms, they were the first to treat the apartment house as a unified whole from sidewalk to summit. The building rose on its own like an organic growth, unencumbered by demarcations of house line or balustrades or cornices. Even the stylized portal blended into the surface. The vertical lines were the strongest element of the building; the setbacks ranked next; and then the windows, which were wide and uniform and so arranged behind the webbing of the facade that it looked as if maybe the building were made of glass and then wrapped in brickwork for protection. It was a twentieth-century habitat in which form, height, and light, all by-products of the new technology, counted most. Old architectural habits had been sloughed off much as the skin of old social habits. Inside the apartments, there was evidence of an honest and economical mind at work. The gracious basics were there—a large entrance gallery, a

55 Central Park West, built in 1929 and designed by Schwartz and Gross, looked as if it belonged to the city of the future.

living room, a dining room, bedrooms, good closets, maid's rooms—but no hall, no extras, no surprises, no conspicuous waste, no historic debris. The architects' attitude might be said to have been embodied in their decision to set the living room two steps below the other rooms, which created a feeling of spatial change without sacrificing real space. As for the mental space, the upper floors, with their nine-room, four-bath apartments, had narrow terraces that incorporated into home the whole vast spectacle of the city.

The building at 55 Central Park West was neither the most sophisticated nor the most explicit example of the modern ideology to appear at the end of the twenties, but the very naiveté of its winged setbacks and soaring water tower made it the most passionate. Emory Roth had designed Art Deco apartment houses too, but his buildings were as classical as they were moderne, for he had mixed feelings about the starkness of the future. Fine architects like Roth might well have gone about their romantic ways for years, easing away from opulence gradually, if the stock market had not crashed in 1929, and with it the market for palatial residences. As fortunes and styles changed overnight, architects and the population at large had new reason to consider something said fifty-odd years before by William Morris, from whom the modern movement in large part descended. "Believe me," he wrote, "if we want art to begin at home, as it must, we must clear our houses of troublesome superfluities that are forever in our way; conventional comforts that are no real comforts, and do but make work for servants and doctors; if you want the golden rule that will fit everything, that is it: have nothing in your house that you do not know to be useful or believe to be beautiful."

No example could be a clearer illustration of sobering up than the Majestic at 115 Central Park West, which was originally designed with a New World exterior of sleek sharp lines, dramatic corner windows, twin tower tops molded as abstract sculpture, and an Old World interior of lavish eleven- to twenty-four-room apartments. When its steelwork was partly erected, the market fell and the architects frantically reworked their building into an assortment of units from three to eleven rooms. The following year, like a confirmation of basic facts, the architects Chanin and Delamarre designed a companion building, the Century, at 25 Central Park West, which offered fifty-two varieties of accommodations, ranging from a one-room unit with wraparound terrace to an eleven-room unit with a private street entrance. All the technical ingenuity of the times was brought to bear on the specifics of the building: a new form of concrete construction that obviated the need for beam drops in ceilings, cantilevered floor slabs to eliminate corner columns and thus provide wraparound windows and wider terraces, special window glass capable of transmitting the ultraviolet rays of sunlight.

The Century was a high-spirited Art Deco tower. Irwin Chanin, who also built six Broadway theaters and a movie palace, the Roxy, saw the whole modern city in theatrical terms. His apartment building looked as if it had been built of children's blocks, systematically and scientifically

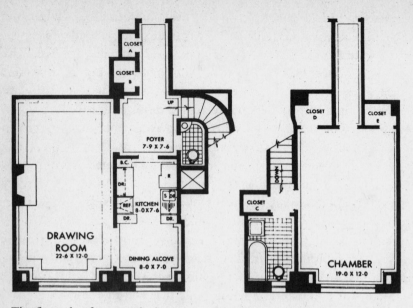

The floor plan for a one-bedroom semiduplex apartment in the Century, 25 Central Park West, built in 1930. It is streamlined, stylish, and functional.

assembled. Its surface was horizontally striated between window panels, as if by a mechanical process, and its tower tops finished off in a sort of collage of machine parts. What the Century promised on the outside was delivered without apology within; the architects had used technology as a collaborative agent in redefining the apartment. They had organized its elements with an eye to the practical expression of the function to be encompassed. This was clearest in the three-room duplex, which had a generous foyer, a drawing room with fireplaces, a dining alcove, a streamlined appliance-dominated kitchen, and, up a spiral staircase, a large bedroom and bath and many closets—but it could also be observed in large apartments, where kitchens were efficient, and sunken living rooms and wide archways had become metaphors of incidental space.

The Majestic and the Century proposed new ideas about how the affluent could live. Their apartments were planned to activate a gracious but simpler life, within the bounds of conventional conduct but without ceremonial clutter. Their layouts were pared down and at the same time extended to include everything within view. Even on the lower floors, and most dramatically in the towers, there was a powerful sense of home as the foreground and the whole community as background. The apart-

ment, the floor plans said, was not a closed, comprehensive environment, but a sensible foothold in a larger, exciting one. Luxury was not
sheer excess or outdated ritual, but coherent, useful form, sunlight, and
perspective. Economy, which once signified niggardliness, provided the
means for collective largesse.

Ironically, the Great Era of Luxury Apartment Building ends here,
with the apartment emerging as a genre of its own, with virtues of its
own. In the thirties, a few more apartment houses like the Majestic and
the Century were completed before the Depression brought the construction industry to a halt in 1932. It resumed, briefly, near decade's
end, and then stopped again for World War II. After the war, the vision
seemed to dim, economics impinged, energy flagged, and the luxury
apartment house, with only a few exceptions, began to resemble a very
businesslike affair. In the thirties, a handful of sumptuous old-style apartment houses went up, too, as if expressing confidence in the way things
were. Such buildings were, and still are, referred to as "throwbacks."
River House, a twenty-six-story limestone-and-brick tower at 447 East
52nd Street, was the most lavish of them, and it sat on the edge of the
river like an exclusive resort. It had its own formal gardens, its own yacht
mooring, and maintained the private River Club, which had squash
courts and tennis courts and a grand ballroom. The building was seques-
tered from the still transitional neighborhood of Sutton Place, and as a
tenant or a visitor passed through its elegant gates, into the private
courtyard with its automobile turnaround, and on into the black marble
lobby, he effectively left the city behind.

In 1936, the playwright Sidney Kingsley seized upon the idea of
River House to create the setting for *Dead End,* a play of social protest.
"Strange sight," the stage instructions read. "Set plumb down in the
midst of slums, antique warehouses, discarded breweries, slaughter
houses, electrical works, gas tanks, loading cranes, coal-chutes, the very
wealthy have begun to establish their city residence in huge, new palatial
apartments." *Dead End* ran on Broadway and then was made into a
successful movie, adapted to the screen by Lillian Hellman, starring
Humphrey Bogart, Marjorie Main, Sylvia Sidney, and Gabriel Dell. It
depicted the hopeless lot of a gang of street kids who lived in the
tenements beneath a magnificent white structure called the East River
Terrace Apartments. To the kids, who swam in the river and made
trouble for the doorman, the building represented class, sophistication,
and wealth—a literal elevation from the streets. Ground level was their

reality, from which they gazed up in wonder and envy at a beautiful young woman on her terrace in the sky. The metaphor at the heart of *Dead End* was poignant, but it was also historically noteworthy, for it made the apartment house, once a place for the poor and the déclassé, into an ivory tower. The message came like an epilogue, to reflect on the close of an era.

In 1929, the *American Architect* devoted a whole issue to the apartment, and at least one critic had a negative say: "At its highest pitch, city life is no longer the life of the family, but one of shifting crowds, of restaurants and theaters, offices and subways—an existence in which the individual is lost in the mass. Of necessity, its architecture will represent a kind of common denominator of its mass requirements; it will be semi-public, hard, intricate, and vast; an architecture of speed, precision, and movement. It will afford privacy without individuality; it will be social without being intimate. . . . In all these qualities, it will reflect the essential structure of cosmopolitan life." Inevitably, the promise of the apartment was connected to the promise of the city, for the apartment owed its raison d'être to the city, and in many ways was a scale model of it. Like the city, the apartment reflected the struggle to find a harmonious balance between old and new, between the individual and the collective, based on cultural priorities. Like the city, it raised problems that were as significant as the solutions.

OPPOSITE TOP: The entrance to River House, which has risen out of waterfront slums. This view is reminiscent of the movie set of *Dead End*. OPPOSITE BOTTOM: River House, New York City, 1931.

West End Avenue at 89th Street, circa 1920.

APPENDIX:
EXTANT BUILDINGS

―――――――――

Of the many apartment houses mentioned by name in this volume, the following eighty-five are still standing on the street. They are arranged here geographically, from south to north, for convenience rather than chronology, although in general, the uptown movement suggests the course of history. Some of the buildings seem small and unstylish now, and would be overlooked but for a stained-glass transom or an unlikely name carved in stone. Others are still big bold presences—as surprising to behold as they were at the beginning of the twentieth century.

The other buildings have been torn down. It was an era of experimentation, after all, and New York has always been quick to rebuild. The very name of New York suggests its changeable nature, as the author of a book titled *New New York* was already pointing out in 1909. By then, a generation of French flats and bachelor apartments was giving way to larger Beaux-Arts buildings. Hubert and Pirsson's amazing Central Park, or Navarro, Apartments was demolished in 1927, the same year the Clark and the Vanderbilt mansions came down. The historic Stuyvesant, still on Stuyvesant family land after three hundred years, lasted until 1957, when it was replaced by a fourteen-story developer's building. In the surge of postwar development, the residential palaces of Park Avenue between 42nd and 59th streets were razed too, leaving behind only number 417 to attest to the style in which the rich had once kept house.

THE EAST SIDE FROM GRAMERCY PARK TO 42ND STREET

The Gramercy, 24 Gramercy Park
36 Gramercy Park

121 Madison Avenue
The Nottingham, 35 East 30th Street

THE WEST SIDE FROM GREENWICH VILLAGE TO 42ND STREET

The Washington Arms, 328 West 11th Street
The Chelsea Hotel, 222 West 23rd Street
The Bryant Park Studios, 80 West 40th Street

THE EAST 50S

417 Park Avenue
The Ritz Tower, 465 Park Avenue at 57th Street
River House, 435–47 East 52nd Street
One Sutton Place

THE WEST 50S

140 West 57th Street Studios
Carnegie Hall Studios, 160 West 57th Street
The Osborne, 205 West 57th Street
The Alwyn Court, 180 West 58th Street
The Gainsborough, 222 Central Park South

THE UPPER EAST SIDE TO 96TH STREET

Fifth Avenue to Park Avenue

825 Fifth Avenue
845 Fifth Avenue
907 Fifth Avenue
925 Fifth Avenue
960 Fifth Avenue
969 Fifth Avenue
998 Fifth Avenue
1030 Fifth Avenue
1035 Fifth Avenue
1107 Fifth Avenue
The Verona, 32 East 64th Street
14 East 75th Street

The King, 56 East 87th Street

535 Park Avenue

570 Park Avenue

635 Park Avenue

660 Park Avenue

740 Park Avenue

770 Park Avenue

775 Park Avenue

778 Park Avenue

960 Park Avenue

1185 Park Avenue

Lexington Avenue to the East River

131–35 East 66th Street

130–37 East 67th Street

Cherokee Flats, 507–23 East 77th Street

120 East End Avenue

THE UPPER WEST SIDE TO 125TH STREET

Central Park West to Columbus Avenue

The Century, 25 Central Park West

The Prasada, 50 Central Park West

55 Central Park West

The Majestic, 115 Central Park West

The Dakota, 1 West 72nd Street

The Langham, 135 Central Park West

The Kenilworth, 151 Central Park West

The San Remo, 145–46 Central Park West

The Beresford, 211 Central Park West

241 Central Park West

The St. Urban, 285 Central Park West

336 Central Park West

The Central Park View, 414 Central Park West

Hotel des Artistes, 1 West 67th Street

The Central Park Studios, 11–15 West 67th Street

The Cooperative Studios, 25 West 67th Street

The Atelier Building, 33 Central Park West

44 West 77th Street

Broadway

The Dorilton, 171 West 71st Street
The Ansonia, 2109 Broadway at 73rd Street
The Belleclaire, 250 West 77th Street
The Apthorp, 2207 Broadway at 79th Street
The Belnord, 225 West 86th Street
The Astor Court, 205 West 89th Street
The Clayton Arms, 215 West 92nd Street

West End Avenue to Riverside Drive

The Chatsworth, 346 West 72nd Street
The New Century, 401 West End Avenue at 79th Street
The Orienta, 302–4 West 79th Street
The Hyperion, 320 West 84th Street
The St. Elmo, 170 West 85th Street
The Clarendon, 137 Riverside Drive at 86th Street
The Georgian Court, 315 West 94th Street
The Clifden, 265 Riverside Drive at 99th Street
The Bertha, 515 West 111th Street
The Cathedral Studios, 610 West 111th Street
The Arizona, 508 West 114th Street
The Tennessee, 514 West 114th Street
The Graham Court, 1923–37 Adam Clayton Powell Jr. Boulevard at 116th Street
The Sophomore, 21 Claremont Avenue
The Colosseum, 435 Riverside Drive at 116th Street
The Paterno, 440 Riverside Drive
The Stadium View, 445 Riverside Drive
The Grant, 514 West 122nd Street
The Ogontz, 509–15 West 122nd Street
The Marimpol Court, 521 West 122nd Street

UPPER MANHATTAN TO HARLEM

The Mannados, 17 East 97th Street
The Zenobia, 217 Central Park North

NOTES

===

Abbreviations

AABN	*American Architect and Building News*
AForum	*Architectural Forum*
AR	*Architectural Record*
NYT	*New York Times*
RER	*Real Estate Record and Builders' Guide*

Chapter 1   IRVING PLACE, 1869

5   The construction of the Stuyvesant, begun in 1869, was completed in 1870.

7   "a certain public frenzy": see Lewis Mumford, *The Brown Decades: A Study of the Arts in America, 1865–95* (New York: Dover Publications, 1971), 6.

Various critics suggest that the Stuyvesant may not be the first apartment house in America, noting that the Hotel Pelham in Boston, an apartment hotel designed by Alfred Stone of Arthur Gilman's firm, was erected in 1856–57, and Boston's Hotel St. Cloud, designed by Nathaniel J. Bradlee, was erected in 1869. Despite this competition, the Stuyvesant was the first American building to be recognized as such. See Sarah Bradford Landau, "Richard Morris Hunt, Architectural Innovator and Father of a Distinctive American School," in Susan R. Stein, ed., *The Architecture of Richard Morris Hunt* (Chicago: University of Chicago Press, 1986), 62; and Paul R. Baker, *Richard Morris Hunt* (Cambridge, Mass.: MIT Press, 1980), footnote p. 499.

"This substitute . . .": George Templeton Strong, *The Diary of George Templeton Strong, Post-War Years, 1865–75*, ed. Allen Nevins and Milton Halsey Thomas (New York: Macmillan Co., 1952), 339.

8   "Another material change . . .": ibid., 97ff.

9   25,000 vacant lots: *A History of Real Estate, Building, and Architecture in New York During the Last Half of a Century* (New York: Arno Press, 1967), 33.

10   "unconscious vandals": Montgomery Schuyler, "The Small House in New York," *AR* (April–June 1899), 368.

"straight up-and-downness": Edith Wharton, *The Age of Innocence* (New York: Charles Scribner's Sons, 1968), 77.

11   "brown sandstone . . .": ibid., 13.

12   "recalled scenes . . .": ibid., 29.

"burglaries, highway robberies . . .": Strong, op. cit., 241.

13   Jefferson, Emerson, and Melville are discussed and quoted in Morton White and Lucia White, *The Intellectual versus the City* (Cambridge, Mass.: Harvard University Press and MIT Press, 1962).

Chapter 2   RICHARD MORRIS HUNT

15   "There is no place . . .": Baker, op. cit., 62.

16   "If other countries teach you . . .": ibid., 49.

"to make a capital of Paris": From Baron Haussmann's *Memoires* of 1891, displayed in an exhibition at the Musée d'Orsay, Paris, France, April 1987.

17   "Paris now had the space . . .": Roger Shattuck, *The Banquet Years* (New York: Vintage Books, 1968), 5–6.

19   On Hunt's early work, see Landau, op. cit., 58.

20   On Roman apartments, see Jerome Cariopino, *Daily Life in Ancient Rome,* trans. E. O. Lorimer (New Haven, Conn.: Yale University Press, 1940), 24–25; and Talbot Hamlin, *Architecture through the Ages* (New York: G. P. Putnam's Sons, 1940).

22   "I was astonished . . .": G. F. Bradby, *The Great Days of Versailles* (New York: Charles Scribner's Sons, 1906), 12. On Versailles, see also Jacques Levron, *Daily Life at Versailles in the 17th and 18th Centuries* (London: George Allen and Unwin, 1968), 68–70.

24   "American ladies . . .": Calvert Vaux, "Parisian Buildings for City Residents," *Crayon IV* (July 1857), 218.

On the design sources of the Stuyvesant, see Landau, op. cit., 62–64.

Chapter 3   THE TRADITION OF HOUSES

25   See Anthony Trollope, *North America* (Philadelphia: J. B. Lippincott, 1862), 219–20.

26   See Constance Gray Harrison (Mrs. Burton), *Recollections Grave and Gay* (New York: Charles Scribner's Sons, 1911), 281.

27   "dressmakers, bird-stuffers . . .": Wharton, *The Age of Innocence,* 68.

"These scattered fragments . . .": ibid., 102.

"Two or three flights . . . avoid": Vaux, op. cit., 218.

28   "for the proper appreciation . . .": Baker, op. cit., 109.

29   "When the Civil War broke . . .": Mumford, *The Brown Decades,* 49.

"gaily and rapidly . . .": ibid., 49–51.

30   "It has long been . . .": *Harper's Weekly,* April 30, 1859, reprinted in John Grafton, *New York in the Nineteenth Century* (New York: Dover Publications, 1977), 43.

"On the first of May . . .": Frances Milton Trollope, *Domestic Manners of the Americans* (London: Whitaker, Treacher & Co., 1832), 177.

31   Colonnade Row: According to M. Christine Boyer, *Manhattan Manners: Architecture and Style, 1850–1900* (New York: Rizzoli, 1985), 52, Colonnade Row was turned into a hotel in 1844.

32   "the tendency to live in herds . . .": Lloyd Morris, *Incredible New York* (New York: Random House, 1951), 7.

Chapter 4   FRENCH FLATS AND OTHER FIRST THOUGHTS

35   Architectural historians are uncertain whether the Haight House was reconstructed from one or two dwellings, since its lot measured 80 by 150 feet.

Landau suggests that the Stevens House looked like Haussmann's buildings.

36   "the most truly picturesque . . .": Baker, op. cit., 208.

For critiques of the Stevens House, see *RER* (January 20, 1877), 42; and *RER* (December 30, 1882), 32.

37   In "The New Homes of New York," *Scribner's Monthly* (May 1874), James Richardson stated that it was difficult to judge numbers because of the nature of the records kept by the superintendent of buildings, but he estimated that approximately fifteen permits for new or reconstructed French flats were issued per month, many of high grade. These specific figures come from "A Word to Large Capitalists," *RER* (July 8, 1876), 500.

38   "300 boarding houses . . .": quoted in Charles Lockwood, *Manhattan Moves Uptown* (New York: Houghton Mifflin, 1976), 293.

"The internal history . . .": Richardson, op. cit., 69.

"it is no wonder . . .": "Vacant Lots in the Fashionable Quarter," *RER* (April 12, 1879), 287.

40   "watching calmly . . .": Wharton, *The Age of Innocence,* 27.

42   Barbara Goldsmith offered the observation about the back wall of Grand Central.

The Vancorlear was referred to as the Van Corlear in the *RER.*

43   "everything requisite . . .": "The Knickerbocker," *RER* (January 22, 1876), 66.

44   See "Is the Apartment System a Failure?" *RER* (April 14, 1877), 281–82.

45   "an absolute perfect homelife . . .": "Apartment Hotels," *RER* (January 20, 1877), 42.

"possessing wealth, culture . . .": Richardson, op. cit., 69.

46   "The discomfort of his rooms . . .": E. Littell, "Club Chambers," *AABN* (February 19, 1859), 59.

"No grander field . . .": *RER* (October 6, 1877), 766.

48   "pure Renaissance . . .": *RER* (August 30, 1879), 689.

"there was hardly any limit . . .": "The City of the Future," *RER* (December 27, 1879), 1056.

49   ended the Victorian Age: Isaac Newton Phelps Stokes, *An Iconography of Manhattan
      Island, 1498–1909* (New York: R. H. Dodd, 1915–28), 1964.

      "the unparalleled advancement" and "Nothing so grand in scale . . .": See Russell
      Lynes, *The Tastemakers* (New York: Harper & Bros., 1955), 112.

      "There never was a time . . .": Lynes, ibid., 116–17.

50   "as they dressed . . .": *RER* (suppl., December 30, 1882), 4–6.

      "The new streets . . .": ibid., 6.

      "We are like children . . .": *AABN* (July 29, 1876), 289.

51   "a cultivated and traveled class . . .": *RER* (December 30, 1882), 6.

      "Gentlemen will never . . .": Morris, op. cit., 110.

      "Those who were willing . . .": *AABN* (May 31, 1879), 175.

Chapter 5   THE COOPERATIVE EXPERIMENT

54   "a number of gentlemen . . .": "All About Home Clubs," *RER* (December 30, 1882),
      147.

      For details of cooperative planning, see "Cooperative Apartment Houses," *AABN*
      (February 19, 1881), 88.

56   "A very important cause . . .": Edward Bellamy, *Looking Backward: 2000–1887* (New
      York: Modern Library, 1887), 126.

57   "fairy tale of social felicity . . .": see Mumford, *The Brown Decades,* 22.

      Much information on the Chelsea comes from notes kept by Juliette Hamelcourt, who
      lived in the building in the twentieth century, and also from running notes in the
      AABN and the *RER*.

60   "in . . . novelty . . .": see *RER* (April 14, 1883), 145.

61   "striking a mean . . .": ibid.

63   Each one of these buildings outdid the others in one way or another—space, revenues,
      plans for household management. The St. Catherine, for example, a relatively small
      building that had seven floor-through apartments of twenty-one rooms each, prided
      itself on its appointments, which included French Renaissance frescoed ceilings,
      flocked and gilded wallpaper, French porcelain washbasins, and elaborate speaking
      tubes (with rubber attachments that allowed the summoning of servants without the
      bother of rising from the bed, as it was explained).

      "We are feeling our way": "The Future of the Apartment House: A Talk with George
      W. Da Cunha," *RER* (November 10, 1883), 881.

63–   people who "like to live in a crowd" and "The very fact . . .": *RER* (April 7, 1883),
64   136.

67   "both a fulfillment and a prophecy": Mumford, *The Brown Decades,* 47.

Chapter 6   THREE NEW MANSIONS

72   "the plum of the season" and other details: Baker, op. cit., 274–84.

      "The Electric Light": Morris, op. cit., 157.

74   "with a hired chef . . .": Wharton, *The Age of Innocence,* 337.

76   "Must I show you . . .": Louis H. Sullivan, *Kindergarten Chats on Architecture, Education, and Democracy* (New York: Scarab Fraternity Press, 1934), 140.

      "what the people are *within* . . .": ibid., 16.

77   "If we don't all stand together . . .": Wharton, *The Age of Innocence,* 48.

78   On New York's "public possessions," see David Chase, "Superb Privacies," in Stein, ed., *The Architecture of Richard Morris Hunt,* 169.

80   "superb privacies": Henry Van Brunt, one of Hunt's first studio pupils, spoke of "superb privacies" in an essay titled "Richard Morris Hunt," *Architecture and Society: Selected Essays of Henry Van Brunt* (Cambridge, Mass.: Belknap Press, 1969), 336.

      "a visual summary": Nathan Silver, *Lost New York* (New York: Schocken Books, 1971), 120.

      The Bourbon exception is cited in Lynes, op. cit., 132.

      Chase, in "Superb Privacies" (Stein, op. cit.), recounts that Alva Vanderbilt chose the oak leaf and acorn as the family crest.

      Paul Bourget's remarks were collected in *Outre-Mer: Impressions of America* (New York: Charles Scribner's Sons, 1895), 22–53.

81   On the popular response to such extravagance, see Chase, op. cit., and also E. L. Godkin, "The Expenditure of Rich Men," *Scribner's Magazine* (October 1896), 497–500.

82   The sailing vessel simile and an abundance of other details are provided by Leland M. Roth, *McKim, Mead & White, Architects* (New York: Harper & Row, 1983). This fine biography and monograph gives a full and compassionate account of the firm's beginnings.

84   "It was a dream . . .": Robert Koch, *Louis C. Tiffany: Rebel in Glass* (New York: Crown, 1964), 61.

      "It is a style of its own . . .": Marianna Griswold Van Rensselaer, "Recent Architecture in America, V: City Dwellings," *Century Magazine* (February 1886), 553.

85   Villard's remarks were published in "The New York House of the Future: An Interview with Henry Villard," *RER* (December 31, 1881), 1208.

      See Sarah Bradford Landau, "The Villard Houses and the New York Rowhouse," in *The Villard Houses,* ed. William Shopsin and Mosette Broderick (New York: Viking Press in Cooperation with the Municipal Arts Society of New York, 1980), 13–18.

86   On the Villard Houses design, see Roth, op. cit., 86–88, and Shopsin and Broderick, op. cit., 45–55.

90   "a chaste simplicity": *Artistic Houses* (New York: Benjamin Blom, 1971), 163.

91   "Most nineteenth-century millionaires . . .": Brendan Gill, introduction to Shopsin and Broderick, op. cit., 11.

Chapter 7   Two Communal Palaces

92   "they created an atmosphere . . .": Nathalie Dana, *Young in New York: A Memoir of a Victorian Girlhood* (Garden City, N.Y.: Doubleday, 1963), 99.

94   "There are but few persons . . .": "The City of the Future," *RER* (November 8, 1879), 1056.

96   "A visitor is lost . . .": *RER* (March 7, 1885), 232.

      "Suits of Apartments . . ." and "This meant that . . .": Stephen Birmingham, *Life at the Dakota* (New York: Random House, 1979), 35–36.

97   "to make money": ibid., 32.

      According to Birmingham, the cost of the Dakota was $1.5 million to $2 million.

      "Like a sewing machine . . .": ibid., 30.

100   "Fashionable, to me, . . .": ibid., 223.

102   "The future of the west side . . .": *RER* (March 28, 1885), 228.

104   Statistics on development are from "Vacant Lots on Manhattan Island," *RER* (May 15, 1886), 636.

105   "design by inflation": see foreword by Harmon H. Goldstone in Andrew Alpern, *Apartments for the Affluent* (New York: McGraw-Hill, 1975).

      For details on building the Osborne, see "The Vertical Village," *Connoisseur* (December 1987), 153; and Davida Deutsch, "The Osborne, New York City," *Antiques Magazine* (July 1986), 152–58.

      "the most magnificently . . .": *NYT* (October 3, 1885), 7.

109   "to stand a steel bridge . . .": Morris, op. cit., 198.

110   "the intricate social questions" and "all meet . . .": Hubert, Pirsson & Hoddick, "New York Flats or French Flats," *AR* (July–September 1892), 61.

111   "Architecture in America . . ." and following remarks: Sarah Gilman Young, *European Modes of Living or the Question of Apartment Houses* (New York: G. P. Putnam's Sons, 1881), 9.

      "the old and barbarous custom . . . disappeared": J. P. Putnam, "The Apartment House," *AABN* (January 4, 1890), 5.

Chapter 8   WILLIAM DEAN HOWELLS IN NEW YORK

113   See John Burchard and Albert Bush-Brown, *The Architecture of America: A Social and Cultural History* (Boston: Little, Brown, 1961), 187.

114   "established repose": Henry James, *Washington Square* (New York: Harper & Bros., 1956), 1.

      "an impenetrable mystery": Edith Wharton, *A Backward Glance* (New York: Charles Scribner's Sons, 1934), 176.

      "I applaud . . .": cited in Leon Edel, *Henry James, 1901–1916: The Master* (New York, J. B. Lippincott, 1972), 6–7.

116   Henry C. Bunner's work is discussed in Van Wyck Brooks's *The Confident Years* (New York: E. P. Dutton, 1952), 13.

      On Howells's realism, see William Dean Howells, *My Literary Passions: Criticism and Fiction* (New York: Harper & Bros., 1895), 193–283; and John Updike, "A Critic at Large: Howells as Anti-Novelist," *The New Yorker* (July 13, 1987), 78.

118   "Boston seems . . .": William Dean Howells, *Life in Letters of William Dean Howells*, vol. 1, ed. Mildred Howells (New York: Doubleday, Doran, 1928), 413.

"Her virtues, her vices . . .": William Dean Howells, *Impressions and Experiences* (New York: Harper & Bros., 1894), 242. Other remarks are found in the chapters "Glimpses of Central Park" and "New York Streets," 234–81.

119   a society on the move: Howells wrote a short story titled "Flitting," in which he used the image of household furnishings being callously bundled into moving wagons to describe the social distress of moving from place to place.

"We must not forget . . . a light room": Howells, *A Hazard of New Fortunes* (New York: Harper & Bros., 1890), 67.

120   "Think of a baby . . .": ibid., 72.

121   "which had its good points . . .": ibid., 83.

122   "I wear a fur-lined overcoat . . .": Howells, *Life in Letters*, vol. 1, 417.

123   "How far . . .": Howells, *Impressions*, 242.

125   "the greatest meeting of artists . . .": Lynes, op. cit., 143.

126   "the first expression . . .": Henry Adams, *The Education of Henry Adams* (Boston: Houghton Mifflin, 1918), 343.

a pathological aberration: Sullivan, *Autobiography of an Idea* (New York: Press of the American Institute of Architects, 1924), 325.

127   "With the same logical . . .": Ernest Flagg, "American Architecture as Opposed to Architecture in America," *AR* (October 1900), 180.

Chapter 9   GREATER NEW YORK AT THE TURN OF THE CENTURY

129   "No one who will study . . .": *A History of Real Estate, Building, and Architecture*, 589.

131   "primeval venerable things": Franz K. Winkler, "Architecture in the Billionaire District of New York," *AR* (September 1901), 677.

132   See *AR* (May 15, 1902), 22.

See Schuyler's obituary for Richard Morris Hunt, "The Works of the Late Richard Morris Hunt," *AR* (October–December 1894), 97.

"indifference to the stiff and starched . . .": *Harper's Weekly* (April 13, 1895), quoted in Grace Mayer, *Once Upon a City* (New York: Macmillan Co., 1958), 112.

135   The comments on the "Rainy Daisy" come from Mayer, op. cit., 74.

138   "The poorest man . . .": *The New Metropolis*, ed. E. Idell Zeisloft (New York: D. Appleton, 1899), 246.

exclusivity to the masses: see Robert A. M. Stern, Gregory Gilmartin, John Montague Massengale, *New York 1900* (New York: Rizzoli, 1983), 102.

working their will on the city: see Leland Roth, who offers detailed information on McKim, Mead and White's work in New York.

143   "Hardly the faintest hint . . .": Zeisloft, op. cit., 6.

144   "It is a famous highway . . .": ibid., 616.

"The uptown life . . .": ibid., 485.

145 Zeisloft's figures for the classes were the Very Rich, 10,000; the Rich, 10,000; the Prosperous, 20,000; the Well-to-Do Comfortable, 50,000; the Well-to-Do Uncomfortable, 500,000; the Comfortable or Contented Poor, 300,000; and the Submerged or Uncomfortable Poor, 700,000.

146 "a certain fashion . . .": ibid., 284. Other classes and their accommodations are described on pp. 280–85.

Chapter 10 BUILDING THE UPPER WEST SIDE

151 an urban nation: see Burchard and Bush-Brown, op. cit., 208–9.

152 "the gigantic upheaval . . ." and "They are not definite . . .": Edgar Saltus, "New York from the Flatiron," *Munsey's Magazine* (July 1905), quoted in Mayer, op. cit., 1.

154 On the effect of the New Law, see *AR* (July 1901), 477–508.

"complete architectural meals": Wharton, *The House of Mirth* (New York: New American Library, 1964), 168.

155 "a sort of no-man's land" and following quotes: Lewis Mumford, *Sketches from Life: The Early Years* (New York: Dial Press, 1982), 3–24.

156 For details of the Ansonia, see Robert Reinhart, "The Ansonia Remembered," *NYT*, (November 7), 1971, sec. 8, 1.

160 "One is verily tempted . . .": Henry James, *The American Scene,* introduction by Leon Edel (Bloomington: Indiana University Press, 1960), 102.

"they couldn't hope to 'get on' . . .": Edith Wharton, *The Custom of the Country* (London: Constable, 1965), 33.

161 "a panorama of platitude": Franz K. Winkler, "Recent Apartment House Design," *AR* (January 1902), 98.

169 the triumph of hope: A. C. David, "A Cooperative Studio Building," *AR* (October 1903), 248.

On the decoration of the cooperative studios: ibid.

170 The first studio building on West 67th Street had been built too tall for the street and had to be called an apartment hotel to remain legal. Builders and building inspectors were careful to respect housing regulations after this incident, and taller buildings necessarily gravitated to wider streets.

171 "the first great residential style . . .": Herbert Croly, "The Architectural Works of Charles A. Platt," *AR* (March 1904), 181–244.

172 "It was so big . . .": "A Cooperative Apartment House in New York," *AR* (July 1908), 4.

"Studios of first-class artists . . .": Dana, op. cit., 192–93.

173 Numbers 535 and 563 Park Avenue and numbers 24 and 36 Gramercy Park were all important natural stepping stones in the rebuilding of New York. Number 24 was probably the most talked about, because many of its founding tenants were eminent. They included Richard Watson Gilder, the editor of the *Century;* Jules Guerin, the mural painter and illustrator; Francis Wilson, the actor; and Hubert Lucas, the architect of the building.

"fill the social void . . .": *RER* (October 23, 1909), 720.

Chapter 11 · SELLING APARTMENTS

174 "colossal hair-comb . . .": James, *The American Scene*, 139–41.

Only 120 new houses . . .: See Herbert Croly, "The Contemporary New York Residence," *AR* (December 1902), 704.

175 "A lady needs only . . .": "Modernized Existence," *Harper's Weekly* (April 18, 1903), 639.

"We see our homes . . .": Charlotte Perkins Gilman, "The Passing of the Home in Great American Cities," *Cosmopolitan* (December 1904), 137–47.

176 "Bring together . . .": *AABN*, January 5, 1907, 1.

"one a survival . . .": George Santayana, *The Genteel Tradition*, ed. D. L. Wilson (Cambridge, Mass.: Harvard University Press, 1967), 37–64.

177 "Experience has shown . . .": *AABN* (January 5, 1907), 2.

"When planning, mentally, . . .": Professor Fick of Copenhagen, "The Apartment House Up to Date," *AR* (July 1907), 69.

179 See John Taurenac and Christopher Little, *Elegant New York: The Builders and the Buildings, 1885–1915* (New York: Abbeville Press, 1985), for more details on the Alwyn Court.

183 "In the Middle Ages . . .": Edith Wharton and Ogden Codman, Jr., *The Decoration of Houses* (New York: W. W. Norton, 1978), introduction.

185– For a discussion of the mechanical aids available in apartments, see Elizabeth Collins
86 Cromley, *Alone Together: A History of New York's Early Apartments* (Ithaca, N.Y.: Cornell University Press, 1990), 119ff.

185 "The little cage sank . . .": Stephen Crane, "Active Service," quoted in Van Wyck Brooks, *The Confident Years*, 140.

"from within": R. B. L. Lewis, *Edith Wharton*, 140.

186 "They had something . . .": Lewis Mumford, *The Brown Decades*, 16.

"Why should we . . .": Elsie de Wolfe (Lady Mendl), *The House in Good Taste* (New York: Century, 1913), 237.

Chapter 12 · THE CONVERSION OF THE RICH

188 The Fifth Avenue Association had been founded in 1907 "when destructive forces were without a check, either in law or in public opinion." Its program had the single purpose of "safeguarding the highest standards of the section," according to *Fifth Avenue, Old and New,* the publication of the organization, which celebrated the centennial of the founding of Fifth Avenue in 1824.

189 "The process of reconstruction . . .": Herbert Croly, "The Renovation of the New York Brownstone District," *AR* (June 1903), 569.

191 "a building containing seventeen private dwellings": "The Multiple Residence: An Essay with a Description of 998 Fifth Avenue," *Architect and Builder* (March 12, 1912), 91–100.

193 "998 can be called . . .": ibid.

196 "It was thus . . .": Wharton, *The Age of Innocence*, 259.

198 See Wilfred W. Beach, "Some Recent New York Apartment Houses from the Work of J. E. R. Carpenter," *AForum* (May 1919), 127–36.

"If the Strozzi Palace . . .": *RER* (February 18, 1922), 202.

199 *RER*, July 15, 1916, reported that the first busiest area of the city in building was located north of 155th Street—strictly speculative ventures; the second was east of Sixth Avenue from 40th to 96th Street, notably between Fifth Avenue and Park Avenue; and the third from 14th Street to 40th Street, where the business was almost exclusively in altering existing buildings for mercantile purposes.

206 On the Marguery and 300 Park Avenue, see Edward Hungerford, "Housekeeping Deluxe," *Tavern Topics* (October 1921), 6.

"Only the newly-rich . . .": Will Irwin, *Highlights of Manhattan* (New York: D. Appleton-Century, 1937), 219–23.

207 In the first designs, Park Avenue was meant to be a composition of five-story buildings that served as bases for thirteen-story towers, set back from the street. Those height controls, however, were supplanted by a zoning order of 1916 that produced the uniform cornice lines and a more massive and impressive rendering of the ideals of the City Beautiful.

On the whole design of Terminal City, see Elliot Willensky, "Grand Central Terminal, Shaper of a City," in *Grand Central Terminal*, ed. Deborah Nevins (New York: Municipal Arts Society, 1982), 101.

209 Anna Glen Vietor, who offered her reminiscences to Lindsy Van Gelder in "Park Avenue," *Town & Country* (September 1986), 186, grew up in the neighborhood in the 1920s.

"new quarter of the very rich . . .": Irwin, op. cit., 219.

210 "a consolidation for . . .": *AABN* put it this way in an editorial, "The badges of plutocracy consolidated for the sake of convenience."

211 "not merely a neighborhood . . .": Morris, op. cit., 304–5.

212 "the just-before-dawn of a new day": Max Eastman, *Enjoyment of Living* (New York: Harper & Row, 1948), 399.

"hitched to the machine and the stars": Ada Louise Huxtable, *Kicked a Building Lately?* (New York: Quadrangle, 1976), 291.

213 "Hardly four generations ago . . .": Martha Bensky Bruere, "The Flat vs. the House," *Harper's Bazaar* (June 1912), 303.

"This is the age . . .": de Wolfe, op. cit., 237.

"For family life . . .": Jesse Lynch Williams, "Back to Town or the Return to Human Nature," *Scribner's Magazine* (November 1915), 542.

214 "Con men, clergymen . . .": ibid., 540.

"People nowadays were too busy . . .": Wharton, *The Age of Innocence*, 353–58.

"The compact world of my youth . . .": Wharton, *A Backward Glance*, 7.

Chapter 13 APARTMENT-HOUSE ARCHITECTS

217 "New York had all the iridescence . . .": F. Scott Fitzgerald, "Echoes of the Jazz Age," in *The Bodley Head Scott Fitzgerald*, vol. 2 (London: Bodley Head, 1959), 12.

"New York in 1919! . . .": Mumford, *Sketches*, 211.

218   See Henry Collins Brown, *Valentine's City of New York: A Guide Book* (New York: Valentine's Manual, 1920), 361.

"Between the present skyscrapers . . .": Charles Edouard Jeanneret-Gris (Le Corbusier), *When the Cathedrals Were White* (New York: Reynal & Hitchcock, 1947), 85.

219   "If you have not seen it . . .": ibid., 90.

"Literally, there is nothing . . .": Hugh Ferriss, *The Metropolis of Tomorrow* (New York: Ives Washburn, 1929), 15.

220   "It is an indubitable fact . . .": ibid., 37.

After World War I . . .: Henry Hope Reed, *The Golden City* (Garden City, N.Y.: Doubleday, 1959), 141.

221   "Buy, Enjoy": Malcolm Cowley, introduction to F. S. Fitzgerald, *The Stories of F. Scott Fitzgerald* (New York: Charles Scribner's Sons, 1951), vii.

224   "The die is cast . . .": R. L. Duffus, "Upper Fifth to House the 4000": *NYT Magazine,* May 24, 1925, 7.

According to catalogues of the architect's work and Pease and Elliman's review of East Side apartments, Carpenter designed numbers 810, 825, 920, 950, 988, 1030, 1035, 1060, 1115, 1120, 1143, 1148, 1150, 1165, and 1170 Fifth Avenue.

the grandest in the decade: See Christopher Gray, "Apartments by Candela: Grandest of the Grand," *NYT Magazine,* September 3, 1988, 67.

230   "beneficent Alma Mater": Emory Roth, "Autobiographical Notes," 1940–1947, unpublished manuscript, Avery Library.

"Roth's towers": Steven Ruttenbaum, *Mansions in the Clouds* (New York: Balsam Press, 1986).

231   "even the 'professional' New Yorker . . .": Irwin, op. cit., 221.

235   The Ardsley at 320 Central Park West, on the southwest corner of 93rd Street, arrived in 1931 too. It was an elaborately styled Art Deco work, with a stepped-back water tower.

On the work of Schwartz and Gross, see Robert A. M. Stern, Gregory Gilmartin, Thomas Mellins, *New York 1930* (New York: Rizzoli, 1982), 397.

239   See Virginia Pope, "New York Now Has Mansions in Flats," *NYT Magazine,* April 5, 1927, 17.

Chapter 14   A New Beginning

244   "We do not glue feathers . . .": Lewis Mumford, *The Culture of Cities* (New York: Harcourt Brace Jovanovich, 1938), 418.

247   "Believe me . . .": William Morris, quoted in Mumford, *Culture of Cities,* 407.

249   "Strange sight...": Sidney Kingsley, *Dead End* (New York: Random House, 1936), 1. It was the dock at 53rd Street that featured prominently in the play and movie, so the building in question is River House at 52nd Street, or possibly the Campanile at 450 East 52nd Street.

251   "At its highest pitch": Roderick Seidenberg, "Apartment House Architecture," *American Architect* (February 5, 1929), 3.

SELECTED BIBLIOGRAPHY

Books

Abbott, Berenice. *New York in the Thirties*. Text by Elizabeth McCausland. New York: Dover, 1967.

Adams, Henry. *The Education of Henry Adams*. Boston: Houghton Mifflin, 1918.

Allen, Frederick Lewis. *The Big Change: America Transforms Itself, 1900–1950*. New York: Harper & Bros., 1915.

Alpern, Andrew. *Apartments for the Affluent*. New York: McGraw-Hill, 1975.

Amory, Cleveland. *Who Killed Society?* New York: Harper & Row, 1960.

Andrews, Wayne. *Architecture, Ambition, and Americans: A Social History of American Architecture*. New York: Free Press, 1978.

Apartment Houses of the Metropolis. New York: G. C. Hesselgren Publishing Co., 1908.

Artistic Houses. 2 vols. 1883. Reprint. New York: Benjamin Blom, 1971.

Baker, Paul R. *Richard Morris Hunt*. Cambridge, Mass.: MIT Press, 1980.

Balsan, Consuelo Vanderbilt. *The Glitter and the Gold*. New York: Harper & Row, 1952.

Barth, Gunther. *City People: The Rise of Modern City Culture in Nineteenth-Century America*. New York: Oxford University Press, 1980.

Bellamy, Edward. *Looking Backward: 2000–1887*. New York: Modern Library, 1887.

Bender, Thomas. *New York Intellect*. Baltimore: Johns Hopkins University Press, 1987.

Birmingham, Stephen. *Life at the Dakota*. New York: Random House, 1979.

Bok, Edward. *The Americanization of Edward Bok: The Autobiography of a Dutch Boy 50 Years After*. New York: Charles Scribner's Sons, 1920.

Bourget, Paul. *Outre-Mer: Impressions of America*. New York: Charles Scribner's Sons, 1895.

Boyer, M. Christine. *Manhattan Manners: Architecture and Style, 1850–1900*. New York: Rizzoli, 1985.

Bradby, G. F. *The Great Days of Versailles*. New York: Charles Scribner's Sons, 1906.

Brooks, Van Wyck. *The Confident Years*. New York: E. P. Dutton, 1952.

———. *Howells: His Life and World*. New York: E. P. Dutton, 1959.

Brown, Henry C. *Brownstone Fronts and Saratoga Trunks*. New York: E. P. Dutton, 1935.

———. *Fifth Avenue, Old and New, 1824–1924*. New York: Museum of the City of New York, 1924.

———. *New York of Yesterday*. New York: Gracie Mansion, 1924.

———. *Valentine's City of New York: A Guide Book*. New York: Valentine's Manual, 1920.

Burchard, John, and Albert Bush-Brown. *The Architecture of America: A Social and Cultural History*. Boston: Little, Brown, 1961.

Burchell, S. C. *Imperial Masquerade: The Paris of Napoleon III*. New York: Atheneum, 1971.

Cariopino, Jerome. *Daily Life in Ancient Rome*. Translated by E. O. Lorimer. New Haven, Conn.: Yale University Press, 1940.

Chambers, Julius. *The Book of New York: 40 Years' Recollections of the American Metropolis*. New York: Book of New York Co., 1912.

Chase, W. Parker. *New York, The Wonder City*. New York: Wonder City Publishing Co., 1932.

Cook, Clarence. *The House Beautiful: Essay on Beds and Tables, Stools and Candlesticks*. New York: Scribner, Armstrong & Co., 1878.

Cromley, Elizabeth Collins. *Alone Together: A History of New York's Early Apartments*. Ithaca, N.Y.: Cornell University Press, 1990.

Dana, Nathalie. *Young in New York: A Memoir of a Victorian Girlhood*. Garden City, N.Y.: Doubleday, 1963.

Day, Clarence. *Life with Father*. New York: Alfred A. Knopf, 1935.

Desmond, Harry William, and Herbert Croly. *Stately Homes in America from Colonial Times to the Present Day*. New York: D. Appleton, 1903.

de Wolfe, Elsie. *The House in Good Taste*. New York: Century, 1913.

Downey, Fairfax. *Portrait of an Era as Drawn by Charles Dana Gibson*. New York: Charles Scribner's Sons, 1936.

Eastlake, Charles. *Hints on Household Taste in Furniture, Upholstery & Other Details*. London: Longmans, Green & Co., 1869.

Eastman, Max. *Enjoyment of Living*. New York: Harper & Row, 1948.

Edel, Leon. *Henry James, 1901–1916: The Master*. New York: J. B. Lippincott, 1972.

Edgell, G. H. *The American Architecture of Today*. New York: Charles Scribner's Sons, 1928.

Ferriss, Hugh. *The Metropolis of Tomorrow*. New York: Ives Washburn, 1929.

Finney, Jack. *Time and Again*. New York: Simon & Schuster, 1970.

Fitzgerald, F. Scott. *The Bodley Head Scott Fitzgerald*. Volume 2, "Echoes of the Jazz Age," "My Lost City." London: Bodley Head, 1959.

———. *The Stories of F. Scott Fitzgerald*. Introduction by Malcolm Cowley. New York: Charles Scribner's Sons, 1951.

Flanner, Janet. *An American in Paris*. New York: Simon & Schuster, 1940.

Garmey, Stephen. *Gramercy Park: An Illustrated History of a New York Neighborhood*. New York: Balsam Press, 1984.

Gerson, Noel B. *The Prodigal Genius: The Life and Times of Honoré de Balzac*. New York: Doubleday, 1972.

Goldberger, Paul. *The City Observed*. New York: Vintage Books, 1979.

Grafton, John. *New York in the Nineteenth Century*. New York: Dover Publications, 1977.

Hamlin, Talbot. *Architecture Through the Ages*. New York: G. P. Putnam's Sons, 1940.

Harrison, Constance Gray (Mrs. Burton). *Recollections Grave and Gay*. New York: Charles Scribner's Sons, 1911.

A History of Real Estate, Building, and Architecture in New York During the Last Half of a Century. Reprint of 1898 edition published by the Real Estate Record Association. New York: Arno Press, 1967.

Hitchcock, Henry Russell. *Modern Architecture, Romanticism and Reintegration*. New York: Payson & Clarke, 1929.

Howells, Mildred, ed. *Life in Letters of William Dean Howells*. 2 vols. New York: Doubleday, Doran & Co., 1928.

Howells, William Dean. *A Hazard of New Fortunes*. New York: Harper & Bros., 1890.

———. *Impressions and Experiences*. New York: Harper & Bros., 1894.

———. *My Literary Passions: Criticism and Fiction*. New York: Harper & Bros., 1895.

———. *Their Silver Wedding Journey*. New York: Harper & Bros., 1899.

Hubert, Pirsson & Hoddick. *The Central Park Apartments*. New York: New York American Bank Note Co., 1882.

Huxtable, Ada Louise. *Kicked a Building Lately?* New York: Quadrangle, 1976.

In Pursuit of Beauty: Americans and the Aesthetic Movement. New York: Metropolitan Museum of Art, Rizzoli, 1986.

Irwin, Will. *Highlights of Manhattan*. New York: D. Appleton-Century, 1937.

Jacobs, Jane. *The Death and Life of Great American Cities*. New York: Doubleday Anchor, 1958.

James, Henry. *The American Scene*. Introduction by Leon Edel. Bloomington: Indiana University Press, 1960.

———. *A Small Boy and Others*. New York: Charles Scribner's Sons, 1912.

———. *Washington Square and Daisy Miller*. New York: Harper & Bros., 1956.

Jeanneret-Gris, Charles Edouard (Le Corbusier). *When the Cathedrals Were White*. New York: Reynal & Hitchcock, 1947.

Kilby, Frank Berger. *Historical Guide to the City of New York*. Compiled from original observations and contributions made by members and friends of the City Historical Club of New York. New York: Frederick A. Stokes Co., 1909.

Kilham, Walter F. *Raymond Hood, Architect*. New York: Architectural Book Publishing Co., 1973.

King's Handbook of New York City. Edited by Moses King. Boston: Moses King, 1892.

Kingsley, Sidney. *Dead End*. New York: Random House, 1936.

Klein, Carole. *Gramercy Park: An American Bloomsbury*. Boston: Houghton Mifflin, 1987.

Koch, Robert. *Louis C. Tiffany: Rebel in Glass*. New York: Crown, 1964.

Kouwenhoven, John A. *The Columbia Historical Portrait of New York: An Essay in Graphic History*. New York: Harper & Row, 1972.

Lamb, Martha J., and Mrs. Burton Harrison. *History of the City of New York: Its Origins, Rise, and Progress*. New York: A. S. Barnes, 1877.

Levron, Jacques. *Daily Life at Versailles in the 17th and 18th Centuries*. London: George Allen and Unwin, 1968.

Lewis, R. B. L. *Edith Wharton*. New York: Harper & Row, 1975.

Lockwood, Charles. *Manhattan Moves Uptown*. New York: Houghton Mifflin, 1976.

Lynes, Russell. *The Tastemakers*. New York: Harper & Bros., 1954.

Lynn, Kenneth S. *William Dean Howells: An American Life*. New York: Harcourt, Brace and Jovanovich, 1970.

Maas, John. *The Victorian Home in America*. New York: Hawthorne Books, 1972.

Macoy, Robert. *History of and How to See New York and Its Environs*. New York: Robert Macoy, 1876.

Mayer, Grace. *Once Upon a City*. New York: Macmillan Co., 1958.

McAllister, Ward. *Society as I Found It*. New York: Cassell Publishing Co., 1890.

McCabe, James D., Jr. *Lights and Shadow of New York Life, or, the Sights and Sensations of the Great City*. Philadelphia: National Publishing Co., 1872.

Metropolitan Museum Historic District Designation Report. New York: City of New York, 1977.

Middleton, William D. *Grand Central, the World's Greatest Railway Terminal*. San Marino, Calif.: Golden West Books, 1977.

Morgan, Keith. *Charles A. Platt, the Artist as Architect*. Cambridge, Mass.: MIT Press, 1985.

Morris, Lloyd. *Incredible New York*. New York: Random House, 1951.

Mumford, Lewis. *The Brown Decades: A Study of the Arts in America, 1865–95*. New York: Dover Publications, 1971.

———. *The City in History*. New York: Harcourt, Brace, & World, 1956.

———. *The Culture of Cities*. New York: Harcourt Brace & Co., 1938.

———. *From the Ground Up*. New York: Harcourt, Brace, & World, 1956.

———. *Sketches from Life: The Early Years*. New York: Dial Press, 1982.

———. *Sticks and Stones: A Study of American Architecture and Civilization*. New York: Dover Publications, 1955.

Nevins, Deborah, ed. *Grand Central Terminal*. New York: Municipal Arts Society, 1982.

The New York American Fall Renting Guide to High Class Apartments. New York, 1910.

New York Then & Now: 83 Manhattan Sites Photographed in the Past and Present. New York: Dover Publications, 1976.

Norton, Lucy, ed. *Saint-Simon at Versailles*. New York: Harmony Books, 1980.

Norton, Thomas E., and Jerry E. Patterson. *Living It Up: A Guide to the Named Apartment Houses of New York*. New York: Atheneum, 1984.

L'Oeuvre de Baron Haussmann, Préfet de la Seine, 1853–1870. Paris: Presses Universitaires de France, 1954.

Le Parisien Chez Lui au XIXe Siècle, 1814–1914. Paris: Archives Nationales, November 1976–February 1977.

Pease and Elliman's Catalogue of East Side New York Apartment Plans. New York: A. G. Blaisdell, 1929.

Pinkney, David. *Napoleon III and the Rebuilding of Paris.* Princeton, N.J.: Princeton University Press, 1958.

Platt, Charles A. *Italian Gardens.* New York: Harper & Row, 1893.

Pritchett, V. S. *Balzac.* London: Chatto & Windus, 1973.

Reed, Henry Hope. *The Golden City.* New York: Doubleday, 1959.

Rider, Fremont. *Rider's New York City: A Guide-book for Travelers.* New York: Henry Holt, 1923.

Roth, Emory. "Autobiographical Notes," 1940–1947. Unpublished manuscript, Avery Library.

Roth, Leland M. *McKim, Mead & White, Architects.* New York: Harper & Row, 1983.

Ruttenbaum, Steven. *Mansions in the Clouds.* New York: Balsam Press, 1986.

Saltus, Edgar. *Vanity Square: A Story of Fifth Avenue Life.* Philadelphia: J. B. Lippincott, 1906.

Santayana, George. *The Genteel Tradition.* Edited by D. L. Wilson. Cambridge, Mass.: Harvard University Press, 1967.

Schuyler, Montgomery. *American Architecture and Other Writings.* Edited by William H. Jordy and Ralph Coe. Cambridge, Mass.: Belknap Press, 1961.

Scully, Vincent. *American Architecture and Urbanism.* New York: Frederick A. Praeger, 1969.

Sexton, R. W. *American Apartment Houses, Hotels, and Apartment Hotels of Today.* Foreword by Raymond M. Hood. New York: Architectural Book Publishing Co., 1929.

————, ed. *Apartment Houses of Today.* New York: New York Architectural Book Publishing Co., 1926.

Shattuck, Roger. *The Banquet Years.* New York: Vintage Books, 1968.

Shopsin, William C., and Mosette Glaser Broderick, eds. *The Villard Houses.* New York: Viking Press in cooperation with the Municipal Arts Society of New York, 1980.

Silver, Nathan. *Lost New York.* New York: Schocken Books, 1971.

Stein, Susan R., ed. *The Architecture of Richard Morris Hunt.* Chicago: University of Chicago Press, 1986.

Stern, Robert A. M., Gregory Gilmartin, and John Montague Massengale. *New York 1900.* New York: Rizzoli, 1983.

Stern, Robert A. M., Gregory Gilmartin, and Thomas Mellins. *New York 1930.* New York: Rizzoli, 1982.

Stokes, Isaac Newton Phelps. *An Iconography of Manhattan Island, 1498–1909.* New York: R. H. Dodd, 1915–28.

Strong, George Templeton. *The Diary of George Templeton Strong: Post-War Years, 1865–75.* Edited by Allen Nevins and Milton Halsey Thomas. New York: Macmillan Co., 1952.

Swanberg, W. A. *Citizen Hearst*. New York: Collier Books, Macmillan Co., 1961.

Sullivan, Louis H. *Autobiography of an Idea*. New York: Press of the American Institute of Architects, 1924.

————. *Kindergarten Chats on Architecture, Education, and Democracy*. New York: Scarab Fraternity Press, 1934.

Summerson, John. *Heavenly Mansions*. New York: W. W. Norton, 1963.

Taurenac, John, and Christopher Little. *Elegant New York: The Builders and the Buildings, 1885–1915*. New York: Abbeville Press, 1985.

Trollope, Anthony. *North America*. Philadelphia: J. B. Lippincott, 1862.

Trollope, Frances Milton. *Domestic Manners of the Americans*. London: Whitaker, Treacher & Co., 1832.

Van der Bent, Teunis J. *The Planning of Apartment Houses, Tenements and Country Houses*. New York: Brentano's, 1917.

Van Dyke, John C. *The New New York: A Commentary on the Place and the People*. New York: Macmillan Co., 1909.

Van Renssalaer, Mrs. John King, in collaboration with Frederic van de Water. *The Social Ladder*. New York: Henry Holt, 1924.

Wharton, Edith. *The Age of Innocence*. New York: Charles Scribner's Sons, 1968.

————. *A Backward Glance*. New York: Charles Scribner's Sons, 1934.

————. *The Custom of the Country*. London: Constable, 1965.

————. *The House of Mirth*. New York: New American Library, 1964.

————. *Old New York*. London: Virago, 1985.

Wharton, Edith, and Ogden Codman, Jr. *The Decoration of Houses*. New York: W. W. Norton, 1978.

White, Morton, and Lucia White. *The Intellectual versus the City*. Cambridge, Mass.: Harvard University Press and MIT Press, 1962.

White, Norval, and Elliot Willenksy. *AIA Guide to New York City*. New York: Macmillan, 1978.

Wood's Illustrated Hand-Book to New York and Environs. New York: G. W. Carleton, 1873.

The World's Looseleaf Album of Apartment Houses. New York: New York World, 1910.

Wright, Frank Lloyd. *An Autobiography*. New York: Longmans, Green & Co., 1932.

————. *Modern Architecture (The Kahn Lectures of 1930)*. Princeton, N.J.: Princeton University Press, 1931.

Young, Sarah Gilman. *European Modes of Living or the Question of Apartment Houses*. New York: G. P. Putnam's Sons, 1881.

Zeisloft, E. Idell, ed. *The New Metropolis*. New York: D. Appleton, 1899.

Periodicals

The citations are far too numerous to list individually here, for many decades of the *Real Estate Record and Builders' Guide*, the *Architectural Record*, and the *American Architect and*

Building News, as well as a selective viewing of a variety of other sources, helped to inform this study. Where voices or thoughts seemed particularly significant, specific articles are noted. Otherwise, the names of periodicals stand as dependable general sources, and the Notes provide additional references.

American Architect

American Architect and Building News

> "The Apartment Houses of New York," October 27, 1883, p. 193.

> "The Apthorp," January 5, 1907, p. 551.

> Littell, E. "Club Chambers," February 19, 1859, p. 59.

> Putnam, J. P. "The Apartment House," January 4, 1890, pp. 3–8.

Architecture

Architecture and Building

Architectural Forum (also known as *The Brickbuilder*)

> Beach, W. W. "Some Recent New York Apartment Houses from J. E. R. Carpenter," May 1919, pp. 127–36.

> Jones, Elisha H. "The Development of Duplex Apartments," June 1912, pp. 159–61.

> "The Venerable Dakota," March 1959, pp. 122–29.

Architectural Record

> Croly, Herbert. "The Architectural Works of Charles A. Platt," March 1904, pp. 181–244.

> ———. "The Contemporary New York Residence," December 1902, p. 704.

> ———. "The Renovation of the New York Brownstone District," June 1903, p. 569.

> ———. "Rich Men and Their Houses," May 1902, pp. 27–32.

> David, A. C. "A Co-Operative Apartment House in New York," July 1908, pp. 1–8.

> ———. "A Cooperative Studio Building," October 1903, pp. 233–54.

> Fick, Professor, of Copenhagen. "The Apartment House Up to Date," July 1907, p. 69.

> Flagg, Ernest. "American Architecture as Opposed to Architecture in America," October 1900, pp. 178–90.

> Hubert, Pirsson & Hoddick. "New York Flats or French Flats," July–September 1892, p. 61.

> Israels, Charles. "The Planning of New York Apartment Houses," July 1901, pp. 477–508.

> Marcou, Paul Frantz. "The Modern House in Paris," January–March 1893, p. 324.

> Price, C. Matlock. "Pioneer in Apartment House Architecture: A Memoir on Philip C. Hubert's Work," July 1914, pp. 74–76.

> Schuyler, Montgomery. "The Romanesque Revival in New York," July–September 1891, p. 375.

————. "The Sky-Scraper Up to Date," January–March 1899, p. 231.

————. "The Small House in New York," April–June 1899, p. 231.

————. "The Works of the Late Richard Morris Hunt," October–December 1894, p. 97.

Winkler, Franz K. "Architecture in the Billionaire District of New York," September 1901, pp. 677–79.

————. "Recent Apartment House Design," January 1902, pp. 98–109.

Bruere, Martha Bensky. "The Flat vs. the House," *Harper's Bazaar*, June 1912, p. 303.

Burnham, Alan. "The New York Architecture of Richard Morris Hunt," *Society of Architectural Historians*, May 1952.

Deutsch, Davida. "The Osborne, New York City," *Antiques Magazine*, July 1986, pp. 152–58.

Godkin, E. L. "The Expenditure of Rich Men," *Scribner's Magazine*, October 1896, pp. 497–500.

Hungerford, Edward. "Housekeeping Deluxe," *Tavern Topics*, October 1921, p. 6.

The New Yorker

Duplex. "New Apartments," 1925 to 1931.

Penthouse. "New Apartments," 1925 to 1931.

T-Square. "The Skyline," 1925 to 1931.

Updike, John. "A Critic at Large: Howells as Anti-Novelist," July 13, 1987, p. 78.

New York Times

Obituaries: Rosario Candela, October 7, 1953, p. 29; J. E. R. Carpenter, June 12, 1932, p. 30; Irwin Chanin, February 26, 1988, p. 17; Philip G. Hubert, November 17, 1911, p. 13.

"The Avenue Transformed," April 5, 1927, p. 26.

Duffus, R. L. "Upper Fifth Avenue to House the 4000," *New York Times Magazine*, May 24, 1925, p. 7.

"Exit Fifth Avenue," October 8, 1925, p. 21.

Gray, Christopher. "Apartments by Candela: Grandest of the Grand," *New York Times Magazine*, September 3, 1988, p. 67.

"New York's Original Apartment House," September 22, 1957, Section 8, pp. 1, 8.

Pope, Virginia. "New York Now Has Mansions in Flats," *New York Times Magazine*, April 5, 1927, p. 17.

Reinhart, Robert. "The Ansonia Remembered," November 7, 1971, Section 8, p. 1.

New York *World*

Real Estate Record and Builders' Guide

"All About Home Clubs," December 30, 1882, p. 147.

"The Bradley Apartment House," October 6, 1877, p. 766.

"The City of the Future," December 27, 1879, p. 1056.

"The Dakota," March 7, 1885, p. 232.

"The Future of the Apartment House," November 10, 1883, p. 881.

"How Great Apartment Houses Have Paid," February 7, 1885, p. 127.

"The New York House of the Future: An Interview with Henry Villard," December 31, 1881, p. 1208.

"The Rebuilding of Park Avenue," December 4, 1909, p. 991.

"Renew Fight for Apartment Houses above 60th Street," February 18, 1922, p. 202.

"Supplement," December 30, 1882, p. 4.

"Vacant Lots in the Fashionable Quarter," April 12, 1879, p. 287.

Richardson, James L. "The New Homes of New York: A Study of Flats," *Scribner's Monthly*, May 1874, pp. 63–76.

Van Gelder, Lindsy. "Park Avenue," *Town and Country*, September 1986, p. 186.

Van Rensselaer, M. G. "People in New York," *Century Magazine*, February 1895, pp. 534–50.

———. "Recent Architecture in America, I: Public Buildings," *Century Magazine*, May 1884, pp. 48–67.

———. "Recent Architecture in America, V: City Dwellings," *Century Magazine*, February 1886, pp. 548–58.

Vaux, Calvert. "Parisian Buildings for City Residents," *Crayon IV*, July 1857, p. 218.

"The Vertical Village," *Connoisseur*, December 1987, p. 153.

Williams, Jesse Lynch. "Back to Town or The Return to Human Nature," *Scribner's Magazine*, November 1915, p. 542.

Papers and Interviews

Papers and Designation Reports from the Landmarks Preservation Commission, New York City

Interviews: Richard Ferrer, Harry Forster, Caesar Pelli, Richard Roth

INDEX